# Grandmother Moon

# Grandmother Moon

## Lunar Magic in Our Lives

### Spells, Rituals, Goddesses, Legends, and Emotions Under the Moon

Zsuzsanna E. Budapest

HarperSanFrancisco

*A Division of* HarperCollins*Publishers*

TEXT DESIGN BY IRENE IMFELD
ILLUSTRATIONS BY AGÚSTA AGÚSTSSON
AUTHOR PHOTO BY CHRISTINE ELLCINO

FIRST EDITION

**Library of Congress Cataloging-in-Publication Data**

Budapest, Zsuzsanna Emese
   Grandmother moon : lunar magic in our lives : spells, rituals, goddesses, legends, and emotions under the moon / Zsuzsanna E. Budapest. — 1st ed.
      p.     cm.
   Includes bibliographical references and index.
   ISBN 0–06–250114–3 (alk. paper)
   1. Moon—Miscellanea.    I. Title.
   BF1723.B83 1991
   133.5′3—dc20                               90–56443
                                                      CIP

91  92  93  94  95    RRD(H)    10  9  8  7  6  5  4  3  2  1

This edition is printed on acid-free paper that meets the American National Standards Institute Z39.48 Standard.

*I dedicate this book to Luna,*

*the Goddess of the Moon.*

*May she come closer to our souls*

*now than ever before.*

*And to Hilary.*

*. . . While the moon*

*shone at the full*

*the women were at their places*

*circling the altar . . .*

SAPPHO

# CONTENTS

# Acknowledgments

I am very grateful for the help of my researcher and sister priestess Helen Farias, editor of *Octava*, whose knowledge and keen sense of the divine led her to the appropriate information. Many, many deep-felt thanks to Diana L. Paxson, my sister high priestess, novelist, and founder of the Fellowship of the Spiral Path. She not only edited my original material but wrote the sections of the View from the Moon and contributed a great deal to the Festivals of the Moon sections. Thank you Susun Weed for selecting the Moon herbs for me. Thank you Angelica Dawson of the Frauenhof Sira in Austria for her translations from German. Many thanks to Rabbi Leah Novick for the long moonwalks and moontalks.

Woman writers don't have wives to thank for typing and correcting and nurturing writers and manuscripts, so I just want to thank Marcella Paolocci for finding my files when my computer ate them; M. V. Divine, author of *Bruheria*, who sent me lovely greeting cards every week that served as encouragement; and Marli Rabinowitz, whose friendship and support gave me a much-needed sense of appreciation. Harper editor Barbara Moulton handled my work with great sensitivity and for her good editorial advice and work I am also very grateful.

## ABOUT THIS BOOK

# *Women Dominate with Culture and Tradition*

I wrote this book as a companion to *The Grandmother of Time* because the Moon was the first clock, where our first concept of time originated.

Luna, our silvery Grandmother, is teaching us about her holy days and her lore from around the world. She is our constant companion, her ever-changing face is always in our view.

I have discussed the journey of the Moon through the zodiac signs in each chapter, but as you know, the Grandmother goes through many signs in one single lunation, so the advice about a particular sign is valid each month only when that sign occurs.

I have included true stories from my life so that you see how I have dealt with the lunar tides, the Moons of my life. The moontides deal with the feelings we go through in life, and in this book I share witchy moon-spells to manage those feelings. It is a good idea to use *The Grandmother of Time* together with *Grandmother Moon* because together they are a complete resource for metaphysical/magical/practical problem solving.

The Festivals of the Moon reflect more Asian, Egyptian, Middle Eastern, and Native American holy days than European ones. This was my intention because these cultures have preserved their lunar calendars to this day. All I had to do was push aside the patriarchal camouflage and find the gentle Moon behind it all.

The European calendar had been based on an earlier lunar calendar, which is the basis of our own. It is well known that Kalends, the Nones, and the Ides of the Moon were originally identical with the phases of the Moon—New, Waxing, and Full. Waning Moon was omitted early on. Could it be the fear of the Dark Grandmother that made them hide it?

The same cultural denial that occurred to our larger Goddess heritage also occurred to our lunar heritage. The victors rewrote the calendars and took the Moon out but made some effort to translate lunar holy days into solar ones when the people would not give up their Full-Moon revelries. The Assumption of Mary, for instance, used to be the great festival of the Moon Goddess Diana/Hecate at the Full Moon in August. The Christian calendar, however, fixed it at August 15, and we may or may not have a Full Moon on this date.

Some holy days that you saw with new eyes in *The Grandmother of Time* reappear in this book—reclaimed as Moon holy days.

The reclaiming of the Goddess calendar is the most important political and spiritual tool in our times. Having fun, celebrating, feeling good, taking care of business inside and out, taking care of each other, making our lives count, and filling them with pleasure is the best revenge against sorry, war-ridden patriarchy. What you celebrate is what is honored and respected. Women's main tool of winning leadership in this world is culture creating, tradition building. Calendars are the blueprints of culture. Traditions, festivals, cultural events of all kinds are the ways women used to dominate in ancient times, and they are still the ways women will dominate again. Women will be leaders in the coming Information Age because all we need is our natural smarts and heart and a rich, supportive culture.

Already today the number one U.S. export is our culture. Madonna. Movies. Music. Women's spirituality. Create culture furiously and diligently by celebrating the Moon and life and yourself. Be the magical glue that creates meaning for our everyday existence. Lunar primates, now is the time to claim vision and healing for the next century.

# *Moontalk*

You think you know her. You have seen her all your life. You have vivid memories of her. She was always there witnessing your life. She was there at your birth, later she was there at your first kiss, and she was there again when your heart was first broken. Who is she really? Who is the Moon to us?

She is the shining one, the magical one, she who shines on all equally.

She is lovely Diana, the opener of the womb; Selene, Egg Mother; Astarte of the womb; Mother Moon; Star of the Sea; Notre Dame, our mother. She is Hecate, Queen of the Witches; Artemis; Amazon; Callisto; Muse; Yemaya; White Shell Woman. These are but a few names of our beloved Queen of the Night, our Moon.

The Moon was the first clock, calculating her waxing and waning was the original way of reckoning time. She is periodicity, the symbol of change that is constant, the light of the nighttime, birthgiver even before there was birth, dark and light mother. Yet as we regard her white, familiar face, some part of her always remains mysterious. The Moon invented mystery.

Astrologers attribute to her the power of conception, the nine-month-long gestation and birthing, nurturance, home loving, romance, security, sensitivity, creativity, and the constant creation of the flow of feelings.

What, pray tell, is not connected to the Moon, that almighty force with the gentle manifestations? What laboratory walls can keep her in or out? Who can study our Grandmother? Who can measure her, she who was the first measurement, never quite fitting? Who can study her effect on humans when everyone who tries to study her is already under her influence? She is the lover and faithful spouse of the Earth, never leaving her, always encircling her like in a courtship eternal. She is creator in cooperation with Terra of organic life on Earth. She is the Other, from Earth we gaze up at her in admiration, and yet she is also our mirror. It was only when we took pictures of our Mother Earth from the distant

surface of Grandmother Moon that we gained our first visual knowledge
of how precious and finite and fragile we—the Earth—really are.

Who can beseech the Moon so that she will divulge her secrets? How
did she choose us to shine upon? Why does she love us so, and why does
she bother to give us life and light? And how, at the same time, can she
look so cold and immaculate? One night when I prayed to her in a
women's circle (she was in Aquarius), I challenged her again, calling out
to her face, "Reveal yourself to us!" She just started singing in her old-
fashioned way, like a bald-headed, kind-faced woman.

> *The blood of the ancients*
> *Flows in our veins,*
> *And the forms change,*
> *But the circle of life remains.*
> *(traditional Wiccan chant)*

Grandmother Moon sings songs that I know, and she sometimes sings
songs I never heard of and she teaches them to me. I was surprised that
she was singing that night and I taunted her.

"What do you mean singing songs to me and being so alive, floating up
there in the clouds?"

"I am not finished yet."

"Finished with what?"

"With setting things right," came the whispered answer.

"Thank you for not being finished yet. Thank you for still caring."

I lit more candles to her, because it's the custom. I remembered my
seventy-year-old friend Jennifer at the swimming pool, who is afraid to
look at the Moon through the tree branches because she thinks it's bad
luck.

"Do you mind if we look at you through the branches?" I asked the
Moon.

"Look at me through your soul," she whispered.

"What about when someone looks at you over her left shoulder? Do
you mind that?"

"No. Look at me any way you can. Look at me with your eyes closed. See me with your womb."

That's moontalk. I feel moonish when I am out with the Full Moon at Tiburon on the water. She is reflected on the surface of the Bay, as she rises from the East Bay hills over San Francisco. So beautiful.

"What is the most important thing we should learn from you?" I asked again.

"To flow. Don't be afraid to let go. Don't be afraid to come back. Don't be afraid to become full. Don't be afraid."

The women were all talking to her now. One woman set her flickering white candle within the spread of her prayer shawl, shielding it from the wind and whispered to the Moonmother.

"You are the most powerful force in my life. Please help me with my health so that I can regain my balance."

Now another woman stood up and prayed to her.

"My son, dearest Goddess, let me keep my son. I want to guide him through his life, I want to keep custody of him. Please help me in court."

Yet another stood up with her lit candle.

"I praise you and thank you for granting my wish from the last Full Moon."

All of us look like women from ancient times as we pray to the Moon, windblown, crowned with seasonal evergreens. And we are doing it every month. She lives in our bodies and now in the rhythm of our lives. We need her, we need to come outdoors to this magical balmy place on the water and worship. We don't care if it's considered silly. Some of our husbands and boyfriends get jealous. What are we doing together—all women without men—in the middle of the night?

The men just have to get over it.

What we know is that it helps us to pray to the Moon. She is alive and visible, she is a mandala for our innermost selves, she is our benefactress, she is our relative, she is Grandmother Moon. We pray with confidence and satisfaction.

We also offer her mooncakes, which in this case consist of bread baked both in the shape of the stars and round like herself. The breads are buttered and baked with garlic. We offer her wine and we feast in her honor, eating our own mooncakes. Whatever we don't eat and think the wildlife would appreciate, like apples and grapes and seeds for the birds, we toss to the four directions as thank-you notes.

Yet that night I was puzzled. The Moon was up to something. She was singing that song, and she had said she was still not finished righting wrongs. What could she be planning now?

"When the women come to know me, they will no longer weep."

"Who said that?" I turned to the women around me, but none of them were talking. They all hummed gently, gazing into the Moon's silvery face.

"Was it you?" I asked. "Are you talking within my head?"

"Of course," she said.

"Then tell me this. Could you guide us to you, give us a little help, a little maternal nudging?"

"I am doing all of that already. But I will do one more thing . . ."

I was breathless. The Moon was talking in my head, and she was about to tell me the great cosmic secret.

"I will give you moonsight," she said.

"What is moonsight? Is it like foresight? How do I get it?"

"It is a prism of knowledge. You look at everything through moonsight, and all will be clear."

"Like premonition?"

"It is . . ."

"Is it like dream sight? Intuition?"

"It is."

"And prophecy and understanding the language of the animals?"

"It is."

"Is it like—"

"Enough. You will know it when it comes. I have to rise over Hawaii now." The voice stilled.

She climbed higher and higher and the meadow upon which our small group meditated became drenched with her silver light. The waking winds kept blowing out our candles, but we knew she was satisfied with seeing our faces; candles were optional.

That night I finished burning the candles in my bedroom, and today I feel I have a lot more energy and love of life than before the ritual. And that is how it should be.

## *Human Beings, The Lunar Primates*

The image of the Moon has always been my most cherished symbol for the unity of the soul. In many cultures the Moon was viewed as a Goddess because of her kinship to women and all organic life or as a magical god who was the true husband of the women, who opened their wombs. But the Moon and the womb were always seen as related: the Moon governed the earth's waters, the womb's waters created the people.

What was it that separated our species from the other animals? When was the moment of truth when we became humans? When did the gentle hand of the beneficial Fates touch our brain and set us free?

Was it when we stood up erect? There are other animals who can stand up—bears, for example. Was it when we first prayed to the Moon? Or when the first woman in childbirth called upon the force who presides over all the births of the world? We don't know if other animals also pray, but the elephants certainly observe burial rites and mourn their dead, which I consider a religious act. Was it when we created the first tools? Made our flints and arrows? Other animals also make tools and use them to get their food. Some use sticks, some use stones to crack open fruits. No, it wasn't tools. And I don't think it was fire either. I think the taming of fire happened after we departed from our animal selves. We trained ourselves first not to fear fire. That was already a human act.

But what made us human to begin with? When something this important comes up in herstory, I always look at sex. There, I think, lies the answer.

We became humans when we separated the womb-cleansing menstruation (which in other mammals is called estrus, is seasonal, not monthly, and is immediately followed by ovulation and the production of pheromones that attract the opposite sex) from sexual receptivity. We became humans when we became sensitive to the rays of the Moon instead of the changing sunlight, which triggers estrus in all other animals. We became humans when we became the first and only menstruating animals. Or rather we became animals no more.

Animal estrus is triggered by the reduction or increase of the hours of light. St. Valentine's Day, when we honor lovers, comes from the older holiday Lupercalia (see *The Grandmother of Time*), the time when wolves go into heat, around Candlemas. What is happening around February 2? The hours of light are getting longer. Animals, first the smaller ones then the larger, are affected, and the mating season arrives for our animal friends. Animals are not interested in mating as individuals (even though many choose mates for life). They are totally dependent on the amount of sunlight to trigger the changes in their bodies that will make them want to mate in the first place.

I made some phone calls. I called doctors. I called a biologist. I called women and men.

"Is it true that we are the only menstruating species?" I asked. There would be a pause, but the answer was always the same. Yes, we are.

Everybody puzzled over how they never thought of this fact before.

"So can I actually say we are lunar primates?"

"I don't see why not," my doctor friends assured me.

"Why haven't I heard about this before?"

Unfortunately the answer was only too old and familiar. I had not heard about this incredible species-transforming evolutionary development *because it was the women who did it, not the men!*

Because of this change in women, human beings do not go into heat anymore. Equinoxes and solstices are holidays of the earth, but they don't force us to present our sex to the first male who comes by. The only place left where all the females are in a receptive sexual mood at once is a whorehouse. Men love whorehouses because they must remind them of the good old days when we were just innocent animals who all went into heat together. There were no extra requirements placed on the males, no dinner dates or theater tickets. There was no necessity to be nice to us, to buy us flowers and be sensitive (moonish). All this romantic longing comes from women messing up the simple old solar customs. All these new cultural demands come because women humanized the simple primates we used to be.

The advent of menstruation separated us from the other animals; menstruation is what made it possible for us to evolve into humans. The humanization of our species and invention of culture were immediate benefits of women's invention of emancipation from mandatory breeding. Women developed menstruation and freed themselves from the need to mate for procreation only. Reproductively it made our species more successful because now we were available sexually all the time (or none of the time, as we chose), but the probability of pregnancy became higher. The drawback of this new feature took some time to appear. It took patriarchy to ruin it all with the control of women. It is what we see today: we became capable of overpopulation.

How did this occur? How did women switch from responding to the rays of the sun to reacting to the gentle magnetism of the Moon? How could this be done?

Our frequent ovulation probably evolved in warmer climates as the season of the birth was not crucial. Our species developed a lot of internal diversity—we are not as alike as the robins—and birth time diverged. This also went along with the increased helplessness of our babies. Can you imagine a group where all the women give birth at once? A very vulnerable group it would have been.

Because sex is naturally rhythmic, once our ovulation happened more than once a year or several times a year it was easy for it to become Moon influenced, for us to begin to respond to the lunar tidal pull on our tissues. But we are still not too tightly ruled by the Moon. Most of us menstruate during New Moons, but there are those who have their periods at the Full Moon or when it is waning or waxing.

Men did not develop into lunar primates like women. Men didn't have to change their bodies to come along on the humanizing road with the women. They only needed to raise their sexual interest from seasonal to day by day. This is why we sometimes feel that the opposite sex is from another species altogether. In most species the sexual rut occurs in both sexes at the same time. Not so in ours. Men have no such lunar cycles. Because of this, men are always ready to mate no matter when ovulation occurs in women.*

Menstruation (infertility) and ovulation (fertility) are two separate spokes of the same wheel of emancipation. Most women menstruate when the Moon is new. They are fertile when the Moon is full. The other half menstruates when the Moon is full. These women are fertile when the Moon is new. The Moon and the women have worked together and created our species, the only menstruating species on Earth.

From our sexual availability came tribal bonding and societies and eventually civilization. All this is women's achievement, but awareness of all this is suppressed lest women remember their awesome role. The society we have now is the furthest removed psychically from the Moon. We stress values that are solar: logic, left-brain activities, physical prowess, competition. In reaction to our lunar primate essence, men claimed the sun as theirs. The sun, too, used to be female in most societies, as Pat Monaghan, Goddess mythologist, has found.

Patriarchy demands that menstruation be hidden and consigns to it shame. It is treated as a dirty crime; it is despised as a curse. Male mythologists attach to it the stigma of the untouchables; male god religions forbid women in that condition to participate in the sacred rites. We teach our young women to hide their blood, then we teach them to hide their brains.

Men must learn to reidentify themselves with women as a species and stop longing for the old primate/estrus times. Men have to acknowledge the fact that the women of their species are responsible for the creation of Homo sapiens and that it is because of the women that they belong to

---

*A good book about menstruation and its meaning and all its scientific proof is *The Wise Wound: Myths, Realities, and Meanings of Menstruation* by Penelope Schuttle and Peter Redgrove, published by Bantam.

this distinguished species. This should not bruise the primate ego or provoke hatred of women for changing things. Men should be proud of women and grateful for their lives.

Intellectually, however, there has been a strong lunar response from the men. Men's fascination with the Moon and their physical exploration of it showed a reconciliation, a start at making peace with their past disregard of the Moon, beginning their new and powerful involvement with the Moon in the age of technology. Men went to the Moon personally.

Today many women rarely view the Moon or pay any attention to her. We are alienated, removed from our sources of power, and so we have developed menstrual cramps and premenstrual syndromes. The lunar tides that made us so wise and innovative in earlier times are now like old telephone wires, dangling from the poles, whipped about in the storms. We try to make the old connections, but we get our signals messed up.

One thing is certain. What women did with their bodies liberated our species from the incessant burden of breeding and separated the idea of sex from procreation. Sex became a separate cultural factor, for pleasure and enjoyment, for romance and love affairs. Procreation became a choice for women, a choice won millennia ago.

Our bodies still infuriate the male establishment. After so many eons, they are still fighting our achievement, attempting to push back the evolutionary clock. They try to make women solar creatures again, making our bodies a battleground, men versus women, wishing back the estrus times when every sexual contact resulted in babies and every conception was a birth, when no female ever said no. Ultimately the law of nature for human beings is expressed in women's bodies, not men's. No male god, no phony priest, no Supreme Court judge can take that away. We both, men and women, belong to the Moon.

## *Lunar Consciousness*

I invite you, dear reader, to step to your window tonight and search out the Moon. Where is she? What is she doing? Is she new? Is she waxing? Is she full or is she waning?

Now close your eyes and try to see the Moon inside your head. What does that feel like? As your map to the skies you should use a good lunar calendar that notes the many phases of the Moon and also the astrological signs in which they occur. Nightly, or as often as possible, repeat this moonwatch. Look at the Moon as the old ally she is. Talk to the Moon in yourself, as you would to a kindly grandmother.

The energies of the world, the magnetism of all watery things are governed by the Moon. You may want to try to follow a few Moon laws. For example, if you wish to have your hair grow fast and strong, cut it while there is a Crescent Moon in the sky. Pay attention to see if it really made a change. If you need to move, find a new place to live during the New Moon.

When the Full Moon comes around, go out dancing, no matter if it's a weekend or not. Take note of your energy level. You will find you are active till late at night and not tired. The Full Moon is good only for ritual, lovemaking, or dancing. If this energy is repressed, be careful on the streets—fights may break out. Drive carefully because the drivers are also under the influence of the Moon, and she makes them crazier than usual.

At the Waning Moon finish things that you started at the New Moon. Do not begin anything new or it will collapse. Don't make contracts and don't sign them. Wait until there is New-Moon energy. During the Waning Moon cut your toenails to make them grow slower.

When you feel you have started tuning your cells, your tissues, the waters in your body to the Moon, build a Moon altar in your home. The Moon altar can be in your bedroom—mine is—or in any room that you consider your personal space.

Create a nature table with a white cloth, silvery things, sea creatures, such as shells, pictures of the Moon, and images of the Goddess of the Moon. Keep some water in a pretty dish on the altar, put salt in another. Obtain silver candles and use them as your meditation candles. How and which way the Moon altar should be arranged is up to you. It must be pleasing to your own eyes and turn you on when you are facing it psychically. Keep your Moon altar always set up, refresh it daily in your thinking and by putting fresh flowers or decorations on it.

From this time on, watch your own feelings more closely. Your feelings respond to your inner Moon. The tides of the feelings must be respected, they must be attended to. Whether you are angry or joyful, at whichever end of the spectrum of feelings you happen to be, light the appropriate candles or do your affirmations at this Moon altar. As you read about other people's Moon festivals, make them yours. It doesn't matter where on the globe these wonderful festivals have survived. It is one world, one planet, and one Moon. Note the way your heart resonates to different ways of observing the lunar holidays, and observe the ones that move you. Specific ways of celebrating the New, Full, and Dark Moon times are included in the chapter on the thirteenth lunation, the Blue Moon.

Lunar consciousness can grow swiftly. In just a short time you will realize how much more aware you have become of this friendly overhead luminary. You will begin to know without looking what phase the Moon is in. You will be able to tell by the energy in your own body. You will be able to say, "It's the Waning Moon, let's not work too hard" or "It's a New Moon, now's the time to start those projects I was thinking about when the Moon was waning."

The Moon affects us even without our conscious participation. During the Waxing Moon, our bodies bleed more if operated on, our skins break out more easily. Warts come off easily at the Waning Moon. Wounds close easier. There is less bleeding during surgery. With lunar consciousness we may be able to access our deeper intuitions, deeper love, deeper aliveness. With lunar interest we may learn more and more about our world, the invisible laws of nature, the laws that have governed us so far.

## Why Is the Moon So Important?

To discuss all the ways in which the Moon is significant to us as lunar primates would take several books. The Moon and agriculture, for instance, or the Moon and nurturance or a study of the Moon's effects on our eating habits and conception would fill a shelf. Here are some of the ways she affects us.

The Moon rules the time when fertility occurs, through the Goddess Mens, whose name means the "right moment." If you think about it, everything depends on fertility. Nations depend on their fertility for citizens, trade, and business. Animals also need to replace themselves to perpetuate the species. Fertility is the breakfast, lunch, and dinner of all living creatures. We eat plants whose fertility provides food, we eat animals, and animals eat other animals, and everybody is given something to eat. Fertility is dinner.

The Moon and women have an ancient pact. We draw our magical power from the Moon. We drew our knowledge of agriculture from the Moon. We created culture centered around the Moon and prosperity. We have Moons in our bodies. Sixty percent of all childbirths start during the Moon time, at night, and twenty-four hours before the Full Moon the number of deliveries increases dramatically in hospitals. If you plant a garden by the Moon, which is an old custom, you will find that your garden looks better and your crops come up right. Your harvest keeps dry if you gather it on the Full Moon. Your hair will grow faster if you cut it during the Waxing Moon and slower in the Waning Moon.

Our connection to the Moon was so close that in ancient times every move in our lives was planned according to the Moon, and everybody knew what Moon it was. It was like today's media—all-pervasive, dominant, and opinion forming. Activities in the world were governed by the Moon, and it worked. The Moon was there as our special guide, through harvest and beauty care, baby making, and merrymaking. The Moon witnessed our romances, our first nighttime activities, our night life, and our dreams.

The Moon was also our downfall. As we learned to grow food by the Moon, we began to have the first food surplus in history. Surplus food meant we could support a larger population, and the men no longer had to hunt to survive. There must have been some mighty dissatisfaction as the main occupation of the males changed from a necessity to a nostalgic sport. The human male was evolved to be a coprovider, and now there was plenty to eat without the game he brought in.

His basic instinct to hunt was channeled into making war (or trade) because surplus food could support longer excursions from the main lodge. Surplus food became the fuel for militaristic adventures, which increased in scope until the entire society was reorganized to supply them. As Moon farming became more successful, the warring cultures proliferated. The food was used to support the armies rather than the population. Today we see the same misuse of resources, as the military gets billions of dollars to wage wars, and women and children and the elderly get their meager budgets cut.

The increased antagonism within the male population against each other was also an effect of the change from solar estrus to lunar menstruation. Since sexual availability of women was now constant, the competition for females was constant and was expressed in the aggression and violence of men against men (as well as against women).

To some extent, war served as a harsh corrective for another effect of year-round fertility—overpopulation. But while war cuts down the children in their full flower, abortion—women's choice of population control—simply sends back the unborn soul to the universal Mother, where all the unborn reside.

One of nature's most pleasant ways of coping with overpopulation is to increase the number of homosexuals in the community. Rather than producing children, gays provide support for those in the community who do have children. The gay uncles and aunts are the legendary fun relatives we remember as adults. Their productivity is directed into other areas. They have enriched our culture with outstanding works in the arts—theater, dance, music, and so on. They are the emotional and cultural caretakers of the population.

However, there is another, Moon-governed way for the control of fertility through knowledge of herbs and the Moon. Birth control by the Moon is a practice I would like to share.

To practice astrological birth control, you first need to find out what sign your Moon was in when you were born. This is part of any astrological chart, or you can look it up in *Natural Birth Control* by the Aquarian Research Foundation. Let's say you found out that when you were born the Moon was in Libra in the last quarter of the Waning Moon. Now you are armed with lunar knowledge.

To use this information for birth control, you abstain from sexual relations for three and a half days before the exact phase and for half a day after. All this is in addition to using the rhythm method, abstaining for five to seven days in the middle of the menstrual cycle. These two times may coincide, which cuts down on the abstinence time. An alternative to abstinence is using birth control during those fertile lunar times.

According to Anna Kria, who is an astrologer in Los Angeles, for a woman to become pregnant, intercourse has to take place twenty-four hours before the birth phase of the woman. If you were born ten hours before or ten hours after the Full Moon, you should avoid getting pregnant at this time. Children conceived at these times often have birth defects. If you desire to have a baby girl, you need even more information. Abstain altogether during the menstrual cycle's fertile period, and try to conceive on alternate months when the birth phase of your Moon was in the feminine signs such as Taurus, Cancer, Virgo, Scorpio, Capricorn, or Pisces. An astrologer can work out a chart of these times. If you desire a boy, choose the Moon phase of your birth in the masculine signs.

## Herbs and the Moon

This is really very powerful knowledge, so it was suppressed most energetically. Remember that for sixteen hundred years Christians have persecuted women and men and even children for the crime of knowledge. Women were killed after awful tortures for knowing how to take away headaches, how to break fevers, how to deliver a child, how to abort a fetus. Today this battle is raging still, except that now we have the opportunity to reclaim the herbal knowledge of the past, and many good books have been written by contemporary herbalists and doctors (see the Bibliography).

The key to herbal birth control is to act early. Herbal birth control is for the aware, not the sluggish. If you don't follow your menstrual cycle and don't know when you are due, the herbs are not much use. But if you pay attention and know when you are ovulating, a cup of tea from such herbs as pennyroyal, ruta, or black and blue cohosh can bring on your period and prevent unwanted pregnancy.

These are powerful herbs. (Once, at a festival, we simply sat naked on pennyroyal plants that were growing as groundcover and we all got our periods at once!) Just celebrate your Moon time with a cup of tea, don't wait until you are three months pregnant. I have often imagined marches for abortion rights with millions of women carrying rattles to mark the rhythms of our sacred dance and herbs to show the power of nature, which no Supreme Court can outlaw.

"Lunar consciousness will liberate you!" said the Moon at last.

There is an old prophecy that the Goddess goes to sleep and her sons are allowed to usurp her power until they fail miserably at everything. They are beset by corruption and unwinnable wars, bad economy and bad faiths, no satisfaction for the poor or the rich men; their hearts are empty, their beds loveless. According to the story, humanity will cry out in anguish to the gods to be rescued. Then through her women the Goddess will wake up and reveal her plan as the women implement it for her.

There will be no more value put on warring—it is old solar primate stuff. The men have learned their lessons. They too will choose happiness, prosperity, the arts, and women instead of dying for nothing (pride). The military machinery will come to a grinding halt. Men will be happy to be rehabilitated to serve life and not death. At this point the Moon will again invite both sexes to join the new human race. In that not-so-distant future the men and the women will no longer feel they are from two separate species. The battle of the sexes will be over at last.

# FIRST LUNATION

*Time ‹ December–January*
*Sign ‹ Capricorn*
*Lunar Herb ‹ Elder*
*Lunar Animal ‹ Spider*

# Cold Moon

## VIEW FROM THE MOON

*The Cold Moon of Capricorn sails across the southern sky. Her pure light shines on fields white with snow or fields bare and brown, on waters that move slowly with cold or hide beneath an icy covering. The winter world guards its secrets well, but the Cold Moon knows them all. This stillness is not death but sleep, in which the world renews itself, awaiting spring. The Cold Moon knows where every secret seed is resting.*

*This is her wisdom.*

## THE GODDESS SPEAKS
### *Frau Holle*

In the German forest far from the village there lived an old woman called Frau Holle. She was always dressed in black because she was a widow and that was the custom. She lived alone and had animals as her servants. Folks said her cat cleaned her house and the dog hunted for her food. Even in the depths of winter there was green in her garden. The air was scented by the warmth of her baking, and the eyes could delight at the wonderful webs she had spun upon her loom. The villagers did not understand her, but they respected her and accepted the fact that she was unusual.

The priest said she was a witch and would not allow her in the church. Frau Holle didn't care. She always said, "God is not in that building anyhow." God lived in the trees of the wood, and in the sacred mushrooms she took when she kept an all-night vigil for a healing ceremony.

By daylight people avoided her, but protected by deep darkness, folk came to see her from far and wide. Even the priest of the new religion sent his housekeeper to fetch medicine for his sore joints. The midwives came to her for her herbs that eased the pain of labor and helped bring out the afterbirth. Young maidens visited her for love potions, and young men came for herbs to stimulate their vitality. She knew cures for all ills.

After a time, Frau Holle disappeared. But folk said she didn't really die. She rode around on the wind's wings, shaking the snowfeathers down. She was heard singing on the rooftops, she tickled the toes of sleepers at night just for fun. Some say she does so still.

Her name is Frau Holle, the wise spinner. She dwells in the shining Moon, who makes the world go round with her magnetism and spins spells on the great wheel of Capricorn.

## *Frau Holle Speaks:*

You can find me in the still waters of your wells and the cold depths of lakes. Come, jump in and see! You will not die. The deep cool well that reflects your face like a mirror will show you the way to my house. When you dare to follow me into the depths of the earth, you will find that even though the world is cold, there I have sunshine. My womb-shaped ovens are baking fresh bread, making new bodies for souls. My apple trees are fruiting beautifully. The vitality of my abundance is yours if you harvest them. I am working hard to bring my children good fortune.

If you work for me to perform my tasks and accept the responsibilities I bring you, to take out the fresh loaves from my hot ovens, pick the apples from my trees, accept the power that I give you, I will hire you as my personal helper. When you fluff my pillows, the feathers flying will make the ground white with snow. When you water my sacred plants, that will create the blessed rain that is necessary to sustain the life above. I am all work, you see. I am all striving, all that is useful.

When the Moon is full I will come and look at your lifework. What have you woven from the fine threads I have given you? Under the Full Moon I shall examine your relationships, your accomplishments. I shall inspect your house for order, your loom for neatness. If I find your work in inspired order, I shall bring you gold, because my footsteps turn into gold and the touch of my fingertips turns everything into silver. If your life is a mess when I come by, I may mess it up even more just to force you out of your old patterns.

I am the striving, exacting mother, the mother who works and needs your help. My realm is the deep waters within the earth, the deep unconscious places of your soul, and the high mountains upon the earth. All magical creatures obey me, but the water nymphs are my favorite daughters. I am the one who can show you your own feelings, confront you with the results, reward you or punish you.

I am the fairy grandmother, my holy plant is the white elder, the holunder that blooms from spring until fall. I heal all diseases with it; it is my magic wand. Through hard work you can find me, through hard work I manifest to you and reward you. Frau Holle instills in you great creative energy, the ambition to gain further skills and information. I give you the ability to translate spiritual values into practical application, to protect and preserve your own life and that of your society. I give you youthfulness even in your later years and the curiosity to discover and implement new ideas and practices.

Tending my apples, you say, is such a humble task. But my apples are your sexuality, your fertility, your sustenance. My oven is the creative cauldron, where new forms take on life. Shaking my pillows brings my season of changes; your cooperation means you are participating in the divine creation.

When I release you into your own world, above the ground, you will enter it enriched and matured by my gifts. The sacred white Holunder will remind you of my presence. Be kind now to the old and the needy, they could be me in disguise, challenging you.

## *Capricorn Message*

People born at this time of the year are blessed with tremendous creative energy, endurance, and dedication. Some say it's an ambitious Moon. They have not only ambitions but organizational talent, which can make them excellent public officials and leaders in politics. The Capricorn Moon teaches us all to create, to shape and direct our energies into tangible results. Endurance is the skill to be learned here, dynamic efforts are highlighted, preservation of your self and your loved ones is your priority.

Now, when it is cold outside, is the time to busy yourself in the kitchen, making tinctures and salves and herbal preparations, and preserving foods such as the juicy cabbage, which is full of vitamin C and lasts so well through the winter. During the Waning Moon, plant in the greenhouse your winter vegetables and kitchen herbs, winter spinach, and leeks. The holidays are over, and it is time to get back to work. Store and cut wood, but don't cut your hair during the Capricorn Moon or it will turn gray soon, unless you prefer white hair like I do.

## MOONTIDES

# *Joy*

Joy comes to us like a distant relative. We know we belong together, we spring from the same tree of life, yet we don't see each other nearly often enough.

"You should come more often!" we cry. "Come every week! Come daily!"

Society doesn't glorify joy, only drama. We don't hear on the news that somebody's mother had a great day or that somebody in the office laughed his head off. It's hard to know just how often joy visits even our friends. They are sure to tell us if something goes wrong, but if something goes right, all they say is, "I'm OK."

We don't hear about joy often enough. Joy is the natural state of the lunar primates. It is joyous to get up in the morning, to share the first part of the day with one's lovers, children, spouse, animals, to share the breakfast meal. It is a joy to meet the people in one's life, to perform one's duties. It ought to be joy to have meaningful work, to get tired from having made a good effort, to come home, relate to one's friends, relax, rest, and sleep. Joy is actually present when you simply feel good. If you are not in jail or at war or sick, and you have enough to eat, joy ought to be with you.

Take a look at your life and highlight joy. What is good about your life? Write it down on a piece of paper. Confront it. If joy is obvious to you, also think about why you feel this feeling, and see to it that you keep it as long as possible.

You can tell if you are joyous because you have an inner glow. You may not jump up and down shrieking with joy, but you may feel like it. Express your joy as much as possible—it will deepen the experience. You may even dare to say it, "I am so happy today!" Don't be superstitious. The Fates will not punish you if you express yourself. Just add for good measure, "Thanks be to the good Fates!" As long as you give those old Crones credit, you can say anything.

Joy is peeking at you from the natural world around you. Joy is luring you to explore and to have adventures. Joy is what makes your social life interesting. People love to hang out with people who know how to be happy. Joy is contagious, like yawning. Joy can be spread out to include many more hearts than the one that started it. Joy is good medicine.

Flowers are connected to the feeling of joy. Buy flowers, cultivate flowers around you. Flowers really know how to revel in their existence. They are beautiful even in death. They show us how the entire path from budding to fading is still joyous. Flowers remove fear and make you think of fairies and wide open spaces.

## MOONSPELLS
# For Calling for More Joy

Magic to call joy into one's life should be performed at the Waxing Moon. Get three cherry-red candles. Gather flowers, whatever kinds are in season, and decorate your altar with them. When you have viewed the Moon that evening, light your three candles and dedicate them to the Fates. Joy is very much in their domain. Say:

> *Red is my blood and red is my laughter,*
> *Red is the color of life and of love.*
> *Gracious Old Ladies, who weave in deep dark places,*
> *Bless me with joy, and bless me with luck.*

Perform this honoring of the Fates three nights in a row, and burn the candles a little each night. The last night, allow your candles to burn down. For incense you can burn red clover. Once the spell is finished, dispose of it by taking a little bit of the candle dripping, dried flowers, and ashes from the incense to a living body of water, cast them in, turn your back, and don't look back.

# To Dispel Tension

I was in Canada, walking with a woman friend in the pristine woods. We were stepping on fresh green moss, on a pristine island. I could not imagine a more tranquil place on earth than this. But as we were walking together, this is what she told me.

"It's so funny to be simply walking in the woods. I only have time to jog here with my friends. I have so little time, I have to do my visiting and my exercise at the same time."

This young woman was stressed out right there in the woods! Can you imagine how much more stress there is for people who live in the cities? Stress is really a state of mind. I deal with it as a moontide, a feeling, because we generate it with our brains and experience it with our whole bodies. Stress is a twentieth-century disease. Unfortunately it can generate all kinds of other problems, such as short, shallow breathing, high blood pressure, hurried eating, neglect of ourselves. In the long run it can lead to major problems, such as heart attacks, strokes, and organ dysfunction.

To control your own mind (where good health originates), write up your priorities and confront the stress-causing overload. Why do you have to overachieve anyway? Why do you have to run and compete? Who told you you must live your own life only on the weekends? Who is forcing you to conform to stressful behavior? You may want to discuss this with friends or mental health workers to get a grip on your own self-imposed rules, your own expectations of yourself.

To help your body, investigate an herb called scullcap (health-food stores have it) and take two or three capsules a day to calm yourself. Avoid coffee and other irritants. Do some swimming or running or walking, and get out into the natural world without having anything else to achieve.

Burn light blue candles, a color that relaxes, wear light blue clothes, watch the sky a lot when it's blue. When you light your candles, also light some incense, such as sandalwood or rose, with a scent that reminds you of a slower pace. Breathe deeply and say as you light them:

> *I am the conductor of peace in the universe.*
> *My highest value is living my life fully.*

*I do not hurry or bury the moments.*
*I am the conductor of peace in the universe.*

To impress your deep brain with this message, do this twice a day, when you exercise and when you retire to bed.

# FESTIVALS OF THE MOON

Lunar holy days occur as the luminary is new, waxing, full, waning, or dark. Hence there is no firm date attached to the feasts.

### New Moon (any month) — Lithuania

The sun is female in the folk songs of Lithuania, while the Moon is male. The earth is believed to be their daughter. In Lithuanian folk tradition, numerous prayers are addressed to the Dearest Goddess and the Dearest God. Bowing three times toward the New Moon, young men and women pray for good health and happiness.

*Moon, Moon, dear Moon, bright little god of the Heaven,*
*you must become round and I remain healthy.*

### New Moon (any month) — Jewish

Women were given the New Moons to celebrate themselves, relax, visit each other. The New Moon is the Divine Feminine, the Shekinah.*

### New Year, New Moon — China

The ancient lunar calendar of China determines the time of the new year, as the first day of the New Moon as the sun enters Aquarius. In San

*Rabbi Leah Novick recommends *Miriam's Well* by Penina V. Adelman for contemporary women's rituals.

Francisco this day is always celebrated with huge parades. The whole town turns out, with girls' bands and boys' athletic shows. There are ancient musical instruments playing, floats with fancy dancing on top, speakers and representatives from City Hall. I love this holiday because sometimes it falls on my birthday, and then I can pretend it's all for me. At New Year's, the Chinese pay off debts, collect what's owing to them, clear up the books, balance their checkbooks.

The celebration is wonderful, and you don't have to come to San Francisco to observe some of the customs. Light white candles and sprinkle salt on them so they crackle. This is the food for the fire spirits. If you jump over the fire, bad influences can be repelled and your luck renewed. Firecrackers scare away evil spirits, clear the stage for the new. On New Year's, we pray to heaven and to earth, and offerings are made of ten bowls of different vegetables and ten bowls of different kinds of meats (for ten is the perfect number). A feast follows at which the ancestors are remembered.

Decorations include flowers, representing the four seasons. Orchid is for spring, lotus signifies summer, the *olea fragrans* means autumn, the flowering almond means winter. Giving oranges to the spirits is for good fortune, juniper signifies "honor" and endurance. You don't have to be Chinese to celebrate the lunar new year.

## Chang-Mu or Chang-O
### Goddess of the Bedchamber, Protector of Children, Midwife
### Thirteenth Day, Full Moon of January—China

Crafty Chang-Mu once lived on the earth as a woman, married to an archer. The gods preferred him and gave him the drink of immortality. But Chang-Mu snatched it away from him and drank the magical brew herself. The nerve! So Chang-Mu became immortal. She fled to the Moon, and there the Hare of the Moon gave her protection. As the Moon Goddess of the Chinese she is all-important, especially in matters of fertility. In the bedchamber she rules over romance and lovemaking. Her other form is the Toad, symbol of conception. Pray to her to receive blessings of peace and pleasure, powers of continuing life, intuitive aggressiveness in pursuit of wisdom.

### *Pilgrimage to the God of Wealth*
### *New Moon (Second Day) in January — China*

A day of pilgrimage to the shrine of Ts'ai Shen, God of Wealth. When it comes to money and wealth in general, all classes of people come and pay homage to the prosperous one. The iconography of Ts'ai Shen includes a surprising number of Moon Goddess symbols, so I suspect he may have been a she once upon a time. Now the wealth-producing box is part of his worship, whence all good things come, and it never runs out of plenty. The Spirits of Concord (Ho Ho Er Hsien) accompany the box, the good spirits of agreement and good will. But another icon is a three-legged frog, the Moon Goddess symbol minus one leg. What happened? Could it be the trinity number coming up in the number of frog legs?

In the worship of Ts'ai Shen, the Bat, dweller in deep dark caves, becomes a good-luck symbol. Other symbols of this worship include children, coins, and ingots. Surely this is the mother. When you pray for wealth, put some of these symbols on your altar, light lanterns if you can, or candles. The New Moon is a time of new beginnings. Pray and meditate over your finances. You might put your own money on the altar as well. Anoint the coins with your favorite essence and ask them lovingly to come back to you and bring all their relatives with them.

### *Lantern Festival*
### *Full Moon of the First Month (January) — China*

This is a Chinese festival held from the thirteenth to the fifteenth day of the first Moon every year. The lanterns are hung everywhere, on doors, on porches, in backyards, and even on ancestors' graves. Lanterns are colorful and varied, elaborate to simple. Fireworks entertain the folks, mooncakes are eaten, and fairs open where merchants can sell their moon wares to the devotees.

### *The New Year*
### *New Moon of the First Month (January)—Japan*

In both Japan and China, New Year's Day is everybody's birthday (except children under sixteen). Special foods are customary. The Japanese offer a "female" cake to the Moon and a "male" cake to the sun. On the domestic shrines the people offer unleavened cakes made of glutinous pounded rice. These "mirror" cakes represent the male and female principles respectively: the sun and the Moon. They are made up in the shape of a flattened sphere. In the Japanese floral calendar, the plum, bamboo, and pine are assigned to the New Year season, January 1–7 (or 15).

"The plum tree is chosen to herald the new year because it is the first to bloom of all the flowering trees. In Japanese folklore, the companion of the plum is the nightingale, which is a joyous bird in Japan and harbinger of spring" (*F & W*, 875).

Takarabune is the name of the treasure ship, bearing the seven Gods of Luck of Japan, which sails into port on New Year's Eve. Putting the picture of this treasure ship under one's pillow on that day insures lucky dreams. There are seven Gods of Luck, or Shichi Fukujin, which are one woman and six men. The woman is Benten, matron of music, beauty, eloquence, and fine arts. She is also a giver of wealth. What are the men for? you may ask. She covered everything that is important.

### *Pongal, Waxing Moon*
### *Fifth Day of Maugha—India*

This festival, celebrated on the fifth day of the bright half of the Moon, is an early spring festival associated with the beginning of Makara, the sign of Capricorn, which is also the beginning of the Indian new year. Veneration is offered to Jagaddhatri, Goddess of Spring, to Rati, wife of the Love God Kama, and to Lakshmi, Goddess of Wealth and Prosperity. The Spring Song, or *Vasant Rag*, is sung, people wear saffron and yellow clothes, and the cattle are decorated as well. People bathe in the sacred junction of the Jumna and Ganges rivers and where the Ganges flows into the sea. At Allahabad a monthlong fair is held. In South India the festival is called Pongal after the rice boiled in milk that is prepared in new pots for the festival.

### Lesser Dionysia and Haloa Festivals, Poseideon
### New Moon — Ancient Athens

In the Mediterranean two crops a year are possible. In the New Moon after the winter solstice, they celebrated the first tasting of the new wine, which was mostly a feast of the countryside where the grapes were grown, and the Haloa, or Harvest Home, festival, the Feast of the Threshing Floor held in honor of Demeter and Persephone.

At this time give thanks for what the winter season (especially the holidays just past) have brought you. Burn three white candles with your own name on them three times for blessings in the future and thanks for the past.

### Strenia, Kalends of Januarius
### New Moon — Ancient Rome

The first New Moon after the winter solstice, the beginning of the Roman new year, was the date when the new consuls took office. At this time gifts called *strenae* were presented to them to invoke prosperity during their terms. The gifts were named after the Goddess Strenia, since sacred twigs from her grove were carried in the procession down the Via Sacra in the celebration of the new year.

Think of it as Inauguration Day. Even in a year when there is no presidential election, newly elected officers will be taking office. Burn a blue candle in front of the national flag or photos of the new officials, and ask the Goddess to inspire them to do their jobs efficiently, mercifully, and honestly. Do something that promotes the kinds of causes you would like your government to support, such as sending a donation to an environmental organization.

# MOON TALE

## *The Goddess Movement, East and West*

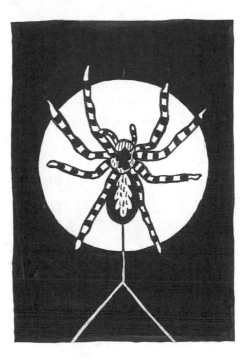

We are sitting in my Aunt Ilona's living room, somewhere on a hill in grape-growing Pomaz, outside Budapest. The New Moon is visible against the mountains and the faraway city. My aunt and her husband, Jeno, live here most of the time now that they are retired, a luxury unheard of in the old regime.

My lover Baker is traveling with me. She doesn't speak any Hungarian, but she is a therapist. She has this idea that she can study people by watching them. If she understands their body language and their voices, language is secondary. I worry a little that she is being left out of the conversation. I cannot keep up with my family and translate to her at the same time.

It seems that everybody in my family belongs to a different political party. Now that we have freedom, we get to choose where we belong and then argue about it.

Uncle Jeno belongs to the conservative democratic party called the Democratic Forum (closest to the American Republicans). Their platform won (through smear campaigning taught them by the American Repub-

lican delegates, according to my brother) in the first free elections in forty
years. The conservatives appeal to the old guard, they remember the old
hurts. They want to give back the land to the original owners, they want
to punish the bad guys from the former regime.

My brother, Imre, belongs to the Free Democrats (more like the Democrats here). Their platform is more modern. They say, "Let's join Western Europe, open up everything, learn to do real business with the real
world." Young people like this party because it is future oriented. They
don't want to go back to an earlier time.

My Aunt Ilona belongs to the Youth Democrats (because she loves kids
and has had many herself). Their platform is to focus totally on the future,
education, and children. Her party has no power either. The argument is,
if the conservatives want to give back the land to the old landowners and
to the church as well, how far do they have to go back to establish
property rights? How far back is back? Before the First World War? The
Second?

My dear little brother, now pushing thirty, how he has grown! I look
at his passionate face as he argues with his favorite uncle. He is lean and
sports shoulder-length dark hair with only a few white strands, the way
the ancient Hungarians used to wear it in historical pictures.

"You cannot go back in time and undo what has been done!" he
argues with his blue eyes flashing. "Will you give back the land to my
sister, who inherited an apartment house from her father but lives in
California?"

"Of course not," mutters Jeno.

I have never known about this apartment house. What apartment
house? Where? But it's too late for my newfound wealth; they are racing
on.

Another uncle joins us now. He has just arrived with his wife. His name
is Bandi and his wife is called Kata. Bandi is the oldest of the group, and
he takes his seat with the dignity of the elder of a tribe. I smell his breath.
He has been drinking already and it's only morning.

"Everything must be given back to the original owners," he declares, "especially what belongs to the church."

"Why to the church and why in particular?" I ask.

"Because it is God's," he says with conviction.

"God doesn't need property in Hungary," I shoot back.

"I was at Recsk for seven years," he says to me sullenly. A meaningful silence follows his statement. I don't understand.

My Aunt Ilona turns to me and whispers, "Recsk was the worst torture camp in the country during Rákosi."

Uncle Bandi was tortured because he was a landowner himself, which was a crime back then. Now I understand. The future ownership of the land is still undecided, but now Bandi wants revenge as well.

"Your party is full of the old regime's obedient pigs!" he accuses Imre, my brother, whose party is supposed to have a clean slate, since they are new.

Imre is hurt that his fledgling party has been singled out as the harbor of the old criminals. All the parties are crawling with turncoats.

"Jenö 's party is run by them!" Imre retorts, angry that his young party didn't win at the elections.

Jenö smiles. He has mellowed a lot. I remember him as a romantic university professor, buried waist high in books.

"The old party-liners are in every new party, grabbing for power. Like Saint Paul on his way to Damascus, they've all had a fundamental change of heart," Jeno says.

Everybody laughs a little, it's a running joke. Yes, reversing one's political position is happening in Hungary now in biblical proportions.

"I don't buy it at all," adds Ilona in her kind manner, serving coffee and homemade baked goods, walnut cookies, poppy rolls. "It's only a change of jobs, not of the heart." It would never occur to any of the men to serve coffee and cookies. It's women's job.

This is so clear that we all agree with it. Yes, the opportunists, the old power figures who have fallen, the bureaucrats, the military—they are all for the new freedom suddenly. It's a moment of reprieve from the tensions in the room. But Bandi is flooded with the old memories now and is getting more excited.

"I want them all lined up in a public square and flogged! And then shot through the eye! That's what they would have done to us!" Bandi cries. Nobody is trying to stop his rage. He leans forward with his eyes bulging out, yelling at me. "Do you know what kind of tortures these men used to do to us?"

Baker is a little nervous now. Obviously I am being yelled at, but she is not sure if I am in serious trouble or not. She waits.

"No," I say simply.

Imre, my "little" brother, jumps in. "You don't have to tell her about your tortures, Uncle Bandi. Zsuzsanna doesn't need to hear that on her first day at home."

"I wasn't going to . . ." Bandi backs away, hurt that his story must stay untold.

"Yes, you were," Kata, the silent wife, speaks up. "You were . . ." Bandi is caught. Yes, he was going to tell me his story. He tells it to everybody he meets.

"Why shouldn't she know about it? Why do we have to protect her?" he demands to know.

"It's her first day home," Imre says kindly.

"All more the reason to catch up with us!" he yells.

My lover moves a little closer to me and presses my hand. "Do you need help?" Kata soothes her husband. She touches his hand, gives him a cup of espresso.

They talk more politics. Politics is my family's main interest.

"What about the women?" I ask. "What is being done for women in all this revolution?"

Bandi takes a superior tone. "Women? What about women?"

I smell a rat. His attitude has suddenly changed from that of a tortured survivor to a that of a long-ruling feudal king.

"It seems to me your male leaders are all morally bankrupt. You ought to tap the fresh reservoir of women leaders."

"Women leaders?" Now Bandi is mocking. "They are worse than the men."

"How do you know? You never had any women in leadership positions before."

But now there is a strange new unity among the men—Bandi and Jenö, even my brother. They were clearly disagreeing before over every detail of their political life, but here there is a sheepish agreement. They have gotten freedom, they have power of sorts, but women—the idea of sharing it with women frightens the men.

"We cannot find any women to run for office," says Imre. "They are not electable."

"Women should get out of the work force and go back to their husbands," offers Bandi, who is obviously out to get my goat.

"Women are not available for leadership," Jenö states, as if it were a divine order.

I look over at Kata. Her face is as still as a deep lake. Ilona and I look at each other too. We are fuming. Ilona's face says, "It's no use."

I am really disappointed in my family. For a moment I wish I hadn't come home.

"You don't deserve peace or justice if you hate women," I say with biting conviction.

Bandi is stung by my words. His face gets red again. Kata looks at me in alarm.

"I don't hate women," Bandi finally says, "I just don't think they are any better than the men."

"You don't want to see them grow into leadership because *you know* they will be better than the men! You fear women making a success out of power. You are just a bunch of male chauvinist cowards . . ."

The last word just slips out of my mouth and I regret it as soon as it leaves my lips. The room chills.

"We are not cowards," Imre now comes back with real hurt in his voice. I almost want to embrace him and apologize. But I did mean it. And they need to hear my anger too.

"Sorry . . ." I back off. "But I get very sensitive about the revolution that I am part of. If you do not see women as possible leaders in your revolution, I cannot support you."

The battle lines are drawn again. Jeno nods. He is the elegant intellectual male in the room.

"She is right. We do hate women. Not the individual women in this room or in our families but women in general."

Ilona rewards him with a special respectful look for his bravery. He has defected from the men's camp. He acknowledged the denial.

I can see that Kata has started thinking this morning. Ilona gets up and takes the empty plates with her, only to return with more cookies. Yes, this is home all right, pastry, coffee, and arguments about politics.

Nothing has been resolved, of course. The land question, the woman question, and the male question all just get abandoned because we are too weary to continue.

Before Bandi and Kata leave, we all sing songs together. They are teaching me the old Transylvanian songs of longing for freedom. Our voices rise in long harmonies originated when Hungarians were still one nomadic nation, and the Transylvanians were the brains and the hearts of that nation. I am relieved that we aren't fighting anymore. We all sing well together. Baker is impressed.

"What a wonderful culture!" she exclaims. "First there is conflict and anger and rage, then there is confrontation and resolution, and then you all sing together. I love it." Secretly I am glad she doesn't speak Hungarian.

"Our mom always said you were a Joan of Arc," Imre tells me on the way home, still thinking of the visit. The mention of our mother makes all feelings of hostility and resentment vanish.

"Masika, why are you dead now?" I say wistfully. "We could run you for some office." No more argument from my brother.

( O )

After this scene and the general feelings about women I was picking up, you can imagine that I didn't expect anybody to show up for my workshop, "Gaia and Her Sisters." In a country where women are invisible, the Goddess must be also.

But through the magical workings of the Goddess I found four talented witches in Budapest. When they wrote to me, they sounded like any new group. They mentioned their desire to publish a magazine. I assumed it would be a modest newsletter. To my surprise they published fifty-thousand copies of *Boszorkány* (Witch) in a thirty-one page, well-researched, and well-written magazine, beautifully laid out with three color plates. Filled with pride in my competent fledglings, I gloat in ethnic satisfaction. Aren't we Hungarians the very best? Jumping two decades of process, *Boszorkány* started in the 1990s as the 1990s.

I am at once impressed by the new political fervor and diversity yet intimidated about doing my Goddess workshop in this atmosphere. The old houses that I remember from my childhood are still pockmarked by bullet holes. They confront me with their stark pain, they dare me to acknowledge them. "Look at me!" they say. "This is what war looked like!" Those images now live in my nightmares, the posttrauma syndromes, my eternal panic, my constant, agitated urgency, my fears that if I slow down, the bullets will certainly hit me. This is the material I still work on at home in my "stop panic" workshops.

My Goddess workshop is in a new building in the suburbs. It is taking place during the last two days of my stay. Good. Maybe more people will hear about it. But there is no mass advertising. Here it's direct mail only and word of mouth. Laszlo, the transcendental therapist turned spirituality organizer, assures me that the mailing list went out and that's all that is needed.

Mingled in striking contrast with the booming tourist trade on the streets we see our ancient cousins, the Transylvanians, dressed in black, selling their embroidery. Tablecloths, blouses, bridal gowns, groom's shirts, runners, white and black lace. Peasant women dressed in black offer them on the streets; they hold them out on their arms, dignified in their utter poverty; they stand silently in the subways; they offer embroidery everywhere. These are the refugees from Romania hunted by the Iron Guard, a fascistic organization still leading pogroms against Transylvanian Hungarians. What was once an ancient national obsession—embroidery—now becomes the number one cash crop.

I look at the stitchery carefully with my Goddess vision. Yes, it is here that the Goddess has maintained her symbolism, her sexy imagery, her colors of importance. The red roses have to have 500 stitches, the blue forget-me-nots only 250. The stems of the flowers look very phallic, the flowers, of course, are all like vulvas. Ancient paganism is hidden in every tablecloth, every pillowcase here. I shop for lacy embroidered blouses, dolls for our friends' little girls, tablecloths for my friend's mother, a black, long, shiny silk pleated skirt for me.

My family meets me at the workshop site. It is a nice big hall, and yes, there are people filing in. I will have an audience after all. My name sounds so grandiose, Zsuzsanna Budapest, the witch from San Francisco. Only kings and queens take on names of cities in my country. But not even they ever take on the name of the capital itself. I feel a little embarrassed, but this is my revolutionary name now. I have to bear it.

My Hungarian is rusty. I ask my audience to help me with words when I need them. Two elderly ladies right away volunteer words for me; they know English too. Words like *sexism, consciousness, oppression, male bias, self-esteem*. The audience encourages me to speak freely, they understand me.

My little nephew, Imre's son, wants to help with the blessings. He shakes my rattle just three times as I told him, and we bless everyone in the circle by singing out their names. Now for the chanting. We have no Hungarian Goddess chants. The Boldogasszony, our Glad Woman, has only Christian songs. We instinctively avoid singing those. Some of my audience make up a chant on the spot. We chant now wholeheartedly. The little old ladies are smiling at me, want to touch me. We embrace.

My Aunt Titi, my mother's sister, is here, surprised at what I do. Nobody in my family has ever seen me work before.

"You are really dancing there," Aunt Titi remarks.

I am also surprised at how well the work is affecting them. All the group is moving, raising energy. Scratch a Hungarian and you'll find a witch just skin-deep.

During the intermission I meet the press. Imagine, Hungarians making a radio show from this event for a special show called "New World." I appreciate these young men. They are not snide or cynical. They ask the right questions and not a word about Satan.

"How are covens organized?"

They are autonomous.

"Is there a strict hierarchy?"

No. How they run themselves is decided locally.

No, I am not the pope of witches.

How often do we gather? We follow the full moons, thirteen times a year for sure.

My nephew, Márton, is blessing the press now with my rattle.

I feel very excited. This is my own country. These forty-five living people are my audience. I thought nobody would come. The Goddess has arrived in Budapest. Maybe I can stop running now. Maybe this time I can accept the idea that the revolution has finally won, last year, and there is no more danger of being shot to death, tortured. Only hard work is ahead of me, and that is fair. I like to work hard.

It will take me some time to relax about the past. Women's liberation is far from being realized in Budapest. It isn't even an issue yet. The women do not see, or are just beginning to see, how they are already being pushed out from the process of democracy. The men don't see how they are shutting their sisters out of the future. It is all unconscious, and some of it is being fortified by the assimilation of values from the West. Pornography has arrived on the streets as the first signs of the "new freedom." All men are equal in using women's images for masturbation.

All men bond against women in pornography. Who is going to point out all these unpleasant facts to the brothers?

The Hungarians. I have had to travel back home to believe that the future is for real. I have to share my knowledge and experience until I make a difference at home too. Only then will I have my old home back, my own integrated identity.

Márton loves circling. He is only five years old, but he loves witchcraft. He wants to go on dancing, shaking the rattle, blessing people, singing out their names. The group has finished, but not him. He is still flying.

I see the future in his green eyes. Laszlo's little girl is in the audience, but she is shy. Next year, if she comes back, I'll teach her.

Magyarország (Hungary) is awake, painfully recovering from long abuse, groping for political answers, searching for fulfilling spirituality. The militant Christians are already evangelizing here. But we sing the old song to the Glad Woman, our Mother Earth.

The Boldogasszony, our ancient Goddess, has claimed us back again.

# SECOND LUNATION

*Time ‹ January–February*
*Sign ‹ Aquarius*
*Lunar Herbs ‹ Usnea, Angelica*
*Lunar Animal ‹ Dolphin*

# Quickening Moon

## VIEW FROM THE MOON

*The Quickening Moon rides through skies of storm and stillness. The upper air is bitter, but now and again a breath of something milder stirs branches beginning to blush with rising sap. Everywhere the snow is melting. In sheltered spots the ground shows the first haze of green. Moonlight shimmers on blossoms white as snowflakes, but softer, as the orchards—apple and plum and pear—begin to bloom. Shyly the world is awakening from winter's sleep, and the compassionate Moon of Aquarius promises that spring will soon come.*

## THE GODDESS SPEAKS
### *Kuan-Yin*

I am Kuan-yin, daughter of the Himalayas. Riding on my sacred dolphin, I have taken my seat among the stars as the greatest constellation,
Aquarius. The original sacred woman, radiant with pure compassion, I
shine for all equally. The poor of the villages still walk the well-beaten
path to my oracular shrines. There is always hardship—the women need
my aid in childbirth and for the health of their families. They seek miracles and visions. I am still the mother who saves the lost and the weak.
In the Himalayas I appear to the lost traveler in the snowstorm as Lung-
nu, the dragon girl. I show the traveler a safe cave away from the winds
and the cold. I banish fear and hardship by sending out my attendant Shan
Ts'ai, the God of Wealth.

I, Kuan-yin, come to the aid of those who call me by name and invoke
my promise to answer the cry for help of every living creature. I can
channel my healing powers through every woman, my voice comes out of
their mouths, my wisdom flows into their minds. Prophecy is my healing
gift to the soul. My shrines are always filled with candles of gratitude. The
Potala is my sacred island, the Ch'ao-yin cave is my sacred home. My
shrines echo with the happy chanting of my women.

I can reach you anywhere in the world. I am always just a prayer away
from you. If you chant my name, I draw near and listen because I am the
Hearer of Cries. The stories of my rescues are endless. I have saved lives
on the seas and in the caves and on the land and in the air. Kuan-yin, the
great Yin they call me. I am the All-Merciful Goddess, the White Moon
is my herald, showing me where to help the creatures of the world. This
was my pledge, and so it is today. I am true to my word. If you practice
compassion, you are my priestess. If you pray to me, I am your compassionate savior.

## Aquarius Message

This lunation brings us selflessness and impersonal love, the ability to care about our fellow humans. At this time we understand that creativity is a problem-solving tool. Violence of all sorts feels especially abhorrent now. The high vibrations of Aquarius filtered through the Moon make us all think of relationships and friendships and our highest and most altruistic values.

Respect and compassion are highlighted by the Aquarian Moon: respect for life, compassion for one's contemporaries, respect for the arts and creativity. This is a good time to practice any artistic talent you may have, read philosophy, debate, and brainstorm. Celebrate this season by doing your share and volunteering for your favorite life-oriented causes.

What is sown when the Moon is in Aquarius will not rot easily; sow and plant everything from which blossoms are taken. Preserve fruit, dry and store fruit as well. Pluck marigold, the healing herb tea for your menstrual irregularities. Aquarian Moon is not a good time to plant trees or cut them. Just pile up wood and store it. Moving to a new house is good now. Do only things that should last a long time. The time is favorable for business deals, correspondence, and writing books. If you are thinking about going on a diet, start it during this lunation in the Waning Moon.

### MOONTIDES

## Conflict

Conflict has another name: life. If you have no conflicts with anybody, you are not doing much of anything. You may not even be alive.

Having said that, I should add that I hate conflicts. My Moon is in Libra and I hate confrontations. But when I haven't had any for a long time, I miss them. Conflicts seem to serve me as well as harmony. In conflict I grow better, although I bloom and bear fruit better in harmony. Conflict is like the New Moon for me—it sparks growth and change.

Since conflict can be either positive or negative, I would like to give you rituals for both affirming conflict and resolving it.

## MOONSPELLS

# *To Postpone a Conflict*

This ritual can be performed if you have a conflict of interest with somebody and you fear you might lose your property or job or there might be a loss of power or influence. This is for conflicts that would take something from you instead of helping you to advance. If you think your situation qualifies, get a black candle (really indigo, there is no such thing as a truly black candle) and write on it a word that describes the conflict. This may require some thought, because you will not have room for a long explanation. Just identify the target and name it. Get some poke root (famous for breaking hexes or averting the evil eye). This herb is sold in occult supply stores or herbal shops, botanicas, and the better health-food stores. Mix it up with frankincense and myrrh (used for balancing energies)—a pinch for a pinch. Also from the botanica or occult store, get some dispelling oil (but olive oil is considered sacred) and anoint (smear) the candle with it. These oils are marketed under a number of names—repelling, dispersing, and so on. Sniff the oils and you will resonate to which is the right one.

Now light the black candle on the altar you have created to honor the Moon, and follow up by sprinkling the incense on self-igniting charcoal that you have already lighted (this is also available in occult or religious goods stores—do not use barbecue briquettes). Take a moment to savor the atmosphere you have created. Then say:

> *Angels of the shadows,*
> *Angels of the Fates,*
> *Ill-timed change sparkers*
> *Now go away from me.*
> *Grant conflict another time*
> *When I will pay my dues.*

> *O Fates, I beseech you,*
> *Let me go free now,*
> *Catch me the next round.*

Repeat this three nights in a row after sundown when you see the Moon rise. The last night, let the candle burn out and dispose of it by throwing it into a living body of water. Do not do this the same night, but choose a convenient time before the next phase of the Moon. Nowadays we take only a little bit of the candlewax left over from the spell, the ashes of the incense, and any flowers that may have been involved — just a small amount of stuff, all biodegradable.

You have not avoided your Fate by doing this, you have simply postponed the spark of conflict to a later date. When conflict comes, life is calling. Constant avoidance of conflict may escalate the problem.

## *For Acceptance of Conflict*

This ritual may be done if you have a fight with a relative or a lover, especially if counseling or discussions with friends has been tried already. Conflicts with your teachers, your place of learning, or about your future are the good and necessary conflicts we affirm and grow with.

For this ritual you need a white candle and whatever kind of incense you have used most successfully (white sage is my choice). Write the word describing your conflict on your white candle. Then write, "Let it be, and may I grow stronger," and say:

> *Humbled I stand before life's challenge.*
> *Angels of the shadows battle me now.*
> *O Fates, weave my life gently as I fight,*
> *May the outcome be a victory for all.*

Burn your white candle for three nights in a row, finishing it the last night, and take a little of all the material things used in the ritual and throw them into a living body of water.

Praying in this manner has a powerful influence on the matter, but nobody — not even a powerful and skilled witch — gets away completely without pain in life. It is good to educate yourself about fair fighting techniques and create safe situations in which to encounter your adversaries. Wear rosemary oil when you face your enemies. Its smell influences the minds around you unconsciously and makes you feel stronger.

## Compassion

The feeling of compassion is very familiar to women. It is the first thing we are taught in kindergarten. Share, play nice, don't hurt each other. We teach this feeling to our kids. The minute they start beating up on each other we start telling them about compassion. So the first rebellion against the mother is the rejection of compassion.

"Johnny, how could you throw that cat out of the second-floor window? Don't you care about the poor thing? How would you like to be thrown down from the second floor?"

"I just wanted to see if it really lands on its feet!"

Compassion is supposed to be practiced in schools. Teachers are big on compassion. They also provide the first examples of the lack of compassion that children are likely to see.

"I really didn't know about that rule," you pleaded as a little girl, intimidated by the flashing of her eyes, hoping that innocence would get you off the hook.

But you were still found guilty. The teacher made an example out of you, and if you really were innocent, you experienced the opposite of compassion—persecution.

Mother Teresa has industrial-strength compassion. She is a trendsetter, she has women followers, all dressed like her. A visit to any of her missions (these days her followers are working not only in India but in American cities like San Francisco) may be a heart opener to those who cannot feel compassion.

We all feel compassionate toward people we love, our pets, and now, we hope, toward our planet. It is people we don't know that we suspect. When we are ignorant, we are willing to go to war, but if we learn about the enemy and see them as humans like ourselves, we may find we are not opposed to each other after all. Sometimes people change. After forty years of cold war, the Soviets are now our buddies and trade partners.

The hardest compassion to feel is toward oneself. When you have no feeling for yourself, no love, no caring, you have no compassion for your loved ones either. You keep damaging yourself. You keep being hurt by self-inflicted wounds. It is not safe to feel this way. Your life energy may be waning. You get tired too soon. Your immune system must have your love. Compassion for the self must be wakened again.

## MOONSPELL

# To Stimulate Compassion in Yourself (for Yourself and Others)

Light a yellow candle (the color of manifestation) in the place where you spend most of your time. Keep the yellow candle burning there, perhaps in a jar, where the dancing flame won't set anything afire, because this ritual is part of your daily life. When the Moon has risen and you have viewed her in the sky, go inside and perform this self-love ritual.

Each night, focus on your dancing flame and say to yourself:

> *I am the child of the Compassionate Mother;*
> *I release compassionate love to myself.*

And now kiss your own hand lovingly. Repeat the words three times altogether, and kiss your own hand three times as well. Kissing your own hand at the Moon's rising is a ritual of unknown antiquity. In biblical times it was strictly forbidden. If you feel foolish kissing your own hand, remember that self-love is not encouraged in our times. If you can work past the taboo on it, more energy will be available to you because of the compassion released to yourself from yourself.

# FESTIVALS OF THE MOON

### *Sarasvati*
### *New Crescent in Magha — India*

This is a festival of the Goddess Sarasvati, apparently called either Besant Panchami or (more rarely) Dawat Puja (worship of the inkstand). This is the festival of the Writing Goddess. She is worshiped by changing the ink in the inkstands. Even if you work with computers, you may want to acquire an inkstand just for this worship.

In Bengal pens, ink, and account books are worshiped to honor the Goddess Sarasvati, Goddess of Learning. Though celebrated throughout the country, she is most celebrated by schoolchildren and university students. Of course Sarasvati is also a river and a river Goddess, who governs the flow of water and thoughts. She is the great flood of energy. Her image is that of the Moon Goddess, a beautiful woman dressed in white, with the crescent Moon upon her forehead, like Diana in Europe. Wisdom and eloquence are her characteristics. Barbara Walker (*The Woman's Encyclopedia of Myths and Secrets*, 894) translates her name as "Flowing One." She says Sarasvati "was also the Queen of Heaven assimilated to Brahmanism as Brahma's wife," but we must remember that she really "predated the cult of Brahma," according to Walker, and "invented all the arts of civilization: music, letters, mathematics, calendars, magic, the Vedas, and all other branches of learning." When kings were baptized in her waters, she conferred divinity upon them. She is sometimes identified with Vach, Goddess of Speech, who caused all words to come into being, including all religious writing (Monaghan, *The Book of Goddesses and Heroines*, 305).

To worship Sarasvati one must clean all writing instruments and dust the books, organize one's diary and personal papers. On this day no writing should be done. Rest. Then go out to see the Crescent Moon and burn some sage to her white image. Address her as the Queen of Heaven and talk to her respectfully, but as you would to a mother. Ask her to give you her energy to study, to write, to accomplish something great. Visualize her holding the pen and writing on small tablets. Pray to her for inspiration.

> *Sarasvati of the pen and of the ink, you have caused words to come to being. Eloquent One, open up my soul to your inspiration. Flow through me as your channel, make my words flow better and more clearly, illuminate my mind.*

### Birthday of Kuan-yin
### Nineteenth Day, Full Moon—China

Kuan-yin is compassion incarnate, the Great Goddess of mercy, healing, rescue, peace, and women. Just as Christianity allowed the worship of the Blessed Virgin Mary after the witch burnings, thereby including a female component in their religion, so Buddhism allowed the veneration of Kuan-yin, and soon she became more respected and remembered than all the other male gods, including Buddha.

Her official mythology is very confusing. She was supposed to have been very virtuous, rejecting marriage and opposing her father by entering a monastery. Some say that her father, still insisting on a profitable marriage, bribed the other women in the monastery to break Kuan-yin's resolve by giving her the hardest tasks. Another story is that the monastery was a hotbed of sex, and when her father heard about it, he burned down the place and Kuan-yin escaped in the form of a bird and flew to heaven. There she chose to remain in human form and help all living creatures attain enlightenment. This is the official story.

According to sacred scholar Merlin Stone, writing in *Ancient Mirrors of Womanhood*, the worship of Kuan-yin is older than Buddhism by far. She was the ancient Nu Kwa. Both Nu and Yin mean woman. The word *K'uai* means "earth." Earth Woman. Mother Nature. The great Tao. Our Lady.

As the Great Goddess of the Orient, Kuan-yin's work seems to be not so much helping people to achieve enlightenment by passing down prescripts or laws or imposing punishments as helping people simply to survive. Stories come to us from the Himalayas, where travelers lost in a storm are led to safe caves by a young girl. At other times women call on her by name when in danger of their lives, and she reduces their attackers to ashes. Healing stories are the most often told. Women pray to Kuan-yin, the great Yin, by offering her oranges and spices, and through unexpected ways healing comes to the poor sick person, providing another proof of her great power and compassion.

To celebrate Kuan-yin on her birthday, create an altar with her image (a woman dressed in flowing gown; she wears golden necklaces and holds a willow branch in her hand, symbol of love and wisdom). Statues of Kuan-yin are often available in Chinese import shops. Offer her fresh fruits, whatever you may have in season, and pray to her by chanting her name.

*Kuan-yin, Kuan-yin, Nu Kwa,*
*Merciful Daughter of Heaven,*
*Kuan-yin, Kuan-yin, Nu Kwa,*
*Bring healing and peace to our world.*

After you have chanted this for a few minutes, you can simply talk naturally to the Goddess about your own situation. Burn sandalwood incense and talk over its smoke so that your breath mingles with the rising smoke and your words get carried heavenward to her ever-listening ears.

Two other beings accompany Kuan-yin, a dragon girl named Lung-nu, her Amazon protector and messenger, and a young boy, Shan Ts'ai, who may be the same as the god of wealth. They figure often in her many rescue stories or when she grants a poor person wealth. Although she is Chinese, people of all races have benefited from her watchful assistance.

## *Lupercalia*
### *Full Moon of February—Ancient Rome*

This is a She-Wolf Moon, the Ides of Februaria, the time of purification and fertility. It is the magical estrus of the she-wolf who suckled Romulus and Remus, so their legend goes, and the season when real wolves go into heat. On this day a representative from the fraternity of Pan (the sacred son of the earth) arrived in the community to facilitate this very important ritual. He was a pagan priest, and he had many mysteries to perform. Upon his official signal the Lupercal began.

First a sacrifice of a goat and a dog was offered up to the gods. Both were fertility symbols. These had to be offered with great sensitivity and great care and respect. When the blood was shed, two noble youths were chosen as the representatives of the younger generation and their foreheads were smeared with wool dipped in this blood to remind them of ancient things. The proper response from the two youths was deep laughter, sacred laughter, a delight in the force of life.

After this they all ate the goat and the dog, because if you kill it, you must eat it, no blame. The skins were used to make whips and some decorative clothing for the priests. Everybody then went outside and tried to stimulate reproduction by whipping the people symbolically with the lashes made from the skins. Being struck by the whip was considered a good-luck charm to conceive healthy babies. The community was excited under this Full Moon, cleansing themselves from the burden of the old year and receiving the power of the new.

If you are infertile or wish to benefit from this ancient fertility rite, eat some goat meat or goat cheese. Smear your forehead with some blood, from meat or your own. Menstrual blood was the original model for this kind of life blood. Get lusty, and feminate (masturbate). If you have sexual partners, make meaningful dates with them. Once a year the mood of the Goddess is especially right for making healthy babies. If you want to participate in the heat, take your chance here.

Laugh a great deal. Go see a comedy. Read the comics. Listen to humorists. Eat a big meal. Party today. When you look up in the sky, see the great She-Wolf going into heat on this day. The Full Moon makes one howl, so merge with the life force.

### Powamu, Full Moon of the Second Month — Hopi

Powamu is the nine-day kachina ceremony held at the beginning of the growing season to encourage the crops. It includes dramatization of the return of Muy'Ingwa, the spirit of the corn and God of Vegetation. He is portrayed sitting within the earth, wearing a mask of clouds of all five colors (yellow, turquoise, red, white, and black). Butterflies, birds, corn, and all kinds of vegetables cover him. The festival also features the grotesque and even obscene antics of the Hopi clowns, painted in black and white stripes. At the festival the clowns act in ways that good manners forbid during the rest of the year, releasing the stresses of the winter through comedy. This kind of license is typical of many cultures at festivals, where a controlled environment allows things to be said and done that provide a catharsis for the community. Perhaps the loosening of restraints has a sympathetic effect on the crops as well, encouraging them to grow.

Seek your own catharsis at the time of this festival by going to see a good gut-splitting comedy.

### Rosh Hoshanah Lailonot (Arbor Day)
### Fifteenth of Shevat — Israel

Tu Bishevat, the New Year of the Trees, is held at the time when in Mediterranean climates the winter is coming to an end. The worst of the rains are over, and things are beginning to turn green. According to tradition, on this day the Creator decides which plants will survive the coming year. In Israel the festival is taken as an opportunity to cherish the natural world and is celebrated by tree planting on a major scale, and those who can't participate in person send money so that trees may be planted in their names.

In northern California the neopagan group Forever Forests holds a tree-planting party every New Year's Day and has reforested many acres of logged-out land. If you bought a live Christmas tree for the holidays, this would be a good time to plant it. This would also be a good time to reflect upon your relationship to the environment and to decide on ways to support efforts to save it at home and abroad. How many acres of forest in your home area have been destroyed in the past year? Who is going to reforest the Amazon?

In arid countries each tree is sacred. It used to be the custom to plant a cedar tree when a boy was born and a cypress for a girl and build the wedding canopy from their wood when a couple married. In ancient times trees had an even deeper significance. The images of the old Near Eastern Mother Goddess Asherah were carved out of tree trunks, and the original form of the Goddess herself was probably a tree. Her tree-trunk images were set up in the courts of the Temple itself and replaced after a discrete interval every time the prophets cast them down.

In Israel the feast for this holiday consists of the fruits of the country—dates, almonds, raisins, figs, and the fruit of the carob tree. If you are celebrating at home, feature foods native to your area. The following grace was written by Helen Farias as an alternative to the Hebrew prayer for the holiday.

> *Our Lady of the Harvest, our blessings on thee,*
> *Who appears to us now as the fruit of the tree.*
> *An apple, a pear, a plum, a cherry,*
> *Any good thing to make us all merry.*
> *The jewel of the branch, the gem of the bee,*
> *Forever the face of our Mother shall be.*

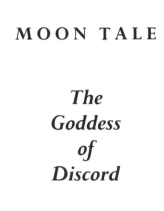

MOON TALE

*The
Goddess
of
Discord*

Once upon a time in my early feminist phase, I thought all women were good and nice, the kind you are yourself, of course—worthy of my trust, always giving space to another, fair, just, hardworking, giving. Being female was equal to being in a constant state of grace. A woman was good, solid, resourceful. I am grateful to those times that actually substantiated this theory for a couple of years.

Then came harsh reality. I started meeting the Goddess of Discord in her many manifestations.

No, she is not going to stand there telling you her name. She is not fond of the likes of us and will always approach cautiously if at all. You say, good riddance. Who needs to confront the Goddess of Discord? Aha! This is where she gets you, because she confronts you without your knowing it. She will sneak up on you when you least expect it, when you are the weakest. If you do not have a working knowledge of her, you are sunk, you are lost, you are toast.

The Goddess of Discord is a phenomenon. She can be manifested by any woman, but often she chooses women who are eternally discontented and then she stays in that form a long time. Certain women become

Discordians by choice, as a backlash to a past filled with servitude to others. No more Ms. Nice Person! Others are born to be Discordians. To be a true Discordian, you can never accept a compromise or even a victory. Your job is forever and ever to disagree, to disobey, to spread discord with vehemence, to foster rebellion. Even if your needs have been met. You have to be that dedicated, that committed to being a Discordian. Only then are you manifesting the Goddess of Discord. Only then are you really traveling on the dark side.

A good example for manifestation of the Goddess of Discord is Phyllis Schlafly. Here is an older woman who has everything—wealth, status, servants. What is her slogan for women all over the country in a similar position? Don't lose your privileges, she advises. Hold on to your female payoffs, whatever they are. You need no equal rights, no power, you need no government help. All you need is a man with wealth and you too will be all right.

She has been credited with having defeated with her organization and lobbying the last big campaign for the ERA. Now, however, the male Republicans have let her slip away into solid obscurity, which only shows you that being patriarchy's good girl never pays. I know that Phyllis wanted some government post as a gesture of gratitude for vanquishing the women's movement for a while, but she got no reward from the boys.

$$\texttt{(\;}\bigcirc\texttt{\;)}$$

The Furies are the triple aspect of the Goddess of Discord. The three old sisters are angered easily, riled up in seconds, their fuses are awesome and short. The Furies have absorbed an enormous amount of abuse historically. They know all the wrongs that have been done by everybody, and their mood is not gracious but vicious and vengeful.

When you pray to the Fates, you are actually addressing the Furies, but they are calmed down for the moment. One remembers the Fates with prayers said in caves and deep holes in the earth. Always offer three things, one to each of them, or they get testy (three candles, three apples, three cups of water or wine). The Fates dwell underneath the earth (in our unconscious selves). They weave the tapestry of life. They create our scenarios. They write our histories.

Alecto, the youngest, starts spinning the thread of life, thus determining birth and the brilliant chart of the stars.

Then Tisiphone, the middle one, picks it up and continues it, develops it, embroiders it.

Of course the oldest, Megaera, snips the thread with her shears. Thus people are born, flourish upon the earth, then die.

If the Fates are aroused to anger, they turn into the Furies. They have to be called down. Some fundamental wrong has to be done in order for them to fly into rage. A murdered child, a raped woman, a butchered mother, a slaughtered son, a wasted husband—these crimes make them care. They are the consciousness of nature herself. If they are then invoked, they hunt down and take revenge upon the wrongdoer. But there must be a spell that calls them down. What if there is no identifiable enemy? They will attack the root of the matter as only they know how.

How do they avenge wrongs?

Insanity, for example, is one of their favorite ways to get even. Or just terrible luck. Luck is the Fates' domain, and to have luck is to succeed, and to have lousy luck is to lose all the time and to be miserable. Sometimes there is talk about the Fates unleashing their red-eared dogs from hell, by whom an offender is torn apart limb by limb. But I think this simply means that the person who offended them is disintegrating, and his own bad natural conscience tears him apart, destroys his personality. Could this be applied to magic? The Furies versus patriarchy. The Furies against wars. I think the Furies must rise to make a place for peace on earth.

Today the Fates are still busy spinning their threads in those deep caves of the unconscious. But often they are transmuted into the Goddess of Discord, not really as vicious as in the old days but simply spreading a bit of discontent, posing challenges, disrupting events, sidetracking programs.

I have known several manifestations of the Goddess of Discord. Any group with more than three members may end up having one. It is good to get accustomed to the Goddess of Discord once identified and to learn her ways, because if you ask the Great Goddess to remove her, she may have to send a new one whom you know nothing about. And this one may be worse.

For years, our local Goddess of Discord used to come to Goddess events and sit in the first row. When we fielded questions from the audience, she would take the opportunity to cleverly trash whoever was speaking at the time. Our Goddess of Discord is fair. She really hates everybody equally. She would pretend to be just an audience member then try to steal the show. If we were not ready for this, the Goddess of Discord would take over the presentation and lay out her own views on the Goddess, which might conflict with those of the speaker. Before you knew what had happened to your presentation, the audience had forgotten you existed. She was that smooth.

I had various speaking engagements at which she did not show up, and I had almost forgotten the warning. I almost started to feel safe. This is when the Goddess of Discord placed herself once again in my path. She took a front seat at a women's conference, in my workshop, and I knew I was in for it. The Goddess of Discord had not been seen lately at anybody else's event, so she was all rested and ready to do her worst to me.

I gave my passionate improvised presentation, "The Temples of the Goddess," with color slides of the Goddess from around the world. I told the mythology of the Goddess that went with the pictures, and save for an occasional lapse of memory about the exact year the objects dated from or the area, I felt pretty secure. The Goddess of Discord's favorite way of goading me was by relentlessly asking about the exact date of the statues in my slides and where they were found. I had never been able to convince her that my primary purpose in these talks was to get across their meaning, not their dates.

But I figured that this time she must have a better plan for disrupting me because she wasn't baiting me about the dates. What could it be? To defend myself, I started telling my audience how sad it is that women have fights and never speak to each other again and what a big waste that is. Everybody in the audience knew someone with whom she had had conflicts. I kept to this theme, and slowly I eased in the concept of the Goddess of Discord. The women had never heard of such a Goddess. So I went on to explain how in every community there is a Goddess of Discord, who is placed there to further growth. But if the Goddess of Discord doesn't produce the positive growth that is the fruit of discord, she is not doing her job well.

The manifestation of the Goddess of Discord sat there serenely and ignored all of this. I explained that our Goddess of Discord is always appearing as a part of the audience, playing on the ignorance of the women at the gathering, and wrestling with the speaker, trying to make her look bad, and how this particular Goddess of Discord had succeeded in disrupting many events.

After this I went on to talk about the international manifestations of the Goddess. We visited visually with the nubile nymphs, splendid maidens, and venerable crones. We admired the colorful pictures of Durga from Burma. We looked at the rainbow-colored winged Isis, we admired Hathor with her horns, we were astonished by the beauty of black Aquaba from Africa.

Then at an odd moment, in the middle of a heroic story about Diana, the Moon Goddess, I heard the Goddess of Discord speak up at last.

"Diana is not only the Goddess of women," she said. I could hear that her voice was loaded with turbulent emotion. There was a lot more to come.

My lifework has centered around promoting the Goddess of the Moon, Diana (Holy Mother), to women. I have been popularizing an old tradition, the Dianic Tradition, which calls women together in all-female circles in women's communities. This reclaimed idea that women must have a spiritual tradition of their own had incited fierce resistance from both the neopagan community and the straight community. The neopagans resisted it because it gave the priestesses a special power, a tradition in which they could attend circles with other women and have a good time. The pagan men felt left out. The straight pagan community, which had a hard time accepting a dominant female divinity, accused me of making up the entire "women only" tradition because I was a feminist. This was a great compliment to me, because Women's Mysteries did exist until the fourth century, and I was only humbly reintroducing them. So this concept of the Dianic Tradition/Women's Mysteries was a very charged theme for me also.

"Diana is the Goddess of the Wild and of women. In her mysteries no man was ever allowed," I stated with all my authority.

The Goddess of Discord now delivered her blow.

"That is not true. There is evidence that men too were Dianic priests, and that men participated very deeply in her mysteries."

The way she said this! Her head was held high now, she stood tall in the room for a short person, and all eyes were riveted upon her. She was now the champion of men's access to women's spiritual stuff. And the way she stated it, she was being fair. She was sharing.

The men's groups have no interest in this, not the slightest. They are not interested in crashing the women's spirituality groups and making them coed. In fact men have started developing their own men-only traditions. But for the Goddess of Discord on this afternoon, men's membership in Women's Mysteries was a matter of principle and research. I was livid.

"Excuse me, but does this mean that according to you there can be no Women's Mysteries at all? That everything always must include men? Why?"

The point she was missing, of course, was that although in ancient times the Goddess was served by men as well as women in some of her aspects, there was a tradition of Diana (as there was for Aphrodite and several other Goddesses) that was for women alone. It is this tradition that is the source of the Dianic Mysteries we practice today.

"The Goddess Diana had a sexual relationship with Endymion, a beautiful youth," she said, as if she had seen them together just a half hour ago.

"You mean Endymion, the guy who was always asleep, even when his eyes were open?"

I had her now. This guy Endymion, whose existence threatened the female-only worship of the Moon Goddess, didn't sound like a hot date to most of the women in the audience.

Always asleep? they whispered. What kind of a lover sleeps all the time? With his eyes open? Is that symbolic of something?

What a clever ploy. She had managed to take control away from me. Some of the audience started debating the issue—Women's Mysteries vs. coed traditions. And then she escalated it.

"The Dianic Tradition is not necessarily a Women's Mystery cult," she said, clicking her tongue on the demeaning word cult *just to goad me. She turned to face my audience, prepared to explain her point of view at length. And I still had fifteen more slides to do!*

At this point she could have just walked away with victory. A speaker cannot be rude to anybody in public. It is an unwritten rule. You cannot fight back. You cannot call on your muscular friends, emit a short whistle between your teeth, and have Amazons carry away the source of your trouble. If you are in public, you have to be patient and kind, lie down, roll over kindly, and die. But never get angry.

What could I do?

"Excuse me," I interrupted her long-winded sentence. "Audience, this is our local Goddess of Discord, and she is demonstrating right now how this concept works. You see?"

A short burst of intense laughter rose from the audience as they understood the concept of the Goddess of Discord. The laughter was part relief, part amusement. The Goddess of Discord turned to me in surprise.

*So that's what you set up for me!* she was clearly thinking. *That's what you set up, and I walked right into it!*

The laughter had disarmed her. The Goddess of Discord had no defense against it. It was splashing at her like bathwater, like water on the fire she had lit. Everybody now saw how quickly discord could be sown among them.

There were moments of self-analysis. The women laughed at themselves, amazed at how quickly they had lost their focus. They good-naturedly acknowledged the Goddess of Discord as a powerful force and then settled back in to the original program.

There was a pause, and I picked up my train of thought on the next slide. As the lights dimmed again I saw the Goddess of Discord slip away through the door. But as she glanced back at me, I could feel her eyes say, *I'll be back!*

# THIRD LUNATION

*Time ‹ February—March*
*Sign ‹ Pisces*
*Lunar Herb ‹ Fennel*
*Lunar Animal ‹ Wolf*

# Storm Moon

## VIEW FROM THE MOON

*The Storm Moon views the world through a shifting sea of clouds, parting to reveal a world ready to burst into bloom. From everywhere comes the music of running water as snowmelt and rainfall gather themselves into rivers to seek their mother, the sea. This is a world in motion; everything is changing, but even as the peace of winter is destroyed, the new song of spring is growing in the air.*

## THE GODDESS SPEAKS
# *Sedna*

Oldest of divine beings, I am Sedna, Queen of the Deep. I gather my creatures around me to protect them from the raging storms. I am the fishtailed Goddess, the sacred whale who gives life to my people, holder and dispenser of all sea foods. I am the one who decides which of my animals can be caught and eaten and which of my animals you must spare or risk my wrath.

Men tell strange tales about me. They say I lived as a woman once on the shores of the northern sea. I was so beautiful that all the Eskimo men wanted to live with me, but I wanted none of them. Not one pleased me. One day a seabird came to offer me a good life among the creatures of the air, and I flew away with him. But the bird lied. It wasn't a good and easy life to which he was taking me but a stinking nest. My father came to fetch me, but the bird people pursued us. My father and I escaped in a boat, but the bird folk raised a great storm by their magic; the boat was low in the water, and it seemed both of us would perish. Then, they say, my father pushed me overboard. Hanging on to the side of the boat with my fingers, I pleaded with him. It was no use. When I tried to get back into the boat, he took out his knife and cut off my fingers. Then he shoved his oar into my eye to send me beneath the icy waters forever.

But that is their story, not mine. My story tells how I rebelled against men's rule, was degraded and defeated, and then found a new kind of power. You should remember this tale and learn from it. Cast down to the bottom of the sea, I made it my home.

My holy fingers touched the waters and created the sea mammals, the winking seals, the sharks, the whales, and all the fish in rainbow colors. My hands hurt when my sea creatures are senselessly slaughtered, and then I withdraw my bounty from the nets of the fishermen. I gather in all the creatures to keep them safe with me.

Look at the simplicity of my body. I lie on my side, and my huge fish tail reaches from end to end of the oceans. I hold in my hand a fish for you to eat, and I hold my woman's breast with the other hand, reminding you that you too came from my life-giving sea. Yes, I am beautiful, and sometimes, if you are lucky enough to spot a mermaid, you may lay eyes on me.

I am Sedna, the Queen of the Deep, queen of storms and tempests and hurricanes. Only magical prayers can please me. Call to me for good luck. When you set out to fish, throw into the sea a copper coin in payment for the fish, and I shall send you many. Call to me when you are caught in my waves and are afraid of being drowned, and I shall send you a dolphin to guide you ashore. Call to me when you need to fall in love, and I shall send you a gentle woman or man to make your heart feel loved and safe.

I am the original Mother, all creatures come from me. I charge you with responsibility for obeying my laws. Don't take more fish from the sea than you can eat. Don't shoot my seals, especially if they have waved at you with their fins. If you take one of those seals, I will take one of your family members with me into the deep. Toss flowers on the waters in my honor. Call out my name to the sea when you feel the need to talk to me. I am in every drop of water. I am in every fish.

## Pisces Message

This time highlights the nurturing feminine instincts and celebrates the watery life-giving powers in nature and women. Intuitiveness, creativity, solving mysteries, psychic occurrences are all part of the ambience now.

Now is the time to let yourself learn the pleasures of life, stop denials of all sorts, indulge in the good life, good sex, good food, good entertainment. Artistic pleasures such as theater, music, and poetry appeal to you now. Make an effort to internalize the Moon's Piscean influences, experience your feelings intensely, express both their positive and negative sides, allow yourself a time of intensity of the heart.

When the Moon is in Pisces, don't preserve vegetables, cut chives, or sow or plant anything from which leaves are taken. Do not store potatoes, bulbs, flowers, or fruit in cellars; they would rot easily now. Taking drugs or narcotics at this time has a greater effect than usual, so be careful. This time is great for getting engaged, getting married, or getting new friends, but be careful with your money. It's a good time for musicians to get together and practice and perform. Brew your own beer, make wine, deal with liquids.

## MOONTIDES

## *Desire*

Feeling desire is actually a very political issue, because patriarchal religions were developed on the premise that desire is not good for you. So if their unanimous paranoia about desire is any guide, it must be very good for you indeed.

The Goddess tradition holds desire sacred; it is yet another way to see the Goddess personally at work. The Goddess has planted desire in our hearts in order to lead us to our destinations. We have many destinations on our journey of life. Desire is the compass that shows us where to go.

I have noticed lately that all the things I desired deeply as a young girl have come to pass. It took a while, but they all eventually happened. Now, there are some that I wish had not come to pass but that made no difference. And I have learned more about myself from watching my desires than any other form of self-examination. Desire is the compass to the Tao, which is itself the movement of energy. The Tao is the flow of life energy. In order to access the movement of the soul, one has to have some desire. We all have the desire to become somebody—a teacher, a writer, a lawyer, whatever, and deep down is the desire to be happy as well. Later in life we become aware of a desire to know, to trust, to love somebody. What a noble feeling desire is!

According to priests and preachers and TV evangelists, we must wage war against desire. Desire is suspect. If it can't be eradicated, it must be stifled. And since the worst desire is carnal, woman and desire are immediately identified. When it comes to this nebulous feeling, this contemptible feeling, isn't woman blamed (remember the apple in the Garden)? The Krishna sect says it is woman who causes the pain in the world (and not men's own dysfunctional economic system) because women bring the souls back to the endless wheel of rebirths. They have the gall to complain about reincarnation!

Desire remains a hot political topic.

The desire for peace has grown in popularity. As more people desire peace, more peace is available. Disarmament is desirable. The desire for no more weapons must grow strong. It's good medicine. So are the desires for cooperation, health, and prosperity. The desire I would like to see stifled is the desire to commit violence, legal or illegal.

Desire is power.

## MOONSPELL

## *To Strengthen a Good Desire*

Burn a candle of a shade of red that makes you feel good. Project your desire into the candle and send it out in the universe with all your emotional energy behind it. Burn some sage or sandalwood or any other incense you are fond of. Pray to the Goddess of the Deep, deep in your psyche, not just the waters, and ask her to increase the desire in your heart. Then say:

> *Beautiful Sedna, Goddess of the Deep,*
> *Make my desire grow.*
> *Make it like a big huge whale,*
> *Let my desire roar,*
> *Let it make me waves.*
> *Beautiful, kind Sedna,*
> *So mote it be!*

When you feel the desire rising in your heart, light your desire candle and work with its energy (feeling it, not denying it) a few more minutes every day until the candle is finished. Make the spell last seven nights in a row or nine nights in a row.

Then comes the hard part. You have to let go of this desire and not think about it for at least a Moon. When you release your desire, it can enter the universe, because it is no longer tied to you, and it can make the necessary contacts to achieve its purpose before it returns. If you do not let it go, it will never leave you, and therefore it can never return and succeed.

## MOONTIDE

# Grief

None of us gets through life without experiencing a large dose of grief eventually. Grief is the result of loss or disappointment, the result of death or severance. Grief is what we feel when we lose a lover, a friend, a parent, a child, or even a pet. But lose them we shall, and we all hate losing. Grief is a deep and bitter emotion, it lives in the very foundation of our being. When we cry, our deep sobs bubble up from this unfathomable place. We shake with grief, we pale with grief, we throw up from grief, we are grief stricken.

Unlike rage, grief is not fuel for anything. Grief is the process of acknowledging an outcome that cannot be altered. Grief is part of growing up because it leads to acceptance of a situation and helps you slowly move on. Depending on the cause of your grief, different rituals can be done.

## MOONSPELLS

# For Venting Grief

The first ritual is to light a black candle and cry. Cry as much as possible, cry every day, call up your grief and cry. When no more tears are there, light a blue candle to calm yourself and just think about eternity. The concept of eternity is hard for us lunar primates, but, after all, we have invented it. Eternity is something we are part of, but only partially. We do die. We are finite. But our souls move past death and actually have another realm in which to gain life again. If you have lost somebody to death, consider—we are going to meet each other on the other side soon enough. "We shall meet again!" is carved over the entrances to many cemeteries.

Those who have died have deep peace. For you it is harder. You will have to live with your grief, for it is an emotion that never really leaves once it has settled in. My mother died eleven years ago, and I still can cry at the drop of a hat when I think of her. Those feelings of grief are barely below my eyelids. But I did get over grieving constantly.

Parents are expected to die first. If you have lost a child to death, that's even harder. That isn't supposed to happen. If a child goes ahead of us, our hearts will grieve deeply. If the child has been kidnapped or murdered or has disappeared, the grief is unbearable. I have talked to the parents of a child who disappeared. They were so stricken with grief that their own friends eventually began to shun them. None but a parent or a child can carry so much grief over a long time.

Grief cannot be channeled into anything else. Grief must be experienced until time—the all-curing medicine—comes to heal it. However, there are rituals that can make it easier to bear. When grief is deep and wrenching, talk to as many friends as possible and spread thin the layers of pain. Keep talking.

If a loved one has died, forty-nine days after the death date you can give a ceremonial dinner in the person's honor. Ancient people believed that the dead sleep for forty-nine days and nights before moving on to the other world, and to give them a nice awakening, a send-off party, is considered good spiritual manners.

Invite friends who stuck with you through the ordeal. This could be a way to repay their kindness to you. Cook the favorite foods of the dead person, set out a place and a chair for that person, with pictures of him or her, and proceed to eat a normal dinner. Leave the food on the dead person's plate untouched, and set it outside as an offering later. Many ethnic groups make the big party very happy, with songs and wine, stories and many toasts. This can be done annually, both to remember the dead person and to give you a chance to feel your pain but not be overwhelmed by it. (For more rituals for the dead, see *The Grandmother of Time*.)

## *For Grief over Separation from Someone Living*

The breakup of a relationship, divorce, a child leaving home, or a conflict over parental behavior—something you cannot change for the moment—requires a different grief process.

Wait until the Moon is full, and light a gray candle (the color gray is to neutralize) with the name of the problem written on it three times (yes, you have to learn to say what's going on very briefly in these spells). Locate a private spot outdoors where you can talk to the Grandmother Moon directly to her face. Hold your gray candle and tell her exactly how you feel. Say something like, "Grandmother Moon, my heart is breaking, grief is with me as a constant companion" and tell your story.

Then pause and take three deep breaths, each time thinking about how your breath connects you to life. Now tell her how you would like to see your situation changed. Talk about it as if it had already occurred according to your desire, saying something like, "Grandmother has understood my feelings and she has set me free of grief. Grief has lifted from my heart like a cloud. Grief has lifted from my heart like a breath. Grief has lifted from my heart like a stone. Grandmother has wrapped this stone up and put it into her medicine bag. Grandmother took her medicine bag to the river of life. She threw the stone into the river and it is now purified. I shall go by the river and pay my respects to the ancestors. I shall walk in the sun and the Moon with a lightened heart from now on." You need to repeat this until you really believe it. First it will be just you talking, but eventually your heart will want a break from grief, and then it will be true.

Do this on the three nights of the Full Moon. Grandmother does listen and she will fix things. However, remember that a completely trouble-free life without any shadows or sorrows is not realistic. All you can do is learn to cope with the troubles that occur. So be patient, and keep up your rituals.

# FESTIVALS OF THE MOON

## *Feast of Hsi Wang Mu*
### *New Moon of the Third Month (March)—China*

Hsi Wang Mu is the Lady (or Mother) of the Western Heaven, formed from the yin principle, which is purely female. Her palace is in the Kunlun mountains of Western Turkistan.

"The right wing, on the shore of the magic brook of the kingfishers, is the residence of the male immortals. The left wing is the residence of the female immortals who are divided into seven categories according to the color of the costumes: red, blue, black, violet, yellow, green, and natural." (F & W, 508).

On her birthday, which falls between the first and the third days of the Third Moon, all the gods visit her. She gives them a great feast: bear palms, monkey lips, dragon liver, and phoenix marrow. The peaches in her garden—female sexual symbols—confer immortality. Chinese women frequently do honor to Hsi Wang Mu on their fiftieth birthdays in gratitude for the menstrual bloods. Hsi Wang Mu is also called Chin Mu. Chin means "Gold," "Precious," or "Excellent," and Mu is "Mother," "Lady," or "Woman." Her consort, Tung Wang Kung, Lord of the West, is the essence of yang, but his role is secondary. Hsi Wang Mu has many children, but their father is rarely mentioned. This, and the fact that all but one of the children is female, suggests that the cult of Hsi Wang Mu is either the product of the matriarchal culture that still survives in parts of China or of women living in a society where, except along the coast, they control all domestic affairs within the compound.

### Feast of Anna Perenna
### Full Moon — Ancient Rome

The Full Moon in March belonged to Anna Perenna, Grandmother of
Time and Fertility. It was a merry festival, where groups of young people
went out into the woods together with romance on their minds. Some
reclined on the grass with their significant others, some built tents from
branches. Warmed by the sun, they shared wine and prayed for as many
years to live as they could drink cups of wine. You can imagine this was
a great excuse to get wild. For those who could still walk, dancing
followed. Anna Perenna was the Goddess who liked bringing sweethearts
together. Her rituals were their kisses and dances and the license extended
to couples to get together. On this Full Moon make sure you do something fun, something sexual if you can. It's a second chance at Valentine's.

### Feast of Holi
### Phalguna Full Moon — India

The Festival of the Goddess Holika is a fire festival. Spring Equinox and
the wheat harvest coincide in western India. Bonfires are built all over the
area, in both the country and the cities. The Holi festival is a mixture of
fertility rites and purification. The people throw colored powder (pollen?)
over each other as they meet on the streets, men squirt women with
colored water (semen?) from bicycle pumps. People wear their oldest
clothes, and the partying can go on all night. Bonfires are burning, sweet
polis are eaten and thrown into the fire as sacrifices to the Goddess.

### Birthday of Ch'un T'i
### Sixteenth Day, Full Moon of March — China

Ch'un T'i is the Goddess of Light. She has eight arms, to accomplish
eight tasks all at once. She is the Taoist Queen of Heaven, Maritchi to
Buddhists, the Goddess whose feast signals the lengthening of the daylight,
ushering in the waxing year in earnest. To celebrate her festival, light a
white candle on this Full Moon, write your name on it three times, and
ask for bright ideas and bright feelings from the Goddess of Light.

## Anthesteria
### Anthesterion Moon—Ancient Greece

The three-day feast that gave its name to this Greek Moon celebrated the new wine. On the first day the casks were opened and all enjoyed the vintage. The second day was the Feast of the Beakers, a public banquet. The major event was the sacred marriage of the Basilissa (the wife of the archon Basileus) with Dionysus, God of the Vine. The ceremony took place in the older of the two temples at Lanaeon, which was opened only for this occasion. The Basilissa (ancient Greek for queen) represented the land itself, and the ritual is clearly a survival of the ancient Great Marriage that renewed the fertility of the earth by sexually uniting the Goddess with the God. Oh, how I would love to have experienced these great sensuous festivals and tell the tale!

## Purim
### Full Moon of Adar—Hebrew

Purim, or the Feast of Lots, commemorates the story told in the Old Testament Book of Esther. Its celebration, however, seems to incorporate elements of the worship of Ishtar, ancient Persian New Year's customs, and Carnival.

According to the Bible, during the period when most of the Hebrews had been carried off by the Babylonians, Ahasuerus, king of the Medes and the Persians, sought a new queen because his previous lady, Queen Vashti, had refused to come into his banquet hall to dance before a lot of drunken strangers. Furious at having his will opposed in public, the king swore to divorce her, "for fear the women of the land would follow Vashti's example." (You can't give those feminists an inch, can you?) The most that can be said for the man is that he too was probably drunk, and the laws of the Medes and the Persians prohibited him from taking back his word once given. In any case, he chose his new queen, Esther (a Hebrew version of the name Ishtar!) by means of a beauty contest.

The prime minister, Haman the Agagite, was from a tribe that was an enemy to the Jews. After he had tricked the king into allowing the

Agagites to conduct a pogrom against them, Esther and her wise uncle Mordecai got the king to allow them to fight back. A three-day bloodbath left the Jews the victors, and Esther, Mordecai, and King Ahasuerus lived happily ever after.

Despite its romantic elements, from the feminist perspective the story is disturbing, but the festival of Purim is one of the most light-hearted in the Jewish ritual year. Today it is usually celebrated with a costume party in which participants take the roles of the story's characters. The tale is read (and sometimes acted out), there is a great deal of horseplay, and lots of food and drink are served. The special dish for this holiday is a three-cornered cake filled with poppyseed. The edges are pinched together so that the cake resembles a yoni.

Although the cakes are associated with Haman, the origins of the festival are probably the ancient New Year's feast celebrated from the New to the Full Moon nearest the Spring Equinox and dedicated to Ishtar, Goddess of the Fertile Crescent. The new year was the time of the sacred marriage between the Goddess (originally Inanna) and her consort, Dumuzi. Inanna was identified with the planet Venus (the morning and evening star), but she was also the first daughter of the Moon God and Goddess Nanna and Ningal. The transformations from Goddess of the Chaotic Storm to radiant queen celebrated in her rituals may have been identified with both the lunar and menstrual cycles.

One of the surviving ritual songs describes the procession (perhaps at dusk when the New Moon and the evening star shine together in the sky). Everyone in Sumer is there to honor her, making a joyful noise with harp and drum and tympani: soldiers and priestesses, respectable couples, youths with hoops, maidens, and male prostitutes fluttering colored scarves. The people compete with jump ropes and colored cords, men and women wear each other's clothing. Then the light of heaven appears:

*My Lady looks in sweet wonder from heaven.*
*She looks in sweet wonder on all the lands*
*And on the people of Sumer as numerous as sheep.\**

As has happened so often, the festival was given a new myth by a new people, but many of the old practices survived. Some friends of mine once attended a Purim party in which the guests had been requested to come as their favorite Old Testament characters. One of them went as Queen Jezebel, who tried to reintroduce Goddess worship to Israel and was killed for it, the other as Gomer. They carried placards saying, "Bring back the Asherim!" "Restore the Sacred Groves!" and the like. Fortunately it was a mixed and mellow party and everyone appreciated the point.

*\*"The Holy One," Inanna, Queen of Heaven and Earth, trans. Diane Wolkstein and Samuel Noah Kramer (San Francisco: Harper & Row, 1983), 99.

# MOON TALE

## *The Tower*

She pours her body into my room in long rays, she assembles herself on a chair with her evening book. Her face is impish, her exquisite white cloak rustles as she spreads her legs out comfortably. She looks at me.

Let me tell you a story about a long, long time ago.

What kind of story? I ask.

A healing story, she says. There is only one kind.

Will it be depressing?

Certainly. But the past is often depressing.

I can tell the Grandmother is already poised to tell her tale, she is ghoulish sometimes in her selections, she likes a good, depressing story. She thinks it's good for you. Her voice lifts softly as she plunges into her tale.

Once upon a time in Transylvania there was a very powerful bishop who had taken it upon himself to find the walls of the most ancient temple in all the land and vowed to build it up again into a new monastery and a church with high towers. It was to be so beautiful and spectacular that people would admire it till the end of time. This was his resolve.

He searched for the right craftsmen to build his church for him and found the ten best masons alive at that time. They were so poor that they hardly had enough to eat and survived only through their neighbors' kindness. Even though they were good workers, the masons were poor because nobody but the church had the wealth to commission anything. Great was the joy of the ten masons when they heard the bishop's plans for building a new monastery, a triumph of the builders' craft, a marvel for all to see.

They set out to see where the new walls would rise. For a week they searched for the old wall that had burned down long ago. They found a little marble piece in the hands of a swineherd; he showed them where he got it and said that the old wall was still there—a little of it, anyway.

The best mason, whose name was Kelemen, and his nine friends walked around the place. They felt great awe, for the Moon was rising above their heads. Surely this was a special place, for they felt the spiritual power that permeated the land and the trees and the rocks around them.

They started their work, and soon they were setting bricks with mortar to put up the wall of the new place of worship. They worked diligently day after day and month after month. But whatever they built up one day they found fallen down by the next morning. Whatever they built up in the morning fell down by noon. No matter how they tried, the wall they built so carefully, so skillfully, would not stay up, would not stand. This went on for three years.

One day the bishop came out to see the work in progress.

"So how is it that the walls are not any higher?" he asked the chief mason, Kelemen. "Why is it that in three years you have not gotten any more work done? Don't you know I need these walls to rise and be huge and beautiful? I want all the world to admire what I have built here for the greater glory of God."

"We understand your noble desire, O mighty bishop," answered Kelemen, "but the truth is that whatever we build in the morning comes down by evening, and whatever we build in the evening falls down by morning, and we don't know why."

"Then I shall pray to my God," said the bishop. "I shall pray to him and tell you what to do."

Evening came and all the masons lay down on their coats to wait. They all looked up at the Waxing Moon and then closed their eyes because they were very tired.

But the bishop prayed with all his heart. Then he lay down to sleep, and in his dream a dark figure appeared to him and it said:

"The wall is falling down because the old walls were cursed by the invaders when they were burned down. The only way the curse against the new building can be broken is by walling up a young woman alive. That will make the new walls hold."

The next morning the masons gathered around the bishop and he told them what he had learned.

"When one of your wives comes to bring you food and water, grab her and put her on the foundation, and quickly build a wall around her, as if it were a joke, and then when she cannot move anymore, finish the wall over her. Then the new walls of the monastery will stand up, and the work you do will show progress, and you will get your reward for a good job." And he left the ten masons to think about this.

These were young men who all had young wives. Many had babies. This job was their very survival. They hated this solution.

Kelemen called them together and arranged bread and salt and the plans for the church on a table in the moonlight. He said to the rest:

"I want you all to take an oath. Swear on the sky and on the salt and the bread and the church picture that the first one of our wives that comes here on Thursday morning through the mist and the dew to bring us food and water we will take and put in the wall and build a new wall around her, walling her in tightly so that she cannot move. You heard what the bishop said. Only if we wall up a young woman like this will the wall stand. Only then can we finish building this church and feed our families."

They decided to do as the bishop and Kelemen told them. Whichever young wife came to visit them first on Thursday through the mist and through the dew, bringing them food and water, they would grab and sacrifice, for the wall must stand for the glory of God.

But they were troubled deeply. Each of the young masons was worried that it would be his own wife who would come first. They all went home that night except Kelemen and spoke to their wives.

"This Thursday, sit at home. Do not come to see us through the fog and the dew. Do not bring us food and do not bring us water. Stay home, do not leave your home."

But Kelemen prayed to the big oak tree. Then he sent this message with a servant to his wife, Piros.

"I lost a bull in the thicket, please find him. Take your time. Then kill him and make me a good soup, bring it to me next Thursday through the mist and through the dew. You are my pride and my dear."

Piros received the note. She got up early in the morning, searched through the briars and found the missing bull. She killed him and made soup from his flesh and started her journey to the mountain. By dawn she was near.

Kelemen was torn with remorse now. It appeared his wife was the only one coming.

"Don't come. Delay, sweet wife. Don't come! Do not come and bring me water! Do not come and bring me food!"

His thoughts reached his good wife, but she heard only that he was thinking of her and wanted to protect her, which made her even more eager to bring the food and water, and she also carried his newborn babe in her arms.

The mason Kelemen watched the road and saw that his wife was on her way. She was the first, she was coming, she was only a mountain below.

Then he prayed to the good oak tree:

"Let there be an angry she-wolf, let the wolf frighten my wife Piros, and let the food and water spill, and let her turn back and go home!"

And behold, an angry she-wolf crossed Piros's path and frightened her, and she spilled her food and water, and her baby cried frightfully, so she decided to turn back and get new food and water.

When Kelemen saw that his wife was turning back, his hope returned that it would not be Piros that must die for their wall to stand. But Piros was a quick woman and lived not too far, she was the fastest walker, and she was in love. Piros felt her husband's thoughts on her and his love for her, and she set out again to bring him food and water with the newborn babe in her arms.

Kelemen prayed again under the big oak tree:

"O spirits, make the path be overgrown by terrible briars, make my wife delay, make the food spill and make her return to our home."

And the spirits heard him and they blocked Piros's path with spiky briars, with the thick growth of the forests. They tugged on her skirts, they delayed her, and she spilled her food and water and almost dropped the babe from her arms.

Kelemen saw that his good wife was going home again to refill her pots with food and water. He was grateful and glad.

But the third time he saw his wife try again, and this time she had brought tools to cut a way through the briars and weapons to frighten away the she-wolf, so he embraced the oak tree and prayed again.

"O spirits, you who granted me my wishes before, please grant me this wish also. Let a dragon block the way, let the dragon breathe fire and frighten my wife so that she spills her food and her water and goes back home."

Piros was suddenly confronted by a huge lizard. It was a very large unusual lizard, and it breathed fire at her, but this time she decided not to back down. She watched her step, quickly passing all the obstacles. She climbed up the mountain, shouting her joy as she saw Kelemen from afar. Shouting her joy, she called his name, Kelemen, to him to help her with the newborn babe.

When she reached the wall she saw that all the men looked grim and sad. Kelemen kissed her but would not touch the food. The others lifted her up and put her on the wall and began building up the wall around her.

She thought it was a mason's joke, but soon the wall became too tight, and she cried out:

"My man, Mason Kelemen, the wall is too hard a joke. It presses on my body, my breasts are flowing with milk, and my babe needs a drink." But the men were not listening to her.

Their hands feverishly reached for more mortar and more bricks, and their hands built the wall stronger all around her, until it embraced her totally.

"My beloved man, Kelemen, help me please! This joke is too hard! I am hurting, my breasts are being squeezed, my body is in pain, and what about my newborn babe?"

Kelemen stood there and he wept. But he did nothing.

Now his wife could hardly be heard, her words were swallowed up by the wall. Brick by brick her voice was no more.

Finally he answered her. "Don't worry about our newborn babe, my dear, he won't be alone. There are good-hearted fairies who will nurse him and hold him, the wind will rock him gently, the rain will bathe him softly and gently until he is grown."

The wall was still ringing with the mother's sweet cries, but after a few days the voice was silent.

The masons built a beautiful big church and monastery on the mountaintop. What they built in the morning didn't fall down by evening, whatever they built by evening didn't fall down by morning, and so they finished the magnificent work, and all came and admired it greatly. The bishop came on his horse with joy in his eyes, and he wandered all around the grounds and was proud. He thanked them richly, by name and by title, and he gave them the promised gold, and even a little bit more for their good work.

But as he stood there, the bishop overheard the masons bragging to each other and to others about how they had walled up Piros, the first wife who came on the Thursday through the fog and through the dew. As he listened he realized that these men would not keep the secret of what they had done and who had told them to do it. So he took away their ladders and their scaffold, he had the structure taken down, and stranded the ten masons on the rooftop with no way to come back down.

High, high among the clouds he left them. He left them there to be drenched by the rain and to starve to death.

On the top of the church they stood yelling and screaming for help, beseeching the bishop, yelling out that it had been his idea to wall up the woman to make the walls stand.

But the bishop was resolute.

"I don't want you to build any more fine buildings," he said. "This is the first and the last! I don't want you ever to touch bricks and mortar again. This church is the only building that will be built by you for the greater glory of God."

And with this he left them on the rooftop, with nothing at all to use to get down.

Kelemen and his nine men talked, and the nine young men listened to Kelemen, and he told them to make themselves wings from wood, and try to fly down from the church's rooftop. They all started working on their wings, they used up all the wood and a lot of the nails, and finally they were ready to come down. They jumped off the rooftop, and down they sailed, but their feet never touched the ground, because in midair they all turned into huge slabs of stone.

Kelemen looked down and saw the nine stones his companions turned into, and he was troubled. He thought about it for five more days, and then he made himself a six-sided wooden plank to glide on.

He kicked off from the rooftop, trying to fly. He was sailing down, but he caught his foot on the wall of the church, or perhaps it was the wall that tripped him and hung him by his toes so that he crashed down. When he reached the ground he hit his head against a stone next to the foundations of the church and died instantly.

They say that a little brook started up from the ground where he fell, a brook with saltwater, and they say that those were the tears of his good wife, Piros, who was still mourning for her newborn babe.*

*Based on a story by Mark Vitez in *Roumanian Folktales,* trans. Kiss Jeno (Bucharest: Kriterion Kiado, 1974), 184.

☾ ◯ ☽

Grandmother Moon is stalking my consciousness. She manifests herself in a shimmering silver gown with pearls in her hair for a crown. She is so beautiful and good smelling. I am sleepy and tired but her presence wakes me up and I open my ears.

How is this story going to heal me Grandma? I ask.

There is much to be learned from this story.

So the men sacrificed a woman just to hold up a wall?

Yes, the wall, which sheltered the bishop's religion.

And how about the other men who went home and warned their own wives? Why did they die?

They killed Piros. Good men when they save only their own relatives are part of the larger evil.

Grandmother, I think this whole idea about a live woman buried in the wall to keep it up is very cruel.

This is going on today, she says with sadness. Women are still walled up in institutions to keep the edifices going, their space taken away, betrayed by all the men—the good ones and the bad ones alike. It is a story of what it takes to hold up patriarchy. It is about the price men have to pay to kill their female sides or the women who love them.

That is not the only price, Grandma. Many women willingly let themselves be walled up, sacrificed, made immobile, in order to support something that is dedicated to death and not life. Survival often dictates to submit to the inhumane jobs, the exploitation of their bodies and souls.

But then the men turn into stones. That is their punishment for participating in killing women. They lose their feelings. Those who cannot feel are the walking dead.

It is a terrible story! I want to yell at her.

But the chair where she has been sitting is suddenly empty. She has sailed away on her last moonbeam. Probably toward Hawaii.

# FOURTH LUNATION

*Time ‹ March–April*
*Sign ‹ Aries*
*Lunar Herbs ‹ Raspberry, Strawberry*
*Lunar Animals ‹ Ewe, Ram*

# Wind Moon

## VIEW FROM THE MOON

*When the Wind Moon rides high in the heavens, her strong winds whirl away the clouds and she looks down upon a world of growing green. As leaf buds burst from bare branches, a veil of varied greens is laid across the forest. New grass in the meadows is already high enough to catch the dew. Shyly folded, the white and purple violets are waiting for dawn to bloom. The energy of spring pulses in the air, and when the moonlight touches each new leaf, it unfurls in ecstasy.*

## THE GODDESS SPEAKS
### *Aradia*

You are seeking me because you are in trouble. You know that you need to learn more about yourself and the world, and you are running around seeking knowledge, going to gurus, taking thousands of seminars, looking for holy men or holy women. Stop. There is no need for this yearning and seeking and unending insecurity. If you do not find the answers within you, you will never find them outside.

I am Aradia, the avatar of the moon. I incarnated as a woman and walked among you. I have seen your poverty, your desperate lives, your need for love and food. I shared your misery for a long lifetime, and when I departed from your world, I left my instructions about what you should do when you need more advice and more power.

Once a month, when the Moon is full, come into my presence again. Gather in some secret place—in the desert, a forest, the mountains or meadows, on the hard rocks of the peaks, on the sands of the beaches, in state parks and national forests, in backyards and empty lots, or even on the rooftops of your houses—wherever you can be alone with me.

Here we shall gather and adore the potent spirit of my Mother the Moon, Diana. She is the true teacher of all magic, from her comes the inspiration that will lead you on your path, hers is the magic that will awaken yours and empower those who are now weak and oppressed.

It was the Queen of the Moon who sent me, because there was so much pain and slavery among you. Diana despises slavery as the death of the soul. Freedom is the teaching she imparted to me, and by me to you, the freedom to live our lives according to her golden rule, "Do as thou wilt and harm none." This is the only rule you need. If you can live like that, you need no more commands.

When you call me into the circle, wear only your skin. Come skyclad, with no clothing to identify you with any time or century. This is the sign that you are really free. You are open to me. You shall be called witches, because you are the Moon creatures who have returned to me. You are the magical folks, those who break the patriarchal rules, those who sow the seeds of the better future. Whatever your trouble is, tell me about it, and it shall be remedied.

Then prepare a feast of cakes and wine, bless every morsel, bless every cup, and make a circle dance that wheels wild and free. Afterward feast in my honor. This will waken your own natural selves, will unbind your chains, will open the cages. Let the Full Moon inspire you while I walk among you, healing you or giving you balm for your ills.

I am still your teacher, the only female avatar, ignored for centuries, but now in free women multiplied. The great teacher lives in you now, in every breath and movement. I am waiting to reveal myself through your actions. "Trust yourself," is my message, trust that your body will know when to say yes and when to say no. The burning times are over, but before the priests lose all their power, they will try their hardest to destroy you once more. You must be steady then, steady within your new-won self. Do not delegate power over your life or your sacred spirit to others.

Heaven's gates open to those who know the way. Death you should not fear, my holy Mother will wait for you there. She takes good care of the dead and the living, she guides reincarnation, she will inspire the unborn to seek willing and loving mothers. Go to her in all matters, and pray to the Full Moon. The ears of the Goddess are open, and her heart listens to yours. Make music and dance, for that is your life. Let the sorrows melt away, let miracles unfold that will answer all your questioning.

I am Aradia, the first teacher and avatar. Welcome to magic, my children, my witches, welcome to the Full Moon's light.

## Aries Message

This lunation's energy is very powerful, filled with sexual energy, the will to make changes and to make love. Leadership is associated with this Moon, a quality always discouraged in women, but it is the female energy that is most pronounced now, because this lunation honors Venus most. Use this aggressive sexuality, this aggressive energy to change circumstances, plans, the world around you. The will of the Goddess is to initiate the ideas, the future, to push forward with inspired leadership, to make love with passion.

The Moon in Aries is a good time for mowing grass or hoeing weeds. Cattle should be taken to pasture, animals will remain calmer at this time. Plant strawberries and beans, sow and plant everything from which fruit or seeds are taken. Plant things that should grow fast and will be used immediately. Cut, pile, and store wood. Trim fruit-bearing trees and bushes in this sign. Don't do anything that may require patience. In Scandinavia the middle of April was considered to be the beginning of the summer half of the year. Its symbol was a green tree. Servants were hired, and shepherds abstained from meat in the belief that to eat it on hiring day would harm the herd.

## MOONTIDE

## *Boredom*

Although it is often not recognized, boredom is one of the major feelings. Even as a child I was afraid of boredom. When I felt it descending upon me, I tried everything to avoid it. In one of these feverish attempts to escape boredom I even taught myself to read. This proved to be a great protection against being bored. We become bored because our spirits are hungry for some stimulation, but we cannot find the one that is appropriate. So we are stuck. We are bored. What can we do with ourselves?

Boredom can be deadly because idle hands often find some mischief to do. Boredom can mess up a perfectly nice person. You do something you know you shouldn't and then you get into trouble. This is immediately followed by other feelings, such as panic, which is certainly a more entertaining feeling than boredom.

## MOONSPELL
# *Against Boredom*

To free yourself from boredom it's good to go hiking, get outdoors, get physical. If you have gone through all your repertoire of activities for escaping boredom and it's still there, light a green candle, burn a little sage, and pray to your most beloved ancestor to lead you back to your path, to help you regain your balance, to show you a new direction. Say:

> *Dearest [ancestor's name], I feel so bored,*
> *please make something move,*
> *make something shake,*
> *let my eyes be open*
> *and see what is really there to see.*

Repeat this three times. Boredom is the mother of invention. Something good will come out of your boredom if you have the guts to stick it out, explore it vigorously. Do not do drugs when you are bored. It may feel as if you are being entertained by your own brain's play, but actually you are wasting your time. Wasting time is not as creative as boredom can be. Treasure your boredom, make it into a teacher as we do with pain in the body, make it tell you where the next excitement will come from.

## MOONTIDE
# *Anger*

Anger is one of the most basic instinctual feelings. Anger is positive because it is not depression. Anger is active. It demands attention, it wants venting, it wants to act out. Anger is blinding, because you are operating from an adrenalin-induced state of mind. Your body can release so much adrenalin that if you weren't expending it in anger, it could kill.

But most of the time anger is useful. At best it shows you where you are most threatened. If you are angry about the same issues again and again, your lunar primate is trying to tell you to make changes, not just simmer in anger. Anger is diffused by expression. Express your anger as soon as possible and name it. Say that you are really angry about this or that. Feeling anger is healthy. Hurting somebody in anger is not. Anger is not a good state in which to conduct negotiations. Use it to identify your problems, but wait until your anger subsides before you make changes. If you are angry a lot, it is a sign that you are not living right. Constant anger is a signal of dysfunction. Investigate, see what's in your past, get some professional help, and change your life, not the lives of others (the latter is impossible anyway).

If you get angry and you have faced it, expressed it, and tried to deal with the cause and there is nothing left to do, but it is still festering in your heart, try the following moonspells.

## MOONSPELLS

## *To Manage Anger*

Take a black candle, anoint it with your own saliva, and write on it "my anger." Burn it each night during the Waning Moon. Burn sandalwood or sage every night and in the morning. Listen to a lot of classical or soothing music. Avoid spicy foods, drink a lot of water. As the black candle burns, so shall your anger burn away. Indigo is a healing color. Watching this candle burn will soothe you. It may even make you cry in relief. Give your anger to the universe, and ask her to use it for the good of all.

## *To Use Anger*

If you are angry righteously at a person or an institution or event, write on your black candle the name of the reason for your anger. The goal of your moonspell must be a remedy that benefits all. Light two red candles as well and place the black one in the middle. Create an altar appropriate to the Fates. Use triple images of the Goddess on it, triple flowers, triple symbols. Use frankincense and myrrh in your incense burner. When the smoke is rising and the three candles are lit, repeat three times:

> *The hurt that I feel,*
> *the wounds that you caused,*

*like a mirror of your soul*
*is three times returned to thee.*
*You will feel the knives,*
*you will feel the pain,*
*you will now absorb*
*what you have sent to me!*

Repeat the moonspell for three nights in a row. When it's done, cast the spell remnants into a living body of water and don't look back.

# FESTIVALS OF THE MOON
## *Hana Matsuri*
## *Eighth Day of the Fourth Month — Japan*

Hana Matsuri, the Flower Festival, is now a celebration of the birth of the Buddha, at which people gather at the temples, and processions of brightly dressed children bring offerings of flowers and hydrangea tea. In an older form of the festival, people climbed hills to gather wildflowers for the family shrine. In Shinto the spirits of the dead dwell in the sacred mountains. At this time wooden markers were placed on graves with prayers for the dead.

In the season of rebirth it is good to remember that without death there would be no room for new things to be born. Death and birth are the two equal and necessary parts of a continuous cycle of transformation.

### Full Moon in Aries
### Dedicated to Venus, the Goddess of Fertility and
### Love and Romance

What a splendid opportunity to cast love spells, to pray for relationships already established, to bless your children, your friends, your gardens, your orchards. Light a white and a green candle on this night with
your name written on them three times for good luck. Those whom you
are blessing should have candles with their names on them as well. Say:

*The world is opened up by love,*
*The world is blessed with love,*
*I bless with Venus power.*
*I bless the children,*
*I bless my lovers and I bless my relatives.*
*Long life, happy homes, good health, and good fortune!*
*Evoe Venus! Lovely evening star,*
*Star and hope of the world.*
*Grant that all these wishes come to pass*
*As the wind blows,*
*As the rain falls,*
*As I have blessed.*
*It is done.*

### Dragon Boat Festival, Tuan Yang Chieh
### Fourth Day, Full Moon of April—China

On this Full Moon there is a dragon boat procession on rivers and lakes
in the moonlight, bringing in the energies of life to the community. People
throw flowers on the waters to float downstream with their blessings and
wishes.

### Feast of the Divine Couple
### Full Moon of April—Japan

This is the time of a three-day festival dedicated to procreation. The
divine couple, O-Yama-no-kami and Kamo-tama-yori-hime, both have

shrines, which get ceremoniously blessed, then the two are brought into the main shrine, where they are allowed to be alone, mating. Children come and offer flowers, fruits, paint brushes, children's toys. Then a hundred men come and they shake the shrines for an hour and a half imitating labor; finally they are thrown from the platforms, which indicates birth. This is a Shinto custom, also dedicated to the Goddess of Midwifery. Make a special evening with your mate honoring your own relationship.

### *Feast of Elaphebolia—Ancient Greece*

The festival called the Elaphebolia, or Deer Shooting, was celebrated in honor of Artemis as Goddess of the Chase and of Game. Deer meat or cakes made in the shapes of deer were offered to the Goddess and shared in the festival. In her capacity as a hunting Goddess, Artemis is the classical Greek version of the Lady of the Beasts who appears in art all the way back to the Neolithic age and as Mother of the Animals in shamanic practice. She is both preserver and destroyer of the animals in her care; but she is the one who knows which species should be controlled and which need protection, and she is merciless to those who kill them irresponsibly.

Eat venison for this feast, or better still, cut out gingerbread or sugar cookies with a reindeer-shaped cookie cutter, and donate the money you would have spent on the meat to a wildlife preservation fund.

MOON TALE

*The*
*Witch*
*in the*
*Library*

I had just returned from visiting my relatives in Europe. My schedule was pretty free except that I was supposed to give a speech to teenagers, set up by a sister who worked in the St. Theresa Library in San Jose. She had asked me if I could talk to the kids about real witchcraft. She said the kids were very interested in the craft, and books on the subject were checked out more than any others. She said some kids asked her if they could talk to a "real" witch. She remembered me and called.

A lot of changes were going on in my life just then. My best friend and longtime lifemate, Kirsten, was getting involved with a new woman, and their romance filled my house and consciousness. They were constantly kissing and hugging and cooing at each other. My friends just referred to them as "the lovers." I was also in the process of putting together a new coven, always an exciting process.

But then the Fates intervened. In order to attract the attention of the rest of the kids who frequented their library, the librarians put out a few leaflets featuring a drawing of a black cat xeroxed from the *Holy Book of Women's Mysteries*, the words *witchcraft* and *Goddess lecture* and my name along with the time and place of the speech. It was a humorous leaflet, not intended to shock or scare.

But one boy, whose mother was a militant Christian, took home a leaflet. The mother of the boy took her leaflet to church, and as the congregants testified about the devil's latest doings, she stood up and showed them the evidence that a witch was going to give a speech in the library to kids. She wanted it to stop.

The preacher recognized a splendid opportunity for publicity and militance, and members of the congregation decided to do something about my speech at the library. They took the guilty leaflet with the black cat to the city council and gave it to their very own fundamentalist councilwoman. She took a look at it, and there was the official stamp of the city of San Jose right above the black cat's head. When she found out that I was going to be paid for my services by the library, she thought she had found a weakness. She claimed the speech should be stopped, because the city, as part of the state, could not sponsor something religious, such as witchcraft. It was a good plan.

But it didn't work.

"We believe the speech does not violate the First Amendment," said the deputy attorney. "The witch can speak" was her ruling (*San Jose Mercury News,* July 13, 1986).

Of course this resulted in some concerted whining from the fundies from Los Gatos, where stopping my speech had now become part of a spirited crusade against Satan. Next the preachers ordered their people to inundate the small library with a letter-writing campaign and phone calls, which tied up all their phone lines for days.

This was when the same librarian sister who had invited me in the first place called.

"Are you aware of what is happening about your speech down here?" she asked.

"No. I am still unpacking my clothes from my trip and interviewing women for the new coven."

"Well, brace yourself. The born-again Christians are up in arms against you. They have threatened to demonstrate against your speech in front of the library. They are calling all the media, and we are getting a lot of calls, both pro and con. Nothing like this has ever happened here before. Of course you can just cancel, Z. I want you to have that option," she said.

"Cancel? Never!" was my immediate gut reaction.

"I have four planets in Aries, including my Mars. I do not back away from challenges," I said proudly. There is always a little extra pride in my voice when it comes to my astrological chart. I am an Aquarian, after all.

"So you are still going to come?" she asked

"I sure am. I think it will be good for the fundies to see a woman talking about the Goddess."

"They'll be there!" my friend assured me. "And so will the media."

Even after she had hung up I still didn't get it. What was the big deal? A small slide show to the kids, explanations about the Goddesses, the earth religions, some historical background. What was wrong with these people? Didn't they appreciate knowledge?

The next few days turned my life into a nightmare.

When the word went out that my speech was going to take place, no matter what, and that the witch was not backing out, the media and my Christian enemies found me. For the next week and half "the witch in the library" made headlines from coast to coast. My brother in Budapest heard about it on the Hungarian radio. He called in panic.

"I heard that the Christians have beaten you up! Is it true?"

"No! Where did get that idea?"

"The Hungarian radio is talking about this Hungarian woman who is being attacked by the fundamentalist Christians."

"They wish," I assured Imre. "Just go to the cemetery and tell our mom that I need her badly. It's time to come to her daughter's aid."

Imagine getting up in the morning and finding that your answering machine has filled up during the night with calls. Curiously you begin to listen to the messages and this is what you find.

"Hey witch, I just want you to know, if you come to San Jose, you will never go home again."

"The Lord despises witches. You are evil, and you don't even know it. Give up your evil intent and leave the little children alone."

" 'Thou shalt not suffer a witch to live,' remember that, witch."

"I am furious. They are banning prayer at school, yet they pay you to come to spread your weird beliefs to little children. Shame on you!"

"The Lord told me to kill you. He talked to me last night, and he told me to kill you."

This was the last straw. I took out the tape and called the San Jose police department. I explained who I was.

"Yes, Ms. Budapest, we know who you are," was the reply.

"I am receiving daily death threats. What shall I do?" I asked naively.

"Cancel the speech," said the good peace officer. "That would be safest."

"I don't want to cancel my speech. I have never ever canceled a commitment, and I am not going to start now. But I am not willing to die for a slide show either. Can I have police protection, please?"

There was a silence on the other line.

"I read in the papers that there will be some hundreds and hundreds of demonstrators bused in for the demonstration from out of town," I said.

"Yes, we heard that too. About five hundred protestors are expected."

"That is a lot of mad people, who wish to harm me personally. I want police protection," I said resolutely. "Can you protect me?"

"I'll call you right back," said the officer.

What if the police were part of the brownshirt mentality? What if they thought I should get what's coming to me for giving a speech about the Goddess. What if . . . I agonized.

The phone rang.

"We can give you fifteen officers, and four snipers," said the voice on the other end. What a fine, deep voice it was. It was the greatest thing I had heard for a long time.

"Thank you, officers! You are all real swell down there!" I was so grateful to him.

"Just let us know your movements, where you are coming in, where you will be getting ready. We will escort you into the building, and we will escort you out of the building, and we'll even drive with you until you have safely left San Jose."

The Goddess had provided!

So it came to pass that I had police protection against the born-again Christians! Times have sure changed since the police were one with the state and could burn or torture anybody accused of witchcraft at their whim. Still, it became very scary as the days passed and the date of my speech drew near.

One TV crew after another marched through my office, mostly news shows. I even did some long-distance radio interviews. This danger had made me more alert and my mind worked faster, and I was able to handle all that came my way. My picture was on the front cover of the *San Francisco Chronicle,* the *San Jose Mercury News,* and of course on tele-vison with every evening news show. Social commentators wrote about the "witch in the library," but they didn't bother to talk to me. But those reporters who did talk with me quoted me correctly, another great blessing from the divine Mother, and one not to be taken for granted.

"The Earth is my Holy Mother," I was quoted. "Beyond nature there is only more nature." "There is no heaven and no hell, both are right here." "Witches don't have a devil, we don't worship male gods in the first place." "The devil and satan are Christian gods."

If only because of this, the ordeal was worth it. It gave me so many opportunities to respond to the charges against witches, the lies, the propaganda, the age-old denial that the darkness they were projecting onto me originated from themselves. Millions of people heard my lines, read my arguments, saw my face. I think it made friends for witches, friends for the Goddess.

The neopagan community also responded with vigor to the newspaper articles, and they decided to show up and give me support. My speech was to begin at 1:00 P.M. The protestors were lined up in front of the library even before it opened at nine in the morning. But so were the blessed neopagans, and they brought their kids along.

The pagans came dressed as they would be at work or any ordinary occasion. The fundamentalist protestors found themselves mingling with the neopagans because they could not to tell by looking that they were the "other." Some of them even sang together before they realized that they were praying with the opposition. The witches enjoyed the shock they created.

While the opposition was giving statements like "We are not interested in what the witch has to say, we are only here to take up seats, so that small children don't get exposed to this" (*Bangor Daily News*, July 14, 1986), others on my side also gave statements. "Everyone here is passing out judgments on everybody else, no one is being very open minded. They are all tripping out because the witch doesn't believe as they do" (*San Jose Mercury News*, July 13, 1986).

Before I left for the library I prayed to my grandmother, who was a famous orator.

"Please, grandmother, if this is too dangerous, if my life is really in danger, please give me a sign. If I can serve you better, I'll back away from this. But if you think I should go ahead, please surround me with your shield, make my senses sharp, my reflexes quick, and my speech good." I listened deeply to my inner voices, and I heard the following: "Take out the naked Goddesses from your slide show."

Was that all? Marvelous! I was not going to be killed. I just had to make sure all the Goddess slides I was showing were clothed!

So I pored over the slides. This was the traveling Goddess temple, my slide show, with two hundred or three hundred slides. I had many choices, so I pulled the ones that showed a breast, a butt, a hip naked. I kept only the fully clothed ones. There were plenty more images where they come from. I was smiling. This was not difficult nor was I compromising any of my principles.

"Ask my great-grandson to help," said the voice after I had finished.

Great idea! My older son was a marine fighter pilot. Would it not be a fine sight if he could come with me, stand there at attention, and break the bones of any fundies who came too near me?

I called Laz.

"Sweetheart, do you remember about five years ago when you buzzed Daytona Beach and got arrested on a felony and had no money, and I breezed into the city and hired a good lawyer for you and got you off practically scot-free?"

"Yeah, Mom. What about it?"

"Do you remember that in a moment of wild gratitude you said to me, 'Mom, I owe you one'?"

"Yeah . . ." He wasn't sure where I was heading. He waited.

"Well, I'd like to collect that favor now."

"Mom, what kind of trouble are you in?"

"The militant Christians have threatened my life. I am getting death threats daily. Many of them. Want to hear some?"

"No, I believe you. Is this about that speech? I read something."

"It is."

"What do you need?" That's my son, bless him. What a fine friend.

"Please come with me to the library, and when I am explaining the slides and turn my back, stay behind me so that nobody can rush up and stab me. And keep an eye out for guns. The lights will be dimmed a little so that the slides can be seen."

"Do you really need to dim the lights, Mom? How am I going to spot guns in the darkness?"

"By instinct my son. Instinct." This seemed to satisfy him.

"You will be not alone," I added. "I have police protection also."

"Police protection?"

"They will escort me to and from the library and surround the audience and look for guns too. You, my love, will be there for me as an emotional support. A personal bodyguard. I feel I can let go of fear if you are in back of me. I cannot give a speech in front of a totally hostile audience, worry about my safety, and do a good job. You will be my peace of mind."

"No problem," he answered suddenly. I felt his warmth, a connection with old times when I was the peace of mind for him and his brother;

when I walked with them to school or picked them up or took them to swim or taught them how to ride their bikes.

One more helper arrived. Phyllis Chesler, my longtime friend, volunteered to face the "vultures" with me. Phyllis has a keen sense of history. She herself has risked her life often for causes she believed in. She opened the Torah and prayed with women at the Wailing Wall. Historical confrontations interest Phyllis.

She drove to the library with me. We sat in the car holding hands, assuring each other of support.

"Now darling, if you need me," she said, "just tell me what to do. I speak to reporters, I speak to crowds."

"How are you at running from gunfire?" I inquired.

Laz was sitting stiffly at attention beside us. He was out of uniform, of course, but his body language would tell anyone he was a marine. Kirsten and the new lover suspended their honeymooning for the afternoon. In fact they looked a bit shaken. I wanted this all to be over with as soon as possible so that I could resume normal life.

What normal life? I never had any, it occurred to me. This is my life—one confrontation after another, some friendly, some not.

As we neared the rendezvous point, four black police cars flanked us, two in front and two in the back. For a moment it felt quite presidential. I was tempted to wave elegantly with just one hand, like Queen Elizabeth, but I controlled the impulse.

As we came to a traffic jam, my son looked out and exclaimed. "Holy shit, Mom! They're all over the place!"

"Who?" I asked, still thinking it was a traffic jam.

"Your demonstrators!"

Phyllis and I poked our heads out of the window and saw the police car slowly clear the way for us. The cops even put on their flashing lights, and the demonstrators parted like the Red Sea. I saw hundreds of angry white faces, no blacks or Asians or Latinas here. The white, born-again Christians were still pouring out of the buses that had delivered them to the library.

"These people are from out of town!" I exclaimed. "Where do they get them from?"

"The Seven Hundred Club was offering them free transportation if they would come to protest," said Kirsten, who was driving. She looked rather pale.

We were usually the ones who did the demonstrating. We were the ones with the protest signs, the flags, the slogans. End the War! Free Women! End Hunger! Abolish the military! Vote for women! ERA Now! Women Choose! The Goddess Is Alive!"

Today we were on the receiving end of this kind of freedom. Well, it was an experience.

My heart started pumping, and my mind flooded with impressions, but deep down I felt I was going to be all right. Now it was a huge challenge. We pulled up behind the library and the police accompanied me from the car to a back door.

I paused before I ducked into the doorway and looked back.

Cameras. TV crews. Reporters shouting as if it were a press conference. Some I recognized from the many home interviews. Some had become friends and they waved encouragingly. And there was another face I recognized, from the leading gay paper in San Francisco. She was also waving and I waved back to her.

This was a miracle. She was the editor with whom I had had an ongoing struggle to give more exposure to women's spirituality in the gay community. For years she had responded that spirituality was not a priority for her. And if it wasn't her priority, the Goddess was never going to be in the paper, since she controlled all that went in.

*Spirituality is not political? Take a look at this uproar,* I thought. *Look how threatened the fundamentalists get when the Goddess is mentioned. Don't you see that the spiritual is the political too?*

I had a sense that she had started to get it. Maybe. Often the leaders are the last to understand that a new phenomenon is afoot. In the ten years I had lived in the Bay Area, never once was my Goddess work discussed in the local gay paper. My events went unreviewed, as did my books.

Inside the library the police stayed with me, waiting for my lecture to start. My son talked to them about F-17s and F-16s, and they started changing their minds about me. After all, I couldn't be a Satanist if my son was a flying marine, now could I?

I was looking at the day's cartoon from the *San Francisco Chronicle*. It was a pyre, with a witch tied to the stake with her back to the reader. But instead of logs, the kindling stacked beneath her was books—all those classic books the fundamentalists tried to ban, like *The Grapes of Wrath*, *Little Red Riding Hood*, *Huckleberry Finn*. Two potbellied guys were chatting to each other beside the witch's pyre in front of the library building. "Good thing we're near a library!" one was saying as other one held a lit torch and smiled. When I looked closer at this cartoon, I could see that the books were already smoking, already burning.

We gave our opposition fifteen minutes to dominate the stage. Unheard-of generosity. I was advised to let them vent their venom—it would help to keep them quiet during the lecture.

For the first time I was in the same room with my accusers. A red-haired, angry priest, frothing at the mouth from too much talking and not enough swallowing, denounced me as a Satanist. He shouted that he was only protecting the innocent children from me. He was the male mother, fighting the evil woman.

I looked around the room. Rows and rows of self-proclaimed Christians were sitting there, staring at the Bibles in their hands, averting their eyes from me. The preacher went on and on. I was nearing the end of my generosity.

"Dearest Goddess," I prayed as my first words. "Find me a place! Put to shame all those who would destroy my good name!" I prayed in front of them, I called on my Goddess for help.

My first slide is always the blue planet Earth.

"This is God!" I said, facing them. They averted their eyes from my slide of the Earth.

"She is the interconnectedness of all life, she is a breathing, living sister, she is part of the universe, and she is the mother of us all. She has created us, she has sustained us, she will bury us and give us new forms . . ."

The fundies were praying aloud so that they could drown out my voice. I was speaking heresies. I felt my son move silently right behind me. I could feel his strong, young body with my back.

I went on to explain the job requirements for being God. You have to be able to create life from small particles and create life so that it perpetuates itself. All of these Mother Earth has done eminently well.

"There is no hell and no heaven." I pointed to the blue planet as she had been photographed by the astronauts from space. "There is only a journey through space, a destination known only to her. We are part of her, but we are also her guests."

They prayed even louder now. Their mumbling and gibberish, which was supposed to be "speaking in tongues," filled the hall. They were feeling their power, they were going to show the witch!

I stopped.

"Is there anybody in this room," I asked, "who is for the Goddess? Please applaud, so I'll know you are here."

To my great amazement, vigorous applause greeted me. Some of the neopagans had gotten in; at least half of the people in the audience were Goddess people, and they applauded loudly. Bless you! The fundies were taken aback. So far they had thought they had this event all sewed up, and they could stop me if they just mumbled their prayers/curses loudly enough. Now they understood that I had support here. So did I. More confidently than before I went on with my slide show, Goddess after Goddess, story after story, the way I usually teach. I presented the Goddess from an international point of view, always my favorite.

At the end I received a great deal of applause. The fundies were still looking at their laps, avoiding looking at the slides of the Goddess, avoiding looking in the face of the Goddess.

The lights went back up and my son smiled at me. This was the first time he had heard my lecture. Oh, good, the boy liked it. It would have been awful if my own son hated the work I had given my entire life to. Then of course I remembered that he burned red candles for a lover when he was lonely, borrowed my altar and my supplies, and he always had a lover. But now a reporter approached him, and this was where he drew the line.

"So how does it feel to be the son of a witch?" the reporter quizzed him.

"No comment," he said presidentially.

Phyllis was darting a watchful gaze from man to man as they approached me, mentally frisking them for weapons.

It was good. What a life. What a sweet, good life it was after all. My many friends were all around, congratulating me, holding me dear, my family, my friends, even the police!

The police car accompanied us all the way to the borders of the city. We honked our horns as we sped off.

The headlines continued for one more day. The *San Francisco Chronicle* devoted editorials and several articles to the "witch in the library," a confrontation of women's spirituality, neopagans, and the fundamentalists. A front-page item was the last report. The local gay paper published nothing.

# FIFTH LUNATION

*Time ‹ April—May*
*Sign ‹ Taurus*
*Lunar Herbs ‹ Catnip, Mallow*
*Lunar Animals ‹ Cow, Bull*

# Flower Moon

## VIEW FROM THE MOON

*The clouds roll away, the wind grows soft and warm. As the Full Moon of Taurus sails the skies, her gentle light glimmers upon a world full of flowers. In the north the last of the fruit trees are filling the air with soft perfume. In the forests primroses spill their pale gold beneath the trees, and the hedges are full of hawthorne bloom. Mustard and cowslips, bluebells and lupine fill the meadows. There are white blossoms, flowers of every shade of yellow, purple, and deep blue, a tide of color spreading northward as the world warms to spring. Now the trees leaf out in full vigor, and youths and maidens go into the wood to lie upon the green grass and bring in the May. All the world is in love, blessed by the smiling Flower Moon.*

## THE GODDESS SPEAKS

# *Hathor*

Come back, O glory that was once my worship among the women! I am ancient Hathor, the Winged Cow Goddess. I wear the horns of the Moon and the orb of the sun. My gentle rays graze upon my most beloved earth, I herd my sacred cows as they nurture and nourish the people. My milk is the food of the young. My skin is their protection. And I have a lot of time to play.

Do you remember how we danced at the revels in Dendera? At Hathor's festivals of intoxication we drank wine. We sang many songs on New Year's Eve, we erupted in passion like the volcanos. Don't you miss the all-night revels when thousands of us danced together, young and old, in holy ecstasy?

Ah, but let me remind you of my serious aspect. I am the spirit that led you to write the first words on paper made from papyrus, my sacred flower. I am the one who urged you to invent music and poetry, dancing, and the arts. I am the culture maker, the community builder, the Festival Goddess.

I am the celestial protector of all bodily pleasures, music for the ears, beauty and costumes, makeup, weaving garlands for our heads, all the joys to the eye. I delight in all the pleasures of touching, dancing, making love. I make you prosperous in your own time, enrich you with home life, children, and good company. I make your crops grow tall, I make your fruit trees bear plentifully, I will dwell with the cat who purrs in your lap at night.

But I have a dark side, and my sacred winged cow nature turns into that of a raging bull when I am angered. I have been known to wade in the blood of men who offended women. I have been known to drink the blood from their skulls and smash those who killed or abused women or children, and that side of me is no longer dormant. Call to me for help when you are in trouble, when male aggression had been directed against you and yours, and I, Hathor, shall rise to the occasion and fulfill your curses, execute your wrath. I am the bloody Goddess when I rise in your defense. I am the terror of men who hate or strike women. Show your power through me, and demand my help, and I shall be there for you with my long arm of destiny and my short arm of immediate retribution. Trust me and trust yourself.

Know this and revel in my nearness. The white Taurus Moon is overhead, sailing across the dark sky. Only the stars are my company. They dance in the heavens. Let you, my dear souls, my daughters, my sons, be playful and love each other, for in doing this you are serving me.

## *Taurus Message*

This fourth lunation gives us energy to focus on our physical manifestation, our bodies, our cycles. Body love and body awareness is the theme. Listen to your body more than ever before and hear her messages as sacred orders. Absorb the love of the body, beauty, prowess, endurance, strength. Then open up to the beloved. Slowly and steadily we channel a love of life.

What you plant in this sign will be resistant to vermin. Sow and plant root crops, preserve fruits. What you plant now will grow slowly. It is a good time for plowing, digging, planting trees. Plants will be robust, trees strong. Work on fences. Cut, pile, and store wood. Wounds could become inflamed and ulcerous. Tend to them with special care. Rest a lot if you are ill.

## MOONTIDES
## *Feeling Like a Party*

It happens to me, and so I am sure it happens to you too. You have been working hard, even your back is aching from all that effort. Think about the past. When did you have your last festive meal? Can't remember? Think again. When did you go to your last party? If once more no picture immediately leaps to mind, you are in need of some serious socializing.

The soul is like any other being. She has needs, and socializing is one of them. Even if you are shy, even if you have no fun at parties, your inner woman/inner man/inner creature will want to hang out with the human village, to be with the tribe.

Call a friend and tell her about this urge to loosen up. Get ideas. Make this a project. Set a date when the Moon is Taurus. Light a purple candle and a pink one for power and happiness. Light candles at your party in the same two colors if you can.

Clean your house and dress up. But the party doesn't have to take place in your house. You can go out. If throwing a party is too much for you, go out dancing. A dance floor already looks like a party. Your inner woman won't know the difference, a tribal dance is a tribal dance. You don't have to dance if you hate it, just hang out with the dancers. Take in that old celebrational vibration. Soak it in like a sponge. Store it up for rainy days.

# *Rage*

Oh, the Dark One has gotten hold of your senses now.

You are filled with high-intensity emotions, you are lit up with fury. Within you the deep-seated reptilian brain is pumping up adrenalin, enough to kill. Does it matter why? You could have been robbed, raped, beaten up, ripped off, humiliated, destroyed. You stand there unable to believe that this is happening to you. How could you have attracted such karma, you may ask?

Stop!

You have not attracted anything. It isn't your fault. You got hit by somebody else's negative energy, somebody else's sickness. Put the blame right where it belongs. Don't internalize the darkness any further. Allow yourself to feel your rage. Rage is good. It is healthier than depression. The organs inside your body are red-hot from rage, your face may be red also. This is how you want to feel it. You don't want to stifle it, hide it, or be ashamed of your righteous rage.

I felt rage when I was arrested for prophesying the future with Tarot cards and put in jail.

I felt rage when I was giving birth and my doctor left me alone for twenty-two hours without once coming by.

I felt rage when after the birth the doctors joked as they were sewing me up, saying, "We are going to make you look like you're sixteen!" And I was only nineteen then.

I felt rage when I got divorced and discovered that all those years I had been married hadn't equipped me to make a living. They were wasted years.

I felt rage when my elder son was sent to fight for oil in the Persian Gulf.

I feel rage when I know that women do 90 percent of the work in the world and own only 1 percent of the wealth. I feel rage when I hear about clitorectomies (cutting off the clitoris, sometimes of six-year-old girls), when I hear about women burned to death for their dowries, or women whose men forbid them to use birth control.

I feel rage when I see the trees disappearing, when I taste the water and it is foul, when I hear about the poor animals who are maimed and killed for some frivolous reason, like cosmetics research.

The list is very long. Rage is a familiar emotion to me. If your soul is awake, you must be angry at all crimes against life.

Now sit down and take a piece of paper and write down what has happened to you. List the reasons you feel rage. Confront your feelings. Keep it personal. Rage is an important feeling. You want to channel it into action. Rage is the best fuel for political action and personal transformation. Make a pledge that you will feel this rage, call it up again and again, and write letters, confront those who hurt you. Plan to fight back!

## MOONSPELLS

# *For Rage*

Now use your right brain. Get a huge black candle and write on it the names of those who have hurt you. Name the targets of your rage. Naming is half the battle. Anoint the candle with your own urine. Place a piece of white paper with the list of your rage underneath the candle, and burn it for nine nights in a row, each night for half an hour at the most. Burn a black incense, something like dispelling or protection or black arts. You are working with the dark side of your soul. We are made of shadows, not only the lights. We are not just nicey nice. We also manifest the Dark One, she who buries things, the Goddess with the shovel.

Over the black candle say three times:

> *I send you my bile, I send you my pain,*
> *I send you a thousand times*
> *What you have sent to me.*
> *I am your own mirror,*
> *I magnify your guilt.*
> *I send you ten thousandfold*
> *What you have sent to me.*

Rage is such a strong feeling, before it dissipates, use it to make some important decisions. Do not swallow rage. It can cause ulcers or internal sickness. Rage is a fuel whose energy can change your life and help you discover your own power.

# *For Revenge*

Revenge is a major theme in our literature, a major theme in our movies. Sweet revenge, we say, a feeling you have when you get even with those who have harmed you.

Revenge is a motivating feeling. It is active. It is entertaining. It is fit food for obsessions. Revenge sometimes takes the place of real life—people postpone their lives just for the process of getting even.

Success is, of course, the best revenge. The only kind of witchcraft revenge I recommend is the one where you reverse the evil sent to you, and send it back tenfold. People who deserve your ire had to have endangered your life, safety, mental health. Revenge is justified if your survival is at stake.

If it's your pride, your ego, your glory, or some other illusion, revenge is not justified. You cannot attack somebody because she took your woman or man away. That's just life, not a crime.

Usually when we take revenge, we return the same bad fortune. But don't fly into the revenge mode just because it's exciting and you feel more powerful. Contemplate the conflict deeply. Sometime's the rash solution you think you need would open the door to an even greater evil.

When you have contemplated your target and have reached a wise decision for revenge, wait until the Dark Moon.

Assemble an altar built to the Kali Ma. She likes bones on her altars — ckicken bones, fishbones. Her symbol is the triangle, her liquid is menstrual blood. Write the name of the person who has harmed you on a piece of paper backward five times, smear it with menstrual blood (if you don't have it anymore, use urine), fold it up, and place it underneath a black candle. Light some black-arts incense or some other baneful scent. Write the name of the person backward on the black candle, with a rusty nail, three times. If you do not know who harmed you, just write "the person who has harmed me."

Burn the incense and the candle and say:

> *I return to you the ills and harm*
> *That you have callously sent to me.*
> *Take back the sleepless nights, terrible danger,*
> *heart's pain, and deep grief.*
> *Back on to you,*
> *Back on to you,*
> *Back on to you.*
> *Spiders' webs will trip you up,*
> *Ensnare you in your own bad luck.*

Repeat this for seven nights of the Dark Moon until your candle is finished. In the last flames of the candle, burn the paper as well. Take the ashes and candle drippings to the person's house or throw it in their path so when they walk by they step on it, and the spell is on. If you don't know where they live or who they are, cast the remnants of this moon-spell in a living body of water and let Kali Ma find the appropriate person.

If you have attacked the innocent, if you have foolishly tried to make your ego feel better, this spell will return to you tenfold, and you will not be able to pray your way out of it.

## FESTIVALS OF THE MOON

### Mugwort Festival, Fifth Day of the Fifth Moon
### New Moon — China

In China, as in Europe, mugwort was a sacred herb. On the fifth day of the fifth month, mugwort was plucked and dolls were made from the tied leaves. These were hung over gates or doors to expel poisonous airs or influences. In Europe mugwort (*Artemisia vulgaris*) was named after Artemis and considered a women's herb. Its leaves were used in baths to bring on menstruation. It was also a witches' herb, whose scent was believed to prevent weariness. Today a tea made from the roots is used to provide a pickup after fatigue. Sleeping on a pillow filled with it could give prophetic dreams. Its leaves were burned in midsummer bonfires to dispel evil.

### Full Moons
### Especially of the Fifth Month — China

Chung K'uei, the "Great Spiritual Chaser of Demons for the Whole Empire," was honored. He was supposed to have freed one of the T'ang emperors from the red demons of emptiness and desolation. He is one of the seven officials in the Taoist Ministry of Exorcisms. At the Full Moon he was given offerings, and his paper image was burned. The fifth Moon, called the pestilential, was particularly hazardous, and so special honor was given to Chung K'uei.

### Munychia
### Full Moon Munychion — Ancient Athens

Munychia was a festival of Artemis as Goddess of the Full Moon. Large round loaves or cakes were baked and surrounded by lamps to symbolize the Moon. These were carried in procession to the temple of Artemis. The Athenians thanked the Goddess for having provided them with the light of the Full Moon during the sea battle of Salamis in which they defeated the Persians.

To celebrate, at the full of the Moon, bake a round loaf (or buy a round of sourdough bread at the supermarket) and place it on a platter surrounded by votive candles or tapers cut into one-inch stubs. Offer it to the Moon and thank the Goddess for helping you to fight your own battles or ask her to illuminate current problems so that you can solve them. Leave part of the bread outside in the moonlight and eat the rest. If you want something to drink, a white wine (a vineyard in California called Chateau Diana makes a good chablis) or springwater in a clear glass goblet would go well.

### Lemuralia
### Full Moon or Ides of May — Ancient Rome

This is not the feast of the lemurs but of the *lemures*, ghosts without surviving family. This was a more serious matter than one might think, since Roman family religious practice honored the ancestors in a way reminiscent of the Orient, and the comfort of departed spirits depended on the honor paid them by their descendants. The ghosts of those whose families had died out required propitiation by the whole community. Participants in the ritual walked barefoot, washed their hands three times, and cast black beans behind them nine times.

This recalls the practices of the third day of the Greek Anthesteria festival, in which offerings of cooked pulse (a kind of pea) were made to the souls of the departed and to Hermes as guide of the dead.

In Rome the Ides of May (Full Moon) was also the Feast of Maia, mother of Mercury (the Roman equivalent of Hermes) and the anniversary of the founding of his temple. Maia herself was probably originally Maia Majesta, a Goddess of growth and spring, but as we have seen in festivals such as the Japanese Hana Matsuri, the old earth religion recognized the necessary connection between death and the new life of spring.

To celebrate this festival, make an altar with pictures of relatives who have passed on. You may include pictures of your spiritual ancestors or the names or pictures of individuals or peoples (such as some Native American tribes) with no descendants now alive. Place vases of spring flowers before them and burn a white candle, honoring their spirits and praying that their good qualities may be reborn.

# MOON TALE

## *Interview with the Goddess of Love*

It happened again. Love came into my life and then left me alone again, furious.

"Who is making these inept arrangements?" I cried. "What kind of Goddess would mess me up again and again, make me fall in love and then ruin everything and take it away?"

To get some answers I decided to make a call on the Goddess of Love. I was naturally apprehensive, since I know she moonlights as Goddess of Death. This was disturbing. I really couldn't show her my anger, lest I trigger hers.

I observed my usual trancing habits. I ate very little that day, and I went out to walk among the tall redwoods in Tiburon. The fresh air and the beauty relaxed me. But I was careful not to exhaust myself, lest I fall too deeply into trance and go to sleep instead.

For the interview I chose the time when the evening star was rising. I decorated my room with fresh flowers and made an altar to Venus. I placed a conch shell in the center of the white, lacy tablecloth. I lit pink and blue candles, her favorite colors. Around my neck I wore a necklace of lapis lazuli, her favorite gem.

After a purification bath with hyssop in my bathbag, I lay down on my bed and closed my eyes. A bathbag is a gauze or net pouch into which you pack special herbs. Myrrh incense, sacred to the female principle of the universe, rose gently into the air, filling my senses. I breathed into my toes, my legs, my knees, my hips, my stomach, my chest, my neck and arms, and finally my head. Each time I breathed I relaxed my body, letting it turn to weightless warmth.

In my hand I clutched a piece of dragon's blood reed, which breaks all hexes, just in case I needed protection. Not that I was suspicious of the Goddess of Love, I told myself. Oh no. It was just the kind of safeguard a witch uses in any trance.

This of course wasn't really true. I have tranced plenty of times without my dragon's blood reed. The reason lies in my relationship with the Goddess of Love. She is my coveted beloved lady, she is also my tormentor, my hated evil stepmother.

The trance descended finally. My spirit left my body, rising like smoke through my head at the spot where the soft skull used to be, the crown. I was surprised that there was no other entity waiting to take me to see the Goddess. I looked down at my body below, to make sure I was out of it, and sure enough I was. But where was my guide?

Already my feelings about the Goddess of Love were starting to make angry vibrations. It was all her fault. Hadn't I been requesting this meeting for three days now, dutifully praying to her each night for an audience? And hadn't I gotten answers through the good omens I saw in the woods? I saw red-tailed hawks, I saw Canadian geese, I saw green-necked mallards all flying westward. Her affirmative omens were abundant.

Then I noticed a bird outside my window. It was a white goose. Not part of a flock, just by herself, sitting on the back porch. "That's it!" I rejoiced. "It's the guide. It must be. Let's go!"

I moved through the wall and the bird sensed me and flew away. I lifted myself to fly after her. This was fun! Flying over my neighborhood is always a great rush. I looked down and there was the corner liquor store where I sometimes buy milk and get my newspaper on Sunday mornings when everything else is closed. But as soon as I made this observation the flight picked up speed, and all familiar scenery receded into a blur. The white bird never looked back at me. She just kept flying, with wings flapping rhythmically. I could hear the way the air hushed through her white feathers.

"White bird, thank you for guiding me to Venus." There was no answer. "Can you send me a thoughtform?" I asked, but there was no answer.

I accepted this. It is a lot to ask from animals to constantly be the links between the will of the Goddess and our requests. I was grateful that she had come at all.

Then the bird decided to sit on a high peak. We might have already been in the western Sierras. The big boulder was rugged, unreachable except by flight. I landed next to the goose.

"So where is she?" I asked the bird again.

The bird looked at me then started to clean her feathers. It was a splendid, beautiful big goose. She was powerful, with gleaming white feathers. In fact the more I looked at her the more outstanding she seemed. Her white feathers shimmered in the night, almost as if they were lit from within. But, I thought, that is just how things look in trance. This was only a goose, not an iridescent bird with a bluish, sometimes pink, shimmer in her feathers. Then the bird tucked her beak under her wing, shook her tail one more time, and went still, as if to go to sleep.

"Wait a minute!" I said, and a terrible thought occurred to me. What if this was not a guide bird but just an ordinary goose? What if I had followed her all the way here with no idea how to get home?

"Wake up!" I said.

No answer. The bird was comfortably asleep. A little wind blew from below, whispering in the trees.

*This is not going to work*, I thought. Venus was just not giving interviews tonight.

"Dearest bird," I said, this time with lots of respect. "Please show me the way back where I came from. I followed you by mistake, I'm sorry.

"No mistake," said a voice.

My heart almost stopped. Who was this? The bird stretched out and I could see that she had human legs!

"I am respectfully asking you, dearest creature, to reveal yourself to me so we can communicate," I said as I would to any apparition met in trance. Now she stretched out two bare arms from underneath her feathers, and the goose became a cover for her—a living blanket.

"Venus!" I cried, bowing deeply. "You are receiving me after all!"

"Don't be so insecure. Of course I'll talk to you!" she said. Her voice was not what I expected. I thought the Goddess of Love would have a voice soft as a nightingale's song, but hers was like a mountain climber's—strong, distinctive.

"Thank you for the gracious opportunity!"

"Oh, don't try to butter me up," she said to me good-naturedly, "I know you are mad at me again."

"It is true," I confessed. "And I'm not the only one. Many of us on earth are mad at you too!"

"Yeah, yeah, yeah," she said, bored now. "What is it this time?"

It was like a mother scolding children who have had the same mishap again.

"It's difficult to really put my finger on it."

"Well, if this is an interview, you'd better have your questions ready."

Venus now emerged from under the goose, who had been sheltering her from the wind. She was a beautiful woman, but not the slim type they always show you in paintings. Venus was fat. She had pink fat, glowing, alive, pretty fat, but she was fat. I was taken aback for a moment. I expected her to look like Marilyn Monroe, or at least like Glenn Close or Meryl Streep. But no. She looked more like Roseanne Barr, but without the bitterness.

"Honor to you, Goddess of Love!" I said sincerely.

She nodded, and I noticed that her hair was braided in cornrows, and now when I looked at her, her skin appeared to be black.

"I like you, Zsuzsanna. Why are you mad at me?"

"It's about my life," I stuttered.

"What's wrong with it?"

"Well, you seem to be sending me lovers, but nobody ever stays long enough, loves me well enough, you know. It's so transient . . ."

"And this upsets you?" This time her shoulders were the color of the yellow sun, her hair long and blowing in the wind. She looked wild.

"I want my true love to stay."

"So stay."

"I mean *them*—"

"There is no 'them.' There is only 'you.' And me . . ."

"I don't understand."

The Goddess of Love chose to stand up now, and this time she was fully clothed, except that her left breast was exposed, her nipple hardened in the wind.

"Transience is natural," she said.

"But . . . but others have life partners for many years, and I am getting too old to play this love game. I want to get married."

"We are not talking about the same things, my dear."

Venus started playing with the snakes that had crawled out from under the big boulder. She made them into necklaces around her neck and bracelets. One python she twined around her waist.

"Why do you keep changing all the time? It's confusing me."

"I am your feelings. I am all feelings. It's my job to change. "

"Can't you ever stay put?" I had lost my temper and I knew it.

Her snakes all glared at me with wild disgust. One of them hissed at me.

"Absolutely not," Venus said. "It would not be me. It would not be life. But you should not marry your feelings, which change, you should marry your intentions, which may remain more constant."

"Marry without love? Isn't that archaic?"

"Marriage is like being roommates. Love is like a fever. I can get you together with your true love, but I cannot stay forever. There are others I have to visit. Right now, for example, youngsters are just learning the thrill of me, and in other places lovers need my heat to create babies."

"Babies! Is that all you care about?"

Venus embraced her fat belly, which now slimmed down miraculously to a flat tummy.

"Just the opposite, my dear. I am interested only in pleasure. Babies are your department. Do you see me with children around? Do I need baby-sitters? No! I had one divine child, Cupid, and he never grows up. He is also in the love business, shooting his arrows into people's hearts. It's a big world. We can hardly manage."

Venus now stretched and rearranged herself into a gymnast with slim limbs and a tiny waist. She flipped around a few times on the boulder; in the air she could hover—she obviously had no mass.

Finally I had had enough. She was so flippant, so self-absorbed. Why would she be in charge of the most treasured feelings in the world?

"Venus, excuse me, but you cause a lot of pain for us people on earth, a lot of pain . . ."

She looked at me and this time she stayed put. She looked like a kindly therapist, with glasses and a pantsuit. She looked ridiculous dressed like that here in the wilderness.

"Would you rather I never visited you again?"

Panic struck me with elemental force.

"Oh no, Mama, that's not what I meant. I mean, please feel free to visit me anytime you want to, please don't drop me from your list. I'll die if you never come again!" This disgusting groveling at least made her smile.

"All right. But what would you have me do instead?"

Here was my chance. I could now solve the problems of the entire world. Venus had asked me how she should handle us and at last I could make my influence felt. This was an all-important moment.

"You could make us fall in love only with people who make us happy," I suggested.

"All of them make you happy at first."

"But later too. Send us lovers who stay lovers, who keep loving us past the beginning."

"But I cannot be there to oversee that," Venus raised her voice in exasperation. "I can only be there at the beginning. The rest is up to you." It started to make sense.

"Only at the beginning, because . . ." I was trying to make her say it one more time.

"—because I have to cover the territory. I have to go around from soul to soul. I have to bind souls together. That's what I do. There are almost five billion of you already."

"Five billion. That's too much," I said suddenly.

"It is!" Venus affirmed. "Can you tell me how I can cover all the hearts and still linger and give my power to continue relationships?"

I was defeated in this one. "Our feelings die. We lose that loving feeling. We break up. We get bored."

"I am only in charge of the beginning. The Queen of Heaven was very explicit on this assignment. At the beginning of the human race, she said, 'You shall bind the hearts together!' And I have been doing it ever since."

I thought about that and realized how cleverly she was putting all the responsibility for broken hearts back in the human race's lap.

"That is not all she told you," I accused her. "Your instructions included dealing the death blow as well."

Venus darkened. She hid away in the feathers, the snakes curled up around her. She stuck out a hand that now was withered and old, the skin like tree bark, she was showing me a handful of maggots.

"You are scaring me!" I complained.

"Don't come to interview me if you cannot take the fear!" she snapped back in a crackling voice

I reached for my trusted dragon's blood reed. It was still in my hand.

"That talisman isn't going to save you from death!" she screamed at me. "Who do you think you are!"

"I am the priestess of the earth!" I recited my witch mantra.

"Well that counts for something!" she softened and made her death aspect disappear. "You are right. It is also my job to take out the old wood, to take home the tired and worn-out souls. It is my job to make you die."

I was at a loss now for what to ask her. If it was her job to take us down, of course she was going to dole out pain.

"Would you like me to leave you alone and not carry you off when it's your time? I could do that, you know."

She was offering me eternal life. Her voice was sweet and conciliatory. She really hadn't meant to scare me as much as she had.

"No! Please—I don't want eternal life that way," I babbled. "I want eternal life as I already have it, the life of my essence, my soul, not my body. When she is ready to go, please take me home gently."

"Don't worry, I will. You have answered wisely," she said, relaxing again. Clearly the fat lady was her favorite form. She transformed into it so often.

Now she started to giggle softly. She could read my mind. I could feel it.

"Just one more thing, dearest Lady . . ."

"Yes?" Venus turned to me and her eyes appeared as deep as the sea, and about the same color.

"Next time when you visit me, you know, and bring me a new love, could it be somebody who is not living out of town?"

"Sure," she said reassuringly.

"Could it be somebody who is loyal and smart, sexy and interesting?"

"Weren't they all?"

"Yes. But . . ."

"But! That's what is wrong with you human beings. You yearn for constancy, but it is you who leave each other. It is you who lose faith, it is you who always want something more or less, something closer or farther, while all the time I am giving you exactly what is yours and you don't seem to realize it. You are hopeless!"

"Then that is my last question: Why are we hopeless like that? What is it with love that is so unsettling, so coveted, and so feared?"

Venus thought about it, this time not impatient as she would be with an inferior, but giving it her deep consideration.

"I think it is because I am the reason for your life. The Queen of Heaven programmed you to make me the top priority. When I am not with you, you are lost like children, you feel betrayed. And when I am there you are fearing my departure. And of course my last visit is the end of all desire."

So there was no way out. My resentment disappeared because I realized that she couldn't help us solve our problems; only we can do that.

"Do you think humans will ever learn to value and appreciate your gifts to us? Will we ever love wisely?"

"No," she answered with a sigh. "If you did, all your poetry, your art, your love songs, and your excitement would disappear. There would be no place to take your date, there would be nobody to write the songs to dance to, you would all be bored."

Peace returned to my heart and I asked the guide to take me home.

The Goddess waved her toes and a flock of Canadian geese burst through the clouds, circling above us.

"They will take you home," she said.

I hesitated, trying to repress my longing for her. But she saw through me.

"You would like to kiss me, wouldn't you?"

"Is that possible?" I asked with my heart fluttering. All the times women had inspired love in me, attraction and arousal, all those feelings were filling my body right now.

"I love you," I whispered to her.

She formed herself into the shape of my lover, the one I was crying over, the one I had to leave for another, the one I missed. She held me in her arms and we kissed deeply. I drank in her kisses. The energy was coming through me like electricity. She held me just the way I like to be held, firmly, kissed with passion and trust. Then she let me catch my breath. I reached for my lapis lazuli necklace and placed it around her holy neck.

"Thank you for all the love I have gotten in my life."

"You are welcome." She stroked the lapis lazuli. I knew it was her favorite stone.

The geese now took up their vee formation, with me in the middle, pulling me along by their own air currents. But my thoughts were still with Venus. I should try to get back to her again soon. She was so nice, and maybe she would kiss me again.

"I kiss you in all the women," I could hear her voice. "All the women are me."

When I woke up, my candles were burned down to the nub. But my altar for Venus was serene, and the flowers had hardly wilted at all. Beauty was everywhere. My body felt refreshed.

I lay thinking of the Goddess and how good it felt to kiss her. Then with a sudden jolt I noticed that the lapus lazuli necklace around my neck was gone!

# SIXTH LUNATION

*Time ‹ May–June*
*Sign ‹ Gemini*
*Lunar Herb ‹ Ginger*
*Lunar Animal ‹ Dove*

# Strong Sun Moon

## VIEW FROM THE MOON

*During this Moon the sun draws ever closer to the earth. Crops are pushing upward; soon the first ripe grain will be here. During the day people seek shelter from too much brilliance, but at night the Full Moon captures the sun's harsh blaze and turns it to pale fire. The radiance of the midsummer Moon transmutes the harsh colors of daylight into the hues of faerie. It transmutes the sun's pitiless illumination into a pure light that blesses all who walk beneath its rays. It transmutes the heat of the day into a gentle warmth that encourages folk to take off their clothes and open their arms to the night sky. The Full Moon is a silver shield of protection for all that lives.*

## THE GODDESS SPEAKS
# *The Shekinah*

Come my beloved people, sing my praises. I have come again this New
Moon to lift your burdens, to lighten your spirits, to make the everyday
dullness disappear. Rejoice! Rejoice! I open the sacred gates of my apple
orchards and set you a fresh festive table underneath the Moon. The
candles are lit. I shall pour fine wine into a cup to refresh you. Come, my
people, partake of the joy that is the Shekinah. No longer hidden and
forbidden, celebrate the feeling of love I bring to you. I am the sacred
Sabbath, the receiving fertile lap, the throne of all authority. Cries and
sighs have ceased now, all pain has disappeared, the spirit of the Goddess
has descended into you. Feel the radiance that is me.

Upon the table I set my braided bread and the round cakes you baked
for me, your Queen of Heaven. Pour your libations upon the ground as
in olden times, return a little of the wine to the earth. Let my women
burn the sweet-smelling incense, for it pleases me to hear your prayers
rising to me like the smoke. My people, behold my face with joy. Euphoria
is rising in your hearts. Come in peace and come in joy, come in jubi-
lation, for your beloved Bride has come.

How will you greet me? How will you love me? How will you seek to
delight me, my beloved?

I shall have my priestesses dance to the most ancient instruments of all,
the cymbals and tiny drums and the playful tinkling of the bells fastened
to their ankles, to the sound of the sistrum and to the clapping of your
hands. Come celebrate with me the joy of life, for the Queen of Peace has
come.

As the midnight hour arrives, my arms open like the gates of heaven,
for I am the delight and joy of both females and males. In me the nations
rejoice. Both old and young are happy. I am the deliverer from pain and
extinction, I am the Law of Love.

## Gemini Message

This sixth lunation will affect our minds with stimulation and a desire for sharing information. In Gemini attention is paid to partnerships, making allies for our projects, attracting those of like mind. Our world opens up, new players appear on the scene, we widen our circle of friends. Life moves faster. This is a good time for gathering our loved ones together, creating family events at which we shine, and entertaining. Awareness of the equality of the sexes and work with both sexes fills our minds.

When the Moon is in Gemini, plant everything that should climb and everything from which blossoms are taken: broccoli, cauliflower, healing herbs, flowers. Cut your hair. Start journeys, close business deals, and catch up on your correspondence. Write to your congressperson, update your journals, write love letters, invitations.

### MOONTIDES

## Bleeding

Listen, daughter, the New Moon is calling you. Now is the right moment. From your depths I call forth your very own red blood. You are tense, you are holding on to it, somebody has upset you, something has depressed you, and now you won't give me the blood that I came to call forth.

Relax, woman.

You have cramps because you are fighting me. It isn't your job to go to the office today. It is your job to dream, to go down deep, yes, and dream. Stop reaching for the pain relievers. They may relax your muscles, but they will also cloud your mind. It is we who are bleeding. I say "we" because at this moment millions of women are with you, bleeding just like you. We are connected not just by our precious blood but because we are dreaming together, many many dreams. Don't take pills. How are you going to dream if you are drugged?

I see that now you are reaching for a glass of scotch or brandy, a beer. Yes, that will make the blood come easier. If you take very little, you can still dream. How about some herbal teas? Make a pot of comfrey tea. Go ahead. Listen to your kettle whistle, pour the hot water over aromatic herbs. Comfrey takes away your pain, yarrow flowers will stimulate your womb to expel the inner lining. Try chamomile tea as well. It will help you sleep. Try raspberry leaves, for they will build up your womb. Sample the many herbs the earth has given us to handle the bleeding.

Lie down now and touch yourself.

Feminate (this means masturbate in postpatriarchal language). Cover yourself to keep warm, sip your drink, then close your eyes and spread your legs wide and feminate.

Now your blood will start trickling out. Think of lovely wet tongues caressing your clitoris. Think of hungry lovers gently eating your sex as if they were nibbling peaches. Think of lovers drinking in your lifeblood. Am I grossing you out? I hope not. You are now my lunar primate. You are acting out millennia-old traditions of menstruating.

Menstruate. Bleed with me. Loll around in bed. Take a nap. I want you to think of images that excite you without judgment. I want you to experience the waves of desire rising, your labia flooding, your heartbeat quickening. Touch yourself with respect and with wild abandon. Your body is yours. There is no frowning judge watching from the corner of your bedroom, but if you think he is, throw your used sanitary napkins at him. Menstrual blood has been known to obliterate the most stubborn judges. Make a date with a lover who likes menstrual blood. Just bleed and relax. If demands are being put upon you by a husband or children, tell them about the mysteries of bleeding, talk about the blood, show them what you have achieved and they will leave you alone. Abdicate from your role as a modern woman. A lunar primate is what you are for a few days. Act like one. Unless it is food, dancing, sex, moonwalks, or sleeping, it isn't your job.

You are connected to all the other women who are bleeding now. A blood-tied global community. Make peace with the blood. Give your blood space. You will come back from your journey through renewal a stronger woman, a happier woman, a more loving woman. Changing woman. On these bleeding days you do not belong to your family, your husband, children, or even lovers. You belong to the silvery Moon alone.

## Sickness

What has happened to you, my dear friend? You are lying in bed. Your aura has shrunk and darkened. You are feeling ill, congested, aching. Your whole body is out of order.

When sickness occurs, there it is a great temptation to assume that something other than the sickness is at fault. Maybe you think you did something wrong, you somehow caused your own illness, your own weakness. Of course, sometimes people actually do. They get sick because they lost the love of a dear one. They get sick because they have not found love at all. Some need their sickness to control others or to get more attention. But most of the time an illness has an organic cause, like a bug, a virus, a broken bone, bacteria. The victim is not the cause. Stop trashing yourself for getting ill.

Here is a moonspell you can use when you're sick to stimulate the life force within you. Burn orange candles in your room (they come in fireproof jars). Place fresh flowers all around you. Wear a scent such as amber or sandalwood to lift your spirits. Complain as much as you like, make a lot of phone calls. If you are too tired, sleep a great deal—deep and satisfying sleep. If you have difficulty getting to sleep, drink St. John's wort tea (available in health-food stores). It will make you relax.

While you sleep, your magical self is working to restore your body's balance. Great dreams can come when you sleep a lot; the brain is not tired and provides colorful spiritual journeys signifying recuperation.

Bathe long and often. Rub your body with herbs, such as mints, sweet balm, and rosemary.

Ask a friend to touch you, to give you foot massages, or just to hold your hand. When you are sick, human touch is powerful medicine.

Talk to your inner self, the wild woman inside; see what she is up to. Chances are your creature inside is moping, holding the injured part of your body, crying pitifully.

Ask a friend to talk to your sickness. First have your friend sprinkle the bed and you with lemon water. Then the friend says,

> *Out, out, sickness! [repeat three times,*
>    *ringing a bell if you have one. Make a noise.]*
> *Repair, O body,*
> *Repair the cells,*
> *Repair the mind,*
> *Repair the will!*
> *You are now free to heal! [repeat three times.]*

Funny thing about faith healing: our creature within—the body, our mass, the wise library of all our ancestors—has the power to heal the body instantly. It only takes a strong message to send to the body parts, to do this or that, and health is quickly recovered. The trick is gaining access to this middle brain. How can we impress this nonverbal part of the brain with a purpose that is stated in words?

The spiritual medicine is a ritual. Raise some power with drums or humming or singing. Use a rattler to drive away evil spirits. Then when you think this middle brain, this ancient one, is listening, quickly say the order, quickly tell her in simple form what you need (as I have stated it above). If she is listening, she will respond. The healing time will be cut in half; sometimes even faster.

If you have cancer, drink a lot of garlic juice. These days they make it without the smell. This is still used by peasants in Hungary to cure cancer. I know of one person who drank a liter of garlic juice a day for three months and was cured.

There are more healing spells in *The Grandmother of Time* and in *The Holy Book of Women's Mysteries*.

# FESTIVALS OF THE MOON

### *Thargelia, Seventh Day of Thargelion*
### *New Moon—Ancient Greece*

This is the birthday of Artemis, the Goddess of the Forests and the Moon in the Mediterranean. With the advent of the patriarchal turnover, Apollo got attached to this New Moon date as the twin of Artemis. But even older and deeper was the celebration on this Moon of the Horae, who were the Goddesses of the divine order in nature, who cause the seasons to change and all things to manifest at the appointed time. Thallo (spring) and Carpo (autumn) were a double Horae in Athens. Sometimes the Horae were a trinity: Eunomia (lawful order), Dike (justice), and Irene or Eirene (peace). It was said that Dike, a younger version of her mother, Themis, the Goddess of Social Instinct, got weary of men and their wars and hid away in the mountains waiting for the better age to come back. Men didn't stop the wars for many eons, and the Goddess of Justice Dike gave up on them. She ascended into the heavens and became the constellation Virgo.

Just because the early summer is a time of rapid growth, it is a period of great vulnerability. If anything goes wrong with the crops at this time, the harvest may be lost. Midsummer customs all over Europe focused on protecting people, crops, and livestock from illness. There is a strong feeling, born of hard experience, that you should walk softly when things are going well, lest by pride you offend the gods. The gods are not so small-minded, but it is a human failing to get cocky when times are good and forget that it will all have to be paid for someday. If we cut forests, we need to replant them; if we take crops from the earth, we must put organic waste materials back in. The order of nature must be observed and protected or we'll hinder the recurring miracle of the seasons.

### Shavuoth
### Waxing Quarter Moon of Sivan — Hebrew

This is the old Hebrew feast celebrating the ripening of the first of the grain. The temple was decorated with greens and flowers. The first sheaves were brought to the temple as an offering, and the story of Ruth was read aloud. One reason given for this is that she was the ancestress of King David, who was born on Shavuoth. More interesting is the fact that she attracted the attention of Boaz while she was gathering up the barley left over after the harvest in his fields. Ruth herself was originally from Moab, not Israel. Is this story another case where a historical incident has been attached to a pagan myth, in this case a Near Eastern marriage of a God and Goddess of the grain? The traditional foods for this occasion are milk and honey and blintzes.

Wherever the holiday comes from, consider it an opportunity to give thanks for all that you have been given. Make an offering of your own firstfruits — put examples or symbols of your work on your Moon altar and thank the Goddess for giving you the strength and skill to do it. Burn a gold or green candle and ask her to help you continue or complete it. Don't be stingy with your abundance. Give all the change in your purse to the first panhandler you see, or make a gift of canned foods or money to a shelter for the homeless.

### Festival of Edfu
### Epiphi 1, Full Moon — Egypt

Hathor, the Goddess crowned with the horns of the cow, was the Egyptian Goddess of Love, Beauty, and Fertility. In the New Moon her image was taken in her boat, the *Neb Marwet* (Mistress of Love), on a journey from her temple at Dendera to celebrate an ecstatic union with the god Horus at Edfu, a journey that would have ended around the time of the Full Moon. Her arrival was celebrated with great festivities, and many couples probably took advantage of the opportunity to follow the example of the Goddess and the God. In Rome this month was considered an especially auspicious time for weddings, especially during the Full

Moon or at a conjunction of the sun and Moon that was a special sign of Hathor.

### Kuan-yin Becomes a Bodhisattva
### Nineteenth Day of the Sixth Moon, Full Moon — China

It is unclear whether Kuan-yin was a Buddhist saint who gradually took over the attributes of earlier deities or an ancient mother Goddess who was euhemerized* as a Buddhist saint. What is important is that she is the ever-compassionate Lady of Mercy who remains close to mortals and continues to be concerned with them. In Buddhist legend she was a mortal who earned Nirvana but refused it until she could help everyone else attain it too. She purposely incarnated as a woman in order to increase her compassion. One prayer to her goes:

> Great Mercy, Great Mercy, oh!
> Thou Take-Away-Fear-Pusa!
> Save from terror, save from suffering
> Through Thy tender woman's heart
> And mighty Buddha's strength!

She is particularly concerned with women and children. Women who desire children offer her a pomegranate or embroidered slippers. She brings souls to children, rescues shipwrecked sailors, and brings rain. She often appears as a helpful old lady, so honor all old women, especially if they are Asian. You never can tell.

### Niman Kachina
### Full Moon of the Sixth Month — Hopi

The ceremony held by the Hopis during the Full Moon, just before midsummer, celebrates the return of the kachinas to their home in Sipapo, the underworld realm. Since the winter solstice, the kachinas have been active in our world, encouraging the forces of growth. By midsummer the first ears of corn are ripening, and it is time for the kachinas to retire to

---

*This term is derived from Euhemerus's theory that the Goddesses and Gods of mythology are simply deified mortals.

rest below. Male and female spruce trees, the tree of power, are cut and set up in the plaza of the pueblo. At dawn of the first day, the masked kachinas come dancing, and their movements portray the broken harmonies of the world. Later that day they distribute gifts to the children. As darkness is falling, they withdraw. Until midwinter they will not be seen again. The Kachina Father offers a parting prayer, asking the kachinas to take with them the wishes of the people that all living things may be renewed by the life-giving rain.

Each region suffers if it does not have the correct amount of rain and sun for its ecology, and human actions have more effect on this than we used to believe. Hopi religious practice is dedicated to helping the people to live in harmony with the cycles of nature; this is the essence of earth religions, whatever their source or symbols. Through the centuries the Hopi have evolved an elaborate system of ceremonies to help them to live successfully on their land. In a delicately balanced environment, it is essential to know how things work and what you can and cannot do. Whether you call it science or religion, respectful appreciation will help you to survive.

Note that the kachinas do not ascend into some distant heaven. Instead they descend into Mother Earth, they go within. Whether you are seeking protection and renewal for yourself or for the world around you, open yourself to awareness of the Goddess within you.

# MOON TALE

## *Dearest Body*

I am dressing for my best birthday party yet, my fiftieth. Standing there naked, fresh from my shower, I survey my closet. I smell of rosebuds and lilies, my armpits have been deodorized, my face has been splashed with witch hazel, and I have rubbed rose cream into it. From the corner of my eye I catch a glimpse of my own naked body in the mirror.

*Don't look*, my brain sends the sensible advice to my eyes. *Go look at your clothes again. Put on your underwear. At least put a shirt on while you're deciding what to wear.* But it's no use. The psychosis has begun. I form the thought, *You are too fat. Much too fat.*

This is how it always starts. Compared to whom am I too fat? I try to combat this line of thinking.

*Compared to . . . statistics.* There is this average woman somewhere, where statistics are spawned like guppies, and she has my height and she is thirty pounds lighter than I.

*Nonsense*, I manage to think. Nonsense. How can women be compared with each other in such an arbitrary fashion? It must have been a man who hated women (because he couldn't get any) who made up these statistics about who should weigh how much in revenge. And we women all believed him because he probably had a Ph.D., and we are suckers for degrees. Women had such a hard time getting higher education, to us it's still a hallowed thing. Professional liars all have Ph.D.'s nowadays.

Slowly I make myself approach the clean pink image in the mirror. It hurts almost physically to even look. It fills me with horror.

*Overweight*. I rush into harsh judgments. *The stomach hangs down . . . it sort of pooches out*. Worse descriptions fill my mind. I suck in my stomach. It sags less. I push my stomach further in with my hands. Better. Maybe I should buy a girdle, but then I would not be able to breathe. I let my stomach out and it pooches out again. Badly.

Who does this fifty-year-old body belong to?

I must confront her. This is my body. My reality. The only thing I have ever really owned.

I remember when my body and I first got together. She was fast and slim. My mother, herself not a fat person, said I was as skinny as a stringbean. Then I hated to eat. Running was my game, fast movements, exhilaration, breathless days. This feeling lasted until my body grew breasts. Then a little soft layer formed on the tummy, just a hint of fat. My thighs, always my main support in jumping and running, now filled out, leaving no space between the two upper legs anymore. My mother said that touching thighs were a sign of beauty. I loved my dearest body then. I had never heard of statistics or *Vogue* magazine. My little breasts were a pride and joy to me. Even my mother's friends admired my budding womanhood. They all predicted that I would grow up to be a pretty woman.

But then came puberty. My body speeded up. She started bleeding. A lot of bleeding. I had to stay in bed for weeks because of heavy bleeding. My body didn't know how to menstruate properly yet. But after a couple of years she worked it out. She menstruated like a clock with the Moon; every New Moon we bled together.

My body. Now I have to come closer and take another, deeper look. This body has a big scar on the belly. It is like a battle wound. The scar of a hysterectomy. Otherwise she is really in nice shape. So what if she doesn't have a flat tummy! She has had two children. I remember the pain and boredom of pregnancy, the stretchmarks I treated with coconut oil to make them go away. The anxious dieting after each baby. My fight against my flesh had begun even as far back as my twenties. That body was size nine and a half, always wishing to be size seven. What madness!

Now I am beholding my breasts. I cup them in my hands as I have seen the Goddess Inanna do in her images. In fact, in the mirror now, I do look a little bit like Inanna, the Queen of Heaven. The breasts are still sort of youthful. I praise my wisdom in shedding the bra in the 1960s. I maintained my muscles. I also swim regularly.

But there she stands now at fifty, my dearest body. Her skin is still translucent. There are good genes in her from great antiquity. It is a Central European peasant woman's body, meant to bend down and gather the wheat, pick potatoes from the moist, rich ground, know the joys of early mornings walking in the wet grass to work, know the secrets of the blueberry patches and raspberry fields in the forests.

Nowadays I use her to work a computer, to move a mouse around with one hand and type with two fingers. She is so patient, she puts up with me. She lets me imprison her, keep her away from the fields of wheat, the fields where animals graze, the mountains and rivers. She types, because my visions are intangible. She cannot gather them in like nuts or blueberries. She has to make marks on disks, a concept totally beyond her understanding. But still she obeys me.

My eyes fill with tears when I think of her now. How cruel and demanding I have been with my body. How unlovingly I have behaved toward her sacred flesh. This achievement of millennia of humankind, this wonderful living library of my people, this beauty, this generous flesh, this loving, warm body. All that I have known and lived is stored in her mass. The embraces of my lovers, the first kiss, the first sex, and the times that followed—my nerves remember every thrill. The smells of foods I ate or desired, the cooking of the national Hungarian dishes, the taste of pastry I adore and associate with well-being.

Why did I ever turn on her? Who made me reject her? What makes us women hate our bodies so much? Whom is this hatred really serving? Who profits from our war on our own flesh? Why are we safe to love only when we hate ourselves?

My list of sins against my body is endless. I put her on diets, in fact most of my life I had to "watch" my weight like an enemy. My weight was her flesh, her veins, her muscles, her blood, her substance. I was out to reduce her and call that my personal "victory."

"If I could only lose ten more pounds. . . ." A dream that was always defeated, because my body always knew better. She never caved in to my insanity. She was always ahead of my game.

I chased her with liquid diets too. She got nothing to eat for weeks but this vile-looking yellow liquid, and she shed the pounds, but I could hear her swear with every swallow of that liquid diet that she was going to fight tooth and nail until she got her mass back and then some, to make sure that next time I attacked her she had something to fall back on. She was hungry so often, and so pitifully.

And I promised her love only if she would get "less." If she would "lose" some more. Especially from her belly, her power center. Both of us looked for love, but we didn't find any more when she was skinny than when she was fat.

After my divorce life changed. I cried and cried over the lost years and learned to appreciate what was ahead of me. I had forgotten about the old signals, the makeup, the plucked eyebrows, dying my hair blond, the high heels that weakened my feet and ruined my spine. I had given up on girdles, bras, stockings, and synthetic fibers. I started wearing natural fabrics, wore my hair as it was designed by my maker, took care of my skin, and let my eyebrows grow in dark and strong.

I was thirty-one years old when I first got a glimpse of what I really looked like, my original design, and it moved my heart. I loved me for the first time. I was all me. I connected with the feminist movement and learned about my history as a woman, learned about others who had to shed even more painful chains than mine. I learned to nurture my inner woman, my spiritual self. I changed my name. I gave birth to myself.

That was twenty years ago. This woman in the mirror is the intended one. This woman is the crowning achievement. This is the woman who went through a lot of hard changes and came out whole at the end. Let's respect her.

*"Dearest body, forgive me!"* I look at her again in the mirror. She is getting more confident, she lets out her stomach even further to test me. I kiss her tummy through the air. *"My flesh is not the enemy. Women-hating culture is, and men and women who make money off women's insecurities,"* I say to her.

*"This from somebody who contemplated liposuction not long ago!"* she scorns me.

It is true. My last dark crime against her. I remember it well. The hatred against my belly was at its highest. It was so intense that I took the first step. I went to a plastic surgeon and asked about liposuction. He cupped his hands over my poor, ashamed belly and pronounced, "What you need is a tummy tuck! We can make you look sixteen! Look at Phyllis Diller, the comedienne!" he pointed out with pride.

I could feel my dearest body shrink from his hands. I thought about Phyllis Diller and didn't see any parallels to my situation. The comedienne was a plastic surgery addict. I saw her on television bragging about how her jaw was broken and reset, so that now at the age of seventy-six she has a new jaw. I wondered if that made her happier. Is a new jaw the purpose of life or even a reason to love oneself?

"How much?" I asked, because the hatred was still very strong in me. I hated it when he said "flab." But deep inside I agreed that he was right.

"Six thousand dollars," he said without batting an eyelash.

The visit to see him cost $145.

I looked at him. He was sitting there with a definite "flab" himself hanging over his belt area. His stomach came from beer and fat foods, not from pregnancy. I had to say something.

"And when are you getting your own tummy tuck, doctor? Your flab is even bigger than mine!"

There was a chilling silence in the room. His reality had been shattered. I was not obeying the rules. I didn't see him as perfect.

"I am not getting any tummy tuck," he said angrily. His face darkened, the good-natured doctor had disappeared. He could have said many things. He could have said that men don't need this operation, they are perfect already. But the truth is that lately men are also oppressed by body image, men also suffer if they are not slim, handsome, blond, or strong.

"Dearest body," I added, "I am sorry. I will never again even consider cutting into you. I promise. That madness is over."

"It is cyclical. It takes different forms, but every six months you end up warring against your flesh." She is not buying my reformation act.

"Dearest body, I'll do more than stop attacking you. I shall treat you like the temple of the Goddess that you are."

"What do you mean?"

"I shall glorify your belly from now on."

"How?"

"I shall wear belly-hugging bejeweled belts and show you off."

"You will?" she is softening up.

"I shall display your belly with pride and wear clothes that decorate it."

Dearest body is now eager. "What about tonight?"

We start with a turquoise silk jumper. She loves that jumper. I am dressing up. I caress her as she slips into her underwear and silk clothes.

"Thank you. Thank you for the flesh," I say.

"You are welcome," she says. "You really love me, you know, you just don't realize it yet." She talks like a patient lover. She will teach me to appreciate her. Fat and all. Or fat in particular. I have such a long road to go. I am so sorry for all the attacks on her, I am so sorry for all the wasted energy we spent working against each other, instead of together. What if all the women in the world decide that fat is beautiful?

"Flabby bellies are desirable," she says.

I remember that all my lovers have loved my belly. Especially the one who loves me now. But I'm the one who has to start loving my own flesh.

In our culture women's fat and womanhood are constantly debated. It is a condition of faultiness, to be corrected, spent money on, worked on.

No woman is born a woman. She has to be made over to male standards. Slimness resembles the male body.

Maybe it is this simple. Patriarchy will fall when all women agree that we all look great and start acting like it. You can already see this conspiracy brewing when the women going to work on the buses and trains and ferries carry their high-heel shoes in a brown bag and slip them on only before they enter the workplace. They slip them off at 5:00 P.M. We know that those heels are not comfortable. Not good for us. It's the memory of footbinding that clings to them.

Men don't get together and exchange ideas on how to eat less, make less mass of themselves, and take up less space in the universe. Men mind their business, corporate affairs, money. What if the requirement that women be thin is only to keep women's energies tied up with hating/fighting themselves? What if it is that simple? An unconscious fear of women having their full energy/belly chakra to use for their own purposes?

Imagine! Not a penny for liposuction! No money to dieting programs and phony diet foods. Everywhere on the posters fat and healthy people having a good time. There are some skinny ones too, and some medium types, but fat people definitely come into vogue, on ad boards, magazine spreads. Roseanne spinoffs on television. But first we have to strike the ad industry with a vengeance and go through the transition that happens when things are changing for the better.

Dearest body is excited about my new revolutionary plans.

"It took millions of years to develop storing fat, you know," she says. "Millions! Those families whose mamas could store fat lived. Those people whose mamas didn't have fat cells in which to store energy died. Now the successful ones are numerous. What's wrong with that?"

My dearest body is getting her hopes up. She swings her hips in the silk jumper, she shifts the gears with gusto, she drives as if she were going to a magical ball. And she is. Already from the street I can hear that the party is in full swing. My lover receives me proudly. She knows she has thrown a great party for me. I hold her in my arms. Her body next to my belly.

"You feel good," she says.

My dearest body presses closer to hers in response.

"I made some resolutions," I confess.

"Good," she approves. "How about a glass of champagne? Everybody else is getting ahead of you."

I look at the huge birthday cake, with my name on it in cream, and I lick my lips.

"Tonight," I say to my dearest body, "you shall be denied nothing. You shall have love, acceptance, and cake."

"Cake? Cake?" she repeats it. I have not given her cake in months. "Really?"

"Really. Cake. Several slices. Eat your fill," I promised.

I wish I could love her more and regard my own and others' shortcomings with good-natured tolerance, fat or muscled. As long as our energies are spent in battle against food and our own flesh, there will be very few activists for women's rights, there will be few of us in leadership, fewer of us able to accept happiness at all.

The dearest body is all we really possess. It is dearest body that makes us feel our own lives. Let's stop the war on our own woman's flesh! Estrogen arise!

# SEVENTH MOON

*Time ‹ June–July*
*Sign ‹ Cancer*
*Lunar Herb ‹ Rose Hips*
*Lunar Animal ‹ Hare*

# Blessing Moon

## VIEW FROM THE MOON

The Blessing Moon moves through the starry sky like a queen among her maidens, serene, radiant, bestowing her favor with equal freedom on beautiful and ugly, on rich and poor. When the light of the Full Moon fills the night sky, all grows still in adoration. A great peacefulness surrounds her. The struggles of the waking world are forgotten. There is only the stillness of the night and the light of the Moon. Her healing light bathes the world, making all things romantic and beautiful.

She fills all creatures with joy.

## THE GODDESS SPEAKS

# *Selene*

I am the White Moon among the stars, silvery and shimmering, dusted with stardust. Your soul is calling me. Are you lovesick or love starved? Have you been forgotten by everyone? Are you as isolated as a machine? Grieve no more, my child. I cannot bear your flowing tears; come and give them to me and I will use them as dewdrops to moisten the grass. Know that everything is transient, love comes and love goes. Do not grieve over lost love or lost lives, for all return to me. Time is an illusion you have invented, it doesn't exist for me. I am constantly changing, and yet I remain the same. I am the original clock. The way you reckon time is based on my fluctuating cycles. Yes, the only thing that is constant is my fluctuation. That is all.

Look at the splendid white horses who are pulling my chariot across the sky! If you look closer, you will see me smiling at you—I, Selene, the mother of the night sky. I am the mother of Hecate, the Witch Queen. Walk beneath my cooling silver rays more often, and I will open your heart. I will open your centers of wisdom, I will dust you off like an old toy in the attic and give you new life.

There, do you feel my embrace now?

I will drip compassion and generosity like ambrosia into your soul, and I will give you children to watch over, I will give you sterling hope for the future and the smells of home-baked bread and homefires burning. Yes, I am home, the Moon, your originator, your protector, your champion.

My influence makes you protective toward all life, for it is my job to watch over all equally, missing none. I am the intelligence that animates the universe. It was my patient magnetism that nurtured the first organic matter, the first cells, inspiring them to divide and multiply. The variety of life-forms are all my artwork. At my prompting the fishes swarm, the guppies spawn, the turtles swim hundreds of miles to mate. It is I who make the reluctant lover more willing. My rays make the lonely soldier yearn for peace. My beauty inspires the minds of men and women to create music and poetry.

Look! A soul is now descending from me to a new mother's womb, my earthly palace. She doesn't know it yet, but this soul was waiting for the right moment to enter her life, and now she is blessed with a healthy new child! Look at all the souls I am harboring in my heart! They are all waiting to reenter life, and I seek out for them willing and committed mothers.

I don't want my children be born into neglect and crime. I don't want my lovely souls to be born to suffering and abuse. I want only those mothers who want to give birth to them. I am against forced motherhood, as I am against forced fatherhood. If you cannot be kind and nurturing to my sweet little ones, send them back to me. Do not hesitate, because I will always offer my infant souls a refuge. It is better to practice wisdom than to accept the care of a soul you cannot love. Give them back to me! I will carry them as I have throughout eternity. In my chariot they will find refuge and bliss. In my silvery bosom they will find the perfect parent that may not exist for them on earth. The Moon Goddess is kind, and the fairies who assist me will lull the babies to sleep or teach them spirit dances or sing with them the sweet songs of life and death and rebirth.

I am the mother of all organic life, but I am not a fool. I have instilled my wisdom in all women. They will remember the messages I have printed on their ancient brains, my DNA codes, and my instincts for survival. Life is precious, so you must treat it with great discrimination and care. Don't abuse my fertility rites, don't abuse my gift of seed. Too many of you can ruin the balance I have so carefully created. Overpopulation is a crime against my gift of life.

Ride easy now. I am watching over you, and you can always pray to me when you are in need. I am the essence of becoming, I am the being who preceded all the gods and their rules, and my women will remember me when I sound my silver trumpets of rebirth. For I am always there within them, and the Moon is the power of life.

## Cancer Message

This is the sign of greatest lunar influence, for this is the home of the Moon, the sign of Cancer. We absorb the nurturing vibrations of the Moon as she stimulates the sense of community in her children, the sense of belonging. Pleasure is very much part of this lunation; life has created a beam of moonlight to hang some happiness on. Eat heartily, sample nurturance, have a massage, get physical in nature. If you wish to have children, this is a good sign in which to conceive. Healthy, talented children will come out of this lunation.

In this sign sow and plant everything from which leaves are taken, but don't plant things that must climb or grow upward. This is not a good time to take journeys, but it is great for beauty treatments and shopping for clothes. Attend to family matters now. Get engaged or married, cultivate new friends, buy silver.

## MOONTIDE

## Envy

Envy is a bad feeling. It gnaws at our hearts, it embitters the sweet, it makes us mean and nasty. We envy people around us because we think we should be like them, and we are not. If they are gifted and are rewarded, we think we are overlooked. If they are happy, we think it unfair, since we are not. The root of envy is low self-esteem. A weak ego. A shaky self-image.

The universe is not unfair, and our turns will come. But our time will not come when it is someone else's turn. To rejoice in other people's good luck is to stimulate our own. To rejoice in other people's good luck is to identify with the lucky. The only psychic use of envy is to stimulate our own efforts to succeed. Envy is a difficult psychic flaw to manage.

## MOONSPELL
### *To Manage Envy*

*Left-brain work to deal with envy*    Write down all the reasons why you are envious and of whom. Go ahead, let it all out on paper. Then, on another piece of paper, explain why you deserve the same good luck as those you envy.

*Right-brain work*    Take the first list and light a gray candle (gray is the color to neutralize), light some purifying incense (bought ready-made at an occult supply store or herb shop or get some hyssop and burn that), and set fire to your envy list. Say:

> *All those I envied,*
> *All those I resented,*
> *I give my envy to the Moon.*
> *Once it burned me,*
> *Once they hurt me,*
> *Now my envy is consumed*
> *By the fire of Moon.*

Take your new list of the reasons why you deserve success and place it on a white cloth in front of your Goddess image (or in front of a vase of flowers, as the case may be). Place a white candle on top of it and light a different incense, your zodiac incense or something you really like to smell.  Say:

> *White Shell woman/Changing woman*
> *Made me wholesome and divine,*
> *She sends me the just and great rewards.*
> *I am wholesome, and I am divine.*
> *I am the best possible [your name] in the universe.*
> *I sow trust in me and grow and I reap,*
> *I work and am always duly rewarded.*

*I am noticed and appreciated everywhere.*
*I am myself, and I am fine.*

The deep mind needs repetitions in order to make a new behavior. Repeat this once a week, on Fridays when your week comes to a close.

## MOONTIDE

## *Awe*

Savor this feeling. It comes to you in sacred times, usually when you are alone in nature or when you witness a miracle of life, such as the rising of the Moon or a sunset, the birth of a baby or a kitten or any living thing. The feeling of awe overwhelms us when we encounter the forces of life, when we have been privileged to glimpse some of the awesome beauty, the awesome power, or the awesome creativity of the Goddess.

When you feel that sense of awe, pray to the Goddess. You are already in an altered state of consciousness, you are already in a state of worship. Assume the classic position of prayer, standing proudly, facing the universe, the mountains, the woods, the green world around you. Arms stretched heavenward as if embracing the whole world, make your affirmations. You may not need to say anything at all. Just allow yourself to experience this state of bliss, of intimacy with the divine. Seek more moments like this, spending time feeling awe. The endeavor will surely lead you to much happiness.

# FESTIVALS OF THE MOON

### Feast of Athena Sciras
### Twelfth Day of Scirophirion, Waxing Moon—Ancient Greece

At this time of year the fierce heat of the sun was dangerous to crops planted in the thin Grecian soil. At a spot outside Athens, Athena was invoked to protect the crops. The priestess of Athena and the priests of Erectheus (founder of Athens) and of Helios made offerings of olives and figs and pears. Do a protection spell upon the matters of your own life during this time. (See *The Grandmother of Time.*)

### Vainikinas, the Binding of Wreaths
### Full Moon of July—Lithuania

Young people celebrate this ancient Lithuanian festival of summer by going to the woods at sunset, where they pick flowers and cut green boughs, which are woven into wreaths and garlands. Two birch or two linden trees are bound together to form an arch, and the girls and boys march through it. When two girls meet two boys, they kiss and sing verses invoking the blessing of a Goddess on sweethearts. It has been suggested that this Goddess is related to the Latvian Laima, "Dearest Goddess." This festival is similar to Beltane customs from warmer lands, where summer comes earlier. One suspects that in earlier cultures where lovemaking was not seen as sinful, the couples that passed through the arch together did more than kissing.

### Bon Festival
### Full Moon of July—Japan

The Japanese festival of the dead is held in July and features elements from both Buddhism and Shinto. Preparation for the holiday involves a complete cleaning of houses, tombs, and ancestral tablets. Buddhist priests and nuns visit houses and graves to recite the sutras and pray for the souls of the dead. Altars and shrines are refurbished and decorated with vases of flowers. Presents of raw fish are given. On the thirteenth day of the month, the spirits of the dead are welcomed back at their graves, escorted back to their former homes, and offered a ceremonial meal. Torches and lamps light their way home. The spirits also wander in the gardens among the flowers. *Bon-adori* soul dances are performed by young women in the moonlight. On the sixteenth day of the month, the spirits are released to return to the otherworld. They are offered gifts, and spirits who have no relatives are honored by little boats bearing paper lanterns. These are set afloat on the Tide of Returning Ghosts to drift out to sea. Pay attention to your loved one's graves. Visit the elderly, make amends, so that good blood is between you and your ancestors.

## Naga-Panchami
### Asarha Full Moon — Bengal, India

Naga-Panchami is the festival of the Serpent Goddess Manasa-Devi, who is especially effective in granting fertility to women. Her serpents, the Nagas and Naginis, control access to spiritual truth, granting it to those who are worthy and keeping it from those who are not. They also prevent such truths from going beyond the material plane. The serpent seems to have been the totem of the ancient Dravidians, and their cult is popular and widespread, especially in southern India. The serpent is, of course, associated with the Earth Goddess in many pre-Indo-European cultures as a symbol of rebirth.

## Feast of the Virgin of Carmine
### July 16, Full Moon — Italy

This is a major summer festival in Italian communities in both Italy and America. The Madonna is honored as a healer of the sick. Candles decorated with images of the diseased parts of the body and models of body parts are offered to her. The offering of such images is a very ancient practice, and carved representations of body parts were thrown into sacred springs and pools as far back as Celtic times. Today the festival features fireworks and illuminations and pushcarts selling all kinds of food.

This practice can be adapted for personal healing rituals involving a problem with a specific part of the body. Depending on your artistic ability, carve a pink candle into the shape of an afflicted limb or organ, or set it on top of a drawing or Xerox. Burn sage incense or any other scent you find soothing, and fan the smoke over the candle and/or picture. Say:

> *By this bright charm*
> *I heal from harm*
> *The [name of part]'s pain.*
> *Consumed by flame,*
> *In the Lady's name,*
> *Come not again!*

Burn the candle for three or nine nights, depending on the size of the problem and of the candle. As the wax melts in the flame, visualize the problem disappearing and the unhealthy limb or body being transformed into radiant health. When the candle is burned down, throw the remains into running water.

# MOON TALE

## *Ecstasy*

When was the last time you roamed on a mountaintop at midnight in the company of garlanded, merry folks, celebrating the Full Moon? We usually spend our evenings trying to get home before it's too late, watching some TV behind locked doors. We may cook a nice meal, call a friend, or just sit down and have a drink. We might go out later to a bar or movie or theater. But on the whole we have little freedom to be ecstatic at night.

We are already living in the twenty-first century, very early in it, but we have been catching up to the next century rapidly as a collective consciousness. We are arriving there as a global village. We are arriving fed up with wars and male violence and the oil crisis. We are arriving with the women all awake at once, with global women's consciousness.

Collective minds used to use drugs to get this kind of synthesis back in the good old pagan days, when we worshiped nature as our mother. When taken properly in ritual, those drugs produced ecstasy as a communal experience. The earth-worshiping traditions all held sacred rituals where ecstasy was shared as sacrament. Millennia went by during which human beings worshiped the forces that kept them alive. All the folk dances, all the ecstatic dancing traditions, all the hypnotic music of the drums and flutes and pipes mingled together were intended to produce religious ecstasy. A diverse global culture sought ecstasy as an expression of the divine.

We don't have such culture anymore. We don't think that prayer is supposed to make us feel ecstasy, the joy of communion with the divine. We only carry a deep-seated hunger for that lost experience. We hunger for ecstasy. We think God is ecstasy. But God isn't ecstasy. God is more like reality.

Ecstasy is far older. Its origins lie in the age of innocence. People back then saw God everywhere. They wanted to play with God, experience the divine, not just hear about it. The Goddess and God of Ecstasy live on only within our ancient memories. Nobody has seen them much lately.

The drugs we take now are no longer supposed to take us into ecstasy. But drug use itself is a form of longing for ecstasy. What we really want is religious ecstasy, which is like a drug itself. Imagine what it would be like if every month all the folks got together and had a celebration about this Goddess or that God and danced outdoors for three days and three nights, often up in the mountains. This kind of religion would gather wide support.

I tried to bring back the old festivals and celebrated the Full Moons for ten years with ad hoc gatherings of anywhere from 17 to 120 people at one time. That makes 210 rituals in 10 years. This figure includes 13 Full Moons and 8 sabbats a year. Rain or shine. Small group or large.

I came close to ecstasy at least three times. How do I know it was ecstasy? The first thing you must realize is that while you are experiencing it, you are not analyzing what it is. You know that something wonderful is going on, but you will not identify that heightened awareness. Altered states reveal themselves later, once you are no longer in them.

The first time I experienced true religious ecstasy was with the Susan B. Anthony Coven Number 1, my old group. I remember that it was an Esbat, a Full Moon. The sabbats (seasonal festivals) were better attended than Full Moons. Esbats were usually attended by only the hard-core witches. And me.

Our group was changing. We had already opened a candle shop on Lincoln Boulevard in Venice, California, and we had started attracting women of color from the neighborhood. Magic in the black community was a totally different world. They all practiced heavy-duty candle burning, sometimes shopping for a full crate of candles at once. Some women had candles going all night and all day. The fire was transferred from one candle to a new one. The flame continued, living on like that for many years sometimes. It didn't matter how long the sacred flame was sustained, it was the effort that counted.

From this community one day we met Lucille. Her real name was Joan, but she had just changed it. But she was thinking of calling herself Isis, because she had just discovered the black Goddesses.

Lucille would come in the morning after she dropped her kids off at school and get a few things. It might be a little incense or scent, because she played around with oils; she loved lavender. Lucille was talkative, and she was informed. She knew about herbs and things we had never even heard of. She tested our dedication by asking us to get her some Devil's shoestring herb and human-looking mandrakes. These were hard items to get. The FDA was busy outlawing our beloved ingredients such as mandrakes and orrisroot powder. But we found them for her, and she was always ready with the next challenge.

Lucille had two wonderful young daughters, ten and eight. They were always very well combed, Lucille liked to brush their hair a lot. She was a doting mother. Gradually she began to bring the kids to the store, first Maddalena and then Martina. The kids helped us make incense packages, they were handy with herbs and stones, and they loved the books. It became a habit that the kids would come to us from school first and wait for their mother to pick them up.

Naturally they were invited to our Full-Moon rituals. Lucille loved rituals and so did the girls. They had their own medicine bundle, their own mojos in it, and their own herbs. Both kids came on the night I'm describing, plus Lucille. We walked up the mountain through the sage-scented night, some twenty-three strong, and we felt very playful after the climb. All that oxygen was enriching our brains.

We formed our circle holding hands and built our altar. On this night Kirsten had her camera with her and she took commemorative shots of the candles burning around the Triple Goddess. All I remember about how things looked that night was the Full Moon that had appeared so close to my face, so huge that it seemed that if I stuck out my tongue I could lick it.

I was filled with happiness. The power raising went very well with the group. They hummed and then chanted freely, generating energy so that our prayers could rise up smoothly. Finally we got to the part when I, as acting priestess, had to offer up the chalice to the Moon. And right there in the middle of holding up my chalice to the Moon, seeing her full roundness resting against the rim of my cup, I suddenly realized where the form and choreography for the consecration of the Catholic communion wafer was stolen from. Of course! It was the Full Moon over the witches' chalice, now appropriated by the church.

I was savoring this night especially. So as I was calling on the Goddess to come be part of our circle, calling her into the liquid of transformation, our wine, I did something unusual. I added a clause to my invocation, and I said to her, "If you please . . ."

Now, usually witches do not pray by abasing themselves like slaves. We don't kneel in prayer, we don't think our Goddess requires us to act like worthless wretches. Many of our invocations are simply calls from equal to equal. But this night I felt humble, I felt the awesome beauty of her heavens. The Moon was so strong that I just couldn't help myself. I said, "If you please."

The circle swayed as usual with the electricity generated by our minds and bodies, but then suddenly a woman, I didn't know which one, yelled out.

"Oh my gaaaaaaawd!" I looked, and the woman who had yelled was

Lucille, but now she was transformed. She looked taller, much taller than before. She stretched to her full height, and she was glowing!

I thought, *Oh, no, Lucille —*. She had wanted to go into ecstasy ever since she met us, she was always talking about it, and now she was doing it. I just hoped that it was genuine and not just theater, because Lucille did like a good show, and she could fake possession if she wanted to and I would never be the wiser.

"Aaaooooo!" Now it was another woman, and the same thing was happening, a woman would yell real loud then get real tall and then glow. What was going on? If we were going to have an Esbat with a bunch of fake possessions, how was I ever going to ground this group? Besides, I didn't know how to handle possessions back then, fake or otherwise. I finished the prayers and had started to set the chalice back down when I too felt it.

It was like an electric current that goosed, literally goosed my behind, goosed the seat of kundalini, the base of my spine, then it proceeded to shoot upward, like heat, as if lightning had struck me.

"Auuuch!" I yelled myself.

It was the sudden unfolding of the kundalini, the female serpent power, the ancient fire. To have this experience most devotees have to go to classes for years!

This rare experience was now sweeping through my small witches' group, one by one. Kundalini, this fire of life, was shooting up to our heads. We all grew to our full height as it did so. Then we held our heads high, and I could feel that I was glowing too. I could have touched my own halo! We looked so divine! Every member of our group experienced this sudden flash of energy. All of us, including the kids, had our kundalini opened up for the first time, and none of us will ever forget it.

Not only did the Moon seem close to my face but so did the stars and so did the faces of all my sisters, black faces and white faces, brown faces, Asian faces, we all glowed together in this uniting ecstasy. Just because we were there at the right time and the right place, Mother Nature extended to us an experience that was certainty, not faith. The heightened sense of reality, the rapture of our happiness in being alive, in being together and part of this spontaneous ecstasy, lasted us a long time.

This circle felt as if we had taken some very fine, very special drugs, but we hadn't even drunk the wine yet. We shared the chalice, passing it from woman to woman, from toast to toast, but it was the elixir of the Moon, it was the fire of the kundalini that produced the altered states of consciousness.

We danced, we feasted, we made up new songs that night, we even played some Goddess games. The kids' presence added a special touch to it all. The new generation was present among us already. They watched the candles, and if one got too close to the quick, they made sure it was safe. When we finished our circle, it was already a pink dawn. We had never circled more than two or three hours before, and I had considered those circles too long. This one felt like it had been going on for only half an hour, yet we saw the golden sunrise together. When the sense of time slips away, just like a visit in fairyland, you know you have been granted an experience of ecstasy with the Moon.

# EIGHTH LUNATION

*Time ‹ July–August*
*Sign ‹ Leo*
*Lunar Herb ‹ St. John's Wort, Rue*
*Lunar Animal ‹ Salmon*

# Corn Moon

## VIEW FROM THE MOON

*All over the Northern Hemisphere the lands that the Corn Moon lights are turning from green to gold. Summer flowers bloom along the roads and in the woodlands; purple asters and blue cornflowers, red poppies like drops of blood against the grass. In the orchards the fruit is beginning to blush with sweetness, and the grain grows high, seedheads swelling with goodness. The light of day lingers long upon the fields, and when the Full Moon rises, she glows a mellow gold. She sees completion and fullness, she sees the reward for all the labor of spring and summer approaching.*

*She blesses the earth with maturity.*

## THE GODDESS SPEAKS
# *Cybele*

I came to you as a black meteorite, a shiny black obsidian butterfly. I rested on your forehead for a moment and you thought that the wind had touched your brow. But it was me, the Goddess Cybele.

When I am among my people, I am the maker of music and games, I am the lovers' sweet bed, I am the ecstasy of the universe. I am the mother of Attis, my male self, I unite with him in the summer's heat and conceive a new son for the future. My priestesses dance for many days in my festivals, they rage down the mountain holding aloft my torch of life, and then with a shriek they extinguish the flame in the ocean.

I am sad then, because I know that my Attis has died again from his self-inflicted wounds. Each year he bleeds to death under my tree of life. My fate is that of many mothers who lose their children to wars or violence. But my powers are magical. When I call his name three times, my voice carries all the way to the realm of the dead. I have buried his lifeless body under my tree of life where he died, and from his blood the violets spring.

I am also the sorrowful mother, the wailing mad mother, the mother who doesn't forget. I am the Pietà, holding my son's dear body in my lap, breathing life back into him so that he will rise in the spring and laugh and drink in a new form. I am all mothers who have shed tears and spent sleepless nights because the sons we bore have gone back to death, and we must claim them again and again so that they may return again through the door of life. I am the Lady of the Harvest, knowing that the grain must be cut down in order to rise once more.

And, oh, when he does, when his sweet laughter is echoing everywhere, when his flawless face fills my eyes again, when he joins the dancing with my priests and priestesses, the Great Resurrection, the green miracle has been accomplished again.

Bring my fierce nocturnal lions and I, Cybele, will take my place in my chariot. Slowly, at a queenly pace, my great sacred cats parade around the city so that my people may see my face. My crown is the four walls of the city itself. I protect it. The Crescent Moon upon my brow is the sign that I am the Mother. Throngs of my people are cheering and waving violet silk flags. Flower petals are thrown in my path. My chariot, like the Moon, rolls majestically across the sky.

Do you frown upon my sacred eunuchs, thinking that they are useless because they have castrated themselves to be more like me? It isn't for you to judge. For many men want to serve me, and in my tradition men may change their sex if they so desire. They are not freaks, they are my sacred priests. Only in your time is it so unusual for a male to want to give up his maleness because of his longing to be a woman.

I am the mother lioness. I rule with justice and unconditional love. I am the one who can claim you from death and draw you back into life's flow. It is I who can bestow a second chance on those who are lost. When you are in your lover's arms and orgasmic feelings shake your body, you are worshiping me. I gave you the ability to feel fully, to be alive fully, to come near me in your ecstasy.

Play flutes for me and feast on my roasted mutton, dance my fierce rounds, and make love in the meadows. No child of mine will ever be devoured by eternal death, for I hold the key to reincarnation.

Cry out, as the priests and priestesses who served me in ancient Rome proclaimed, "Be of good cheer neophytes, for Attis has been saved and so shall we in turn be saved" (in Merlin Stone, *Ancient Mirrors of Womanhood*, 201).

Nobody is condemned in my traditions. No mode of sexuality is dictated to you or required. All my children are equal in love and all are blessed. Join the parade that follows my silver image, carry me to my new place of honor, bathe my image in your rivers and lakes, adore me with violets, burn my incense in rich billows of smoke. Take to the Full Moon's esctasy your open heart and know that the joy of life is safe. The joy of life is me. The joy of life is the natural state for your heart. Rejoice!

## Leo Message

This eighth lunation is filled with queenly energy, the kind we need in times of trouble and times of business. Absorb optimism from this vibration, because to be aware of the light side of life is a particular blessing. It is a good time to interact with your peers, socialize, date a lot, make contracts, rule your world with beneficence and wisdom. A Moon in Leo gives you skill in organizing others into projects, far-reaching goals, visions. Energy is the theme of this lunation, so express your power, save the earth, save yourself, make your world a better place for everybody.

In the sign of Leo, start things that should last a long time, such as studies in philosophy or creative projects. If you deal with the law, now you will be favored. Deal with precious stones, gold, silver. Plant your roses and they will have wonderful scents and colors. Plant everything from which fruits or seeds are taken. Now is also the time to prune your trees and bushes. Paint your house, spruce up your environment.

## MOONTIDE

## Enthusiasm

Enthusiasm is the currency of life, it is gold. If you have enthusiasm for your projects and what is going on in your life, you are going to be successful. Everybody loves a person who has this kind of glowing energy. If you don't have enthusiasm, if you get up tired in the morning, or you never seem to relax deeply, something is not functioning right. In addition to talking to mental-health workers, perform the spell that follows upon yourself in secret, telling no one.

## MOONSPELL

## For Enthusiasm

Under the Full Moon in Leo, go out to a wild place where you can be assured of privacy and build a safe fire, big enough to make you feel warm. (If you cannot make it to the wilderness, build the fire in a hibachi in the backyard or even on a screened apartment balcony.) Prepare an altar by spreading a small white cloth near the fire and place upon it a cup of wine and a cup of water, a beautiful braided bread, and some frankincense and myrrh in a fire-safe dish.

Now pray to the Moon, arms stretched skyward. Praise her beauty, her power. When you feel that you have gotten her attention, take your clothes off so that your skin can absorb the magical vibrations of the Moon. Feel the breath of the night on your skin, feel the freedom of being one with nature, and run around the fire three times yelling something affirmative.

"I love my life!" for example, would be good, or "I bless my life!"

Now that you are all warmed up, still skyclad, jump over the fire three times. Each time you jump you should make a short wish.

"Enthusiasm!" you may choose to call. "Good health!" "More energy!"

The Goddess will grant you whatever you call out as you leap over her sacred fire. This ritual is one of purification as well, because it cleanses you from the past.

When you have finished the three jumps, take a sip of the water and then pour the rest onto the earth, saying, "I salute you, Goddess of All Life!"

Then take a sip of the wine and again pour some of it on the earth, saying, "I salute you, Mother of All Gods!"

Drink some more of the wine if you wish, and give your third blessing: "Honor to the Earth and all those who serve her!" Pour the rest out on the ground. It is a courtesy to return a little of the wine and water to where they come from, to the earth. After this you may linger and visit, talk to the Moon, light candles—it's up to you. But after doing this ritual, starting the next day, you will have more energy than ever before.

## MOONTIDE
## *Shame*

This is a difficult feeling to deal with, for shame is our patriarchal emotional heritage. Our conditioning to be ashamed of being women begins when we are barely out of babyhood. Little girls who are raised as Jews or Christians or Moslems are taught that Eve, the original mother of all, gave away the store. We learn to our horror that she was to blame for losing paradise! Paradise! And we have just arrived in this world and the jig is already up! Who would not feel royally ripped off at this news?

Then we actually do something for which we feel shame. We hurt a lover, a parent, a child. We hurt ourselves. We exercise our sexuality in ways that are not approved by society. We feel we are too fat. We are poor, we cannot provide for our children well enough, we are not good housekeepers. We internalize that shame also. By the time we are grown, we are well accustomed to this shame, we carry it naturally now, pretend it doesn't bother us anymore. But it does.

Shame is a tool men use to rule females. Men are not susceptible to it in the same way. Men don't believe that they should be ashamed of themselves as a sex for being responsible for 90 percent of the crime in the world, making wars, killing women, molesting children. They know they are men, hence they are inherently "worthy." Society assures men of their value all their lives, so if they do something wrong or shameful, they apologize, and that's the end of it. Women, by contrast, feel ashamed just for existing, because of the conditioning they have undergone since birth.

## MOONSPELL
## *To Get Rid of Shame*

If you have done something real that you are ashamed of, apologize to the hurt parties and make restitution. If you still feel guilty after that is done, try this.

Go outdoors to view the Waning Moon and meditate on it for a time. Then return inside and take a long purification bath, with blue bath salts (so that your bathwater looks blue). Afterward rub lemon peels on your heels and ankles, an old gypsy way to purify.

Then light two white candles and place them on either side of a mirror, light some purifying incense, such as sage, and inhale it, taking deep breaths. Stand naked between the candles and face your reflection. This is deep work, because you have to reach to the oldest memories of shame that you have. Look into your own eyes in the mirror and say, "I forgive myself from my deep memory for being female."

Then take a breath without a word. Continue:

> *I celebrate myself for being female. [breathe]*
>
> *I forgive Eve, my foremother, who wisely ate of the fruit of the Tree of Knowledge. [breathe]*
>
> *I celebrate Eve, my foremother, who created my species through inventing menstruation. [deep breath]*
>
> *I forgive the little girl who believed that she was shameful. [deep breath]*
>
> *I celebrate the little girl who survived to become me. I celebrate her! [breathe]*
>
> *I forgive the young woman who was used and oppressed. [breathe]*
>
> *I celebrate the young woman who survived the lies and became the spiritual warrior. [deep breath]*

Here you have to get creative and write your own script, because you alone know the particulars in your life. What else do you need to forgive yourself and celebrate yourself for?

When you come to the part where you actually did something shameful, follow the same procedure. First forgive yourself, then celebrate yourself for having overcome the shame. Do as many affirmations as needed. When you are finished, get dressed and nip off the candles.

Once a month, when the Moon is waning, you can give yourself a booster on shame repelling. Shame is like mold, it creeps back if you are not looking.

# FESTIVALS OF THE MOON

### Meeting of the Herdsman and the Weaver Girl
### Seventh Day, New Moon of the Seventh Moon—Japan

This lovers' festival appears to celebrate the closest approach to Earth of the stars Vega and Altair. Vega is Chih Nu, the Weaver Girl, the daughter of the sun, whose task it was to weave the iridescent seamless robes of the gods. Some say that in her tapestries she wove the changing seasons as well. She was married to the cowherd from across the Milky Way (Altair), and their passion was so overwhelming that they spent all their time making love, and no work got done. So the gods exiled Chih Nu to one side of heaven and her lover to the other. On one night in the year they cross a bridge of branches carried by magpies for an ecstatic reunion. Another version of the story says that Chih Nu's lover was a worthy mortal whom she bought out of slavery through the excellence of her weaving. Chih Nu was the patroness of domestic arts and weaving in particular, to whom young girls prayed in order to gain skill. Young women held needlework contests at the time of this festival.

These stars are the brightest stars in the sky overhead and can be seen most easily at dusk before the other stars appear. With Deneb, they form the Weaving Maid's crown. This is a time to remember long-lost lovers. Invite the one you love to watch the sunset, and look for the Weaver Maid and her lover in the night sky. A nice dinner might follow, and after that, who knows?

### Brauronia, Feast of Artemis
### Hekatombaion, New Moon—Ancient Greece

The cult of Artemis as Bear Goddess originated in Brauron in Attica and was adopted by the Athenians. Sometime between their fifth and tenth year, girls would spend a summer at the Temple of Artemis, learning the rites of the Goddess and practicing the bear dance, which was performed at the Feast of Artemis at the beginning of August. They were called the little bears and wore fringed garments dyed with saffron. At the festival they marched in procession to the temple, accompanied by their mothers, and were commended to the care of the Goddess.

Celebrate this holiday by taking your daughter for a picnic at a park. If you don't have a daughter, borrow one—invite the child of a friend. Even better, make it a joint affair with other women and girls. Give the girls saffron-colored ribbons to wear, and run races, play ball and other games with wreaths for the winners. Pile stones to make an altar, and lay flowers and some of the food from the picnic upon it as an offering. Dance in a ring, and ask the blessing of Artemis upon her daughters.

### Moon Sister Chang-O
### Fifteenth Day, Full Moon—China

On this midautumn night the Moon looms big and bright. It is a time of thankfulness for heaven's bounty, sharing a lantern procession with friends, telling the magical stories of Chang-O the Moon Goddess, eating the sacred mooncakes, dressing up, feasting in her honor.

The Moon Goddess Chang-O ascended into the Moon when she drank the elixir of life, which granted immortality. Her worship rituals are conducted by women only. On her Moon altar the women place a picture of the Jade Palace where Chang-O lives in the Moon, a small figure of the Moon rabbit who protected the Goddess. Thirteen mooncakes for the cycle of the year are offered to her. Then the women light the candles and the incense and each woman steps out, prays to her, and bows. Spirit money is set on fire. Moon music is performed by the Moon sisters, who specialize in songs concerning matters of the heart.

### Feast of Pacha Mama
### Sowing Month, Full Moon—Ancient Peru

For those living in the Southern Hemisphere, this time of year begins the agricultural season. Pacha Mama was the Inca Earth Goddess who was represented by a long stone set in the fields. The Coya (wife of the Inca, who served as chief priestess of Mama Huaca, the mother of the chief of the gods) made offerings, asking the Goddess to protect and fertilize the fields. Offerings were also made to the frost, air, water, and sun.

## Feast of the Plow of Sita
### Sravana Full Moon — India

Sita, wife of the legendary god-king Rama, was an incarnation of the fertility/prosperity Goddess Lakshmi. Her name means "furrow," because she was born from the earth at the touch of the plow. Because of its role in releasing the fertility of the earth, the plow was a sacred symbol, and it was considered lucky to have one present at a wedding ceremony.

After she and Rama were married, Sita was kidnapped by the monkey king Ravan. Rama rescued her, but the people gossiped, questioning her chastity. Even though she proved her purity by appealing to the Fire God, Agni, Rama's honor still required him to exile her. Talk about blaming the victim! Listen to this: Their children brought about a reconciliation, but when Rama began to doubt her once more, Sita appealed to the earth from which she came to prove her innocence by taking her back again. I guess even the Goddess gets fed up! When earth took her daughter back into her womb, Rama was convinced, and sorry. But of course it was too late by then. This male god needs therapy.

This can be interpreted as the return of the harvested grain to the soil or, in more human terms, as a drama of the (feminine) generosity of nature versus self-destructive male pride.

## Assumption of the Virgin Mary
### August 15, Full Moon — Medieval Europe

All over Europe the festival celebrating the ascent into heaven of the mother of Jesus — her transition from human to divine — was a firstfruits festival, incorporating elements of the old celebration in honor of the Goddess. At these festivals Mary is specifically invoked to protect the harvest during the last crucial days before it is gathered in, especially from hail. I remember this festival as a little girl. We had to gather flower petals. My friend Ida and I busied ourselves all afternoon gathering as many flowers as we could and then taking the petals off the stems. We then participated in a procession of mostly women carrying the statue of the Virgin around the fields in the neighborhood, casting these petals in front of the litter of the Virgin.

In *Woman's Mysteries* (109–10) M. Esther Harding quotes from the Syriac text of "The Departure of My Lady Mary from This World," which states: "And the Apostles also ordered that there should be a commemoration of the Blessed One on the thirteenth of Ab [the Hebrew lunar month closest to August] . . . that clouds of hail, bearing stones of wrath, might not come, and the trees be broken, and the vines with their clusters." This is the same purpose for which offerings were formerly made at this time to Hecate and Diana in ancient Greece and Rome.

In Armenia and Bulgaria the feast celebrated the beginning of the grape harvest. In Greece offerings of new wheat and small cakes were made. In Syria the offerings also included small yoni-shaped cakes. Elsewhere the fruit trees were blessed as well. In England herbs were blessed by the priest and afterward used for curing charms. In Scotland this was the great feast of Mary, the time of the Marymass Fair, at which horse races, the oldest in Europe, are held (horse racing is also a part of the festival in Syria). In Elche, Spain, an elaborate three-day drama of the Assumption is presented in the cathedral, which culminates in Mary's coronation as Queen of Angels.

On this day make an offering of your own firstfruits to the Goddess. Set up an altar with fruits and cakes and flowers, and lay upon it a representative sample of whatever projects you are working on. Thank her for making you productive, and ask her help in completing the work.

### Nagyboldogasszony Napja
### Full Moon, or August 15—Hungary

This holiday commemorates Hungary's historical decision to join Europe as a new nation at the beginning of the eleventh century. In order to be accepted, we had to be Christianized, and this was enforced by the mighty arm of the official military. Dissenters who rebelled and wanted to remain part of the Goddess-worshiping Earth religion as they had before were killed, tortured, and maimed.

In order to appease the angry nation, the first king, Saint Stephen, himself a new convert for political reasons, made a huge ceremony of offering up our new Christian nation to the Blessed Mother. The Goddess didn't even have to have her name changed, she was called the Big Glad Woman, and that is what we called Mary. There is a difference—the Big Glad Woman had only a daughter, called Little Glad Woman, not a son called Jesus. But we overlooked this in order to continue the worship of Mother Nature. So today in modern Hungary this is a red-letter day. Nobody goes to work. There are fireworks at night over the river Danube, big feasts, and during the day long processions on the main streets of Budapest carrying the right hand of Stephen in a gilded box. It is said that his hand is still preserved after a thousand years because when he offered up the crown, this hand touched the hem of the cloak of our Queen of Heaven, the Boldogasszony.

# MOON TALE

## *Jumping Over the Broom*

My most enjoyable role in life is to be the priestess, the Medea, the Medicine woman. In my capacity as the Medea I have perfomed memorial services for people who have passed on, house blessings, and blessings on children. I have done many political spells with large groups of women and men and spells and rituals to heal the Earth. My latest project is creating Earth pledge circles, in which we each pledge to recycle our glass bottles, plastic bags, newspapers, and so on as a sacred promise. When somebody has made an enthusiastic promise, we all chant, "What a good Earthling!"

The bulk of my work as a Medea is performing weddings.

Like most women, I love weddings. I love to get dressed up in my purple gown, to decorate my head with flowers, to meet with the wedding party, who are usually at their wits' end, put them at ease, give them their parts, explain the ritual, and then with all the family members perform the ritual—always different for each couple, for each party.

I want to talk about weddings because marriage is the most loaded symbol for women and the most emotionally charged ritual there is. It is sometimes the only outstanding ritual in a woman's life. Patriarchy has

taken away all the others, such as coming of age, the celebration of her
first menstruation, which is certainly as momentous as a wedding and
whose effects last longer than most relationships. No longer has she a
ritual to honor her when she is Queen, a woman in her prime who has
taken on the work of the Goddess in the world. She has been ignored and
certainly is not celebrated when she becomes a crone (age fifty-six) and
enters the wise age, the sage age, the age of wisdom.

But at her wedding a woman is acknowledged as a Goddess. She is
dressed up in the white gown of the Sun Goddess Lucina, at whose
festivals in Sweden all girls and women wear the white gown. Her sacred
veil means she is protected, she is blessed. Her long train, carried by
young women or girls, signifies that she is in the flower of life and is the
head of all the women. Weddings as we know them today still incorporate
many ancient elements. It is these symbols that wake tears in the eyes of
women. It is the lost symbolism, whose importance is dimly remembered
even though its true meaning is unknown, that makes women cry at
weddings.

What is going on?

Love is going on. Not even patriarchy can change that.

Grandmother Moon has enchanted another young or old couple, she
has moved their hearts, and now they want to make a public commitment
to each other. This publicly witnessed commitment is what's really old.
The community witnesses a love bond and treats that couple differently
afterward. The ritual creates a space between what was and what is to be.
It makes the transition from being engaged to being married.

I often ache at these rituals because I also long for somebody with
whom to make this kind of public commitment. My wedding to the young
boy from Hungary whom I married when I was nineteen only worked for
a few years, then we grew up and grew apart. I have no bitterness about
it, I just felt that the state of being married as it exists in contemporary
American culture was not a good place for me or any other woman. It
isn't natural to separate women from each other into their respective
split-level houses, locked in with the identical architecture and indoor

appliances. It isn't natural not to talk to your neighbors. It isn't natural to think that you exist alone in the world with only one man and your kids. Human beings are social beings. We need community. Most species who build societies see to it that the females and babies have plenty of support groups, each other, plenty of information. Isolation is only for those who are preparing to die.

Each new couple starts out with good intentions. They don't have time to realize that one partner, the female, is already disadvantaged because she belongs to the less appreciated caste. Her earning power is only half that of a male equal to her in skills. Women own only 1 percent of the wealth of the world, while we do 90 percent of its labor. This is something that the young woman doesn't want to know or contemplate. It is too depressing. In the West we are individuals, we are different. Western women are not going to be oppressed like the female sex was during the last two thousand years. Rising on the wings of our special love, we will overcome this. Our lives will be different.

If women didn't think like this, if we started having meetings over our plight in the world, started concentrating on our oppression and what to do about it, nobody would dare to get married for many, many years. And the Goddess of Love would not like that. She wants us to be on schedule, she has biological clocks clicking, she has hormones churning, she has young hearts and old hearts yearning. Revolutions have to be fought simultaneously with her plans. That's all there is to it.

Love is now. So are weddings.

Pagan weddings can be elaborate and expensive or very flexible and simple. They also can be legal or not legal, depending on the combination of the sexes involved. Same-sex weddings are still not recognized by any church or state but have always been recognized by the Goddess. I perform a great many lesbian weddings.

The most recent wedding I did here in Berkeley, however, was for a heterosexual couple—Cynthia and Paul.

They were classic examples of the progressive tradition. They met when they were both students at the University of California. One day

Cynthia submitted a poem about some chameleons to the local paper, something about their tongues and lightning, rather long and wise. This poem won an award and was printed in its entirety. Paul read that issue over his coffee and liked the poem with the chameleons. He liked the long discussion and the frightening images Cynthia had thrown onto the page. He liked it so well that he wrote to her in care of the paper. The poem resonated with something in him. He himself liked to write things down, especially about chameleons. She answered the letter and they met. That was twenty years ago. They had been together ever since. They never got married. They didn't believe in it. They were both Jewish, but their relationship was a fiercely private matter to them, not to be messed with by rabbis.

Now their children wanted them to get married. The children were about to get married themselves, and their parents' situation bothered them. But Cynthia and Paul were holding out. They refused to cave in to social pressure. There was only one possibility—Paul and Cynthia had agreed to get married if they could do it in a Goddess ritual conducted by a witch. That would be different. They were willing to get married like that.

The kids tracked me down and told me the story. What a great honor! Of course I agreed.

The wedding was held on top of a hill overlooking the blue Bay, full of fluttering sailboats, with the fog coming in from the Pacific and the city's skyscrapers glistening on the other side of the Bay. Paul was the hardest one to get ready for the ceremony. He didn't want to wear a crown of flowers. He loved the flowers but he had trouble with the crown concept. It was too feudal. I explained to him that wearing flowers on our heads means we identify with the earth. It was also a symbol of respect for the marriage. That was a reason he could understand.

At the beginning of a "tryst," the kind of Goddess wedding ceremony I perform, there is always music chosen by the trystees. Usually it is played by a gentle harp, flute, or piano, a violin, or a couple of violins.

I myself prefer the heartbeat rhythm of drums, round and warm sounds, rising from deep in the belly up to the mind. On this occasion Cynthia had asked a friend called Bob to play his harmonica, but he was so shy he stayed too far away from the audience and we could hardly hear him. But we all knew that he was playing beautifully, even if we could only hear it when the wind blew our way.

It didn't matter.

Paul and Cynthia were led in by their kids, slowly, listening to their inner music. He was dressed in a regular business suit, she in a lavender gown with an amethyst necklace. They were both barefoot, as I had requested, so that they could touch the earth. But they walked on rose petals the kids had scattered in their path. You could tell this was a very beloved couple. They had raised their four kids together, accumulated friends along the way. Now for the first time they were publicly celebrating their union. A very different wedding indeed.

This audience didn't take long to raise energy for the ceremony. I explained the sonic meditation technique, in which the coordinated humming of a group of people aligns their brainwaves, and they did it, just like that. Upon this collective vibration, soft as a bed of mist, I floated the ceremony.

The tray of food was also very special. Roasted almonds (sacred to Venus) and shimmering black prunes, nasturtiums, root vegetables (carrots), the stems (asparagus), and flowers (cauliflower) decorated the tray. In a wedding this is my high altar. Above this humble tray of food, I call on the Goddess of All Life to strengthen the couple's resolve, to make them grow together, to bring forth fruit from their love and labors, and to reach out like branches to their community. Paul and Cynthia had lived my blessings already. I was simply acknowledging their twenty years together.

An important part of the ritual is the point when each partner selects something from the tray and, putting it in the other partner's mouth, says, "May you never hunger."

This is a pledge. It covers hunger of all sorts. They are promising to feed their partners enough to appease love hunger, food hunger, attention hunger, knowledge hunger, experience hunger. It is a big promise.

Then they drank from the silver cups. These are the symbols of pleasure, silver of course, to make them sacred to the Moon. It is important to hold wedding ceremonies in accordance with the phases of the Moon. I chose a Waxing Moon for this wedding, just a day before she grew full. New Moons are best for young lovers, new couples.

Cynthia and Paul used water from the kitchen in their chalices. "May you never thirst," they said, offering each other a sip from the silver chalices. Thirst, like hunger, can be for many things, so this promise covers thirst for affection and love, thirst for recognition and knowledge.

Grandmother Yvonne cried steadily from this point on. She had waited a long, long time for her daughter's wedding. After the kids started coming, she thought it would never happen. But now the day was here, and it was beautiful.

Weddings are always a women's event. The groom, however charming, is really just her escort. This is the only day devoted to celebrating the woman who is a sacred bride. She is the center of adoration (she looks so beautiful), the center of attention (take another picture with her and all the members of the family). She is all dressed up, she is taking vows. Humanity's future depends on these promises. Will she give her gifts of life even in the midst of patriarchy for the sake of love? Will she obey (no way!) or will she be rebellious (you bet!)?

The last act of the ritual is for the couple to crown each other with flowers to affirm respect for each other.

"Thou art Goddess!" said Paul.

"Thou art God!" Cynthia replied.

Paul accepted his crown of flowers without a whimper. They both saw each other as representatives of the divine. Nobody is inferior in this ceremony.

The ending of the ceremony may be the most beautiful part of it, when the couple, as the children of the earth, stand crowned by the Goddess and wait to seal their fate by jumping over the broom. At this point they may say some meaningful words or read poetry to each other.

Cynthia read her chameleon poem. At first everyone listened in shock. Chameleons? Slinging tongues of fire? How disgusting! And her poem was so sad and so depressed, such a contrast to her splendid wedding. And yet this poem was what had attracted Paul. What could be more appropriate?

Then Paul read the letter he had written in reply. It was the letter of a young idealist, full of congratulations and longing for his twin soul. His last line was, "You may find this letter strange, but I promise you if you give me a call, you might find this relationship fruitful."

"Fruitful," he had said twenty years before in one passionate moment of prophecy.

Now I asked the audience to heap upon the couple their personal blessings. Yvonne wanted to say something, but she was still too choked up. So all the kids took turns and wished Mom and Dad many more lovely years of happiness. The daughters were especially moved. They wept openly once Yvonne had started the weeping. Weeping is contagious, like yawning. When one starts, others follow.

The audience called out, "Health," "Vacations," "Deep love," "Happiness." But at the specific request of the couple, absolutely nobody was allowed to throw rice upon them for fertility. They already had enough children.

We placed the broom to the west, because this was already a marriage formed in the eyes of love, and when the last blessing had been said, holding hands the couple jumped and left the earth for a moment. The family photographer immortalized the moment on video as they jumped over the myrrh broom.

When they landed on the other side, they kissed and embraced each other as if they were newlyweds. This ceremony was a celebration of both their past and future years together.

For the reception the wedding party withdrew into the large hall with a skylight and two rubber trees growing right through the ceiling, in harmony with the redwood walls.

"We had another Goddess wedding here yesterday!" whispered the woman who was pouring wine into the cups.

"How wonderful!" I said. "It is catching on!"

Yvonne had had enough tears. She was now beaming, a drink in her hand. I sat and sipped a little champagne, and we talked about the ceremony. This seemed to have been a perfect wedding! Everybody was raving about it.

There was dancing now. A live band playing sixties songs, the rock and roll of the gray set.

Some of the weddings I do are spiritual commitments only, but this wedding was legal, so we signed the papers. I had a hard time fitting my name in the allotted spot. Paul and Cynthia were beaming. Paul had forgotten he was still wearing his crown and ate his dinner in it!

The city was being devoured by the slow creeping fog dragons, but the Golden Gate Bridge was postcard beautiful. I reflected on weddings—my most cherished job—and thought about other couples, living out there in the world without ever celebrating their unions with a ritual. I wanted to call them all: "Hey, you don't know what you are missing! You deserve to be celebrated! Your emotional bonds are important to the community." I feel the world is always safer when the people love each other.

Finally Paul and Cynthia danced a slow dance, the official wedding dance. The way they looked at each other was deeply moving. Paul was still wearing his crown, they had become inseparable. Cynthia had taken hers off but she was adorned by her beatific smile, totally given over to the zen of weddings.

Then one of the daughters took their hands, dancing with them in a group of three, then the other daughters joined in, and the shy son. Now all six of them were dancing together. Then Yvonne, the grandmother, made it seven, and now everybody, relatives close or far, was getting up and joining the couple dancing around them in concentric circles. Later

I overheard the young women talking among themselves about how they would also like to "jump the broom" and how "cool" it was.

"The Goddess is taking over the weddings. It is catching on," I thought. It's about time.

# NINTH LUNATION

*Time ‹ August–September*
*Sign ‹ Virgo*
*Lunar Herb ‹ Wild Carrot*
*Lunar Animal ‹ Pig*

# Harvest Moon

## VIEW FROM THE MOON

*The Harvest Moon rises plump and round as a pumpkin above the shorn fields. Wheat stubble gleams in the moonlight, bound corn shocks stand like worshipers. The trees are still in leaf, but there is a chill in the air, and they are beginning to glow with autumn's gold. Soon the harvest will be gathered in, the autumn leaves will fall. Tonight the sky is clear, glittering with stars, but tomorrow clouds may hide the earth from view. Tonight all is peaceful, but change is in the air. The Harvest Moon is full, but already she is beginning to wane, like the year. She understands that the moment of triumph is the beginning of loss.*

## THE GODDESS SPEAKS
# *Ix Chell*

Round and slow, ringed by a dark circle foretelling tomorrow's storms, I sail from the jungles of Yucatán to come to you. I am the serpent of the heavens who brings the healing rain. You see me overhead, my face silvery and kind, my body lean and strong. I amuse myself with the shooting stars. You hurry home to where warmth awaits you. A child kisses you hello, or a lover, maybe you talk to a cat or a dog, or perhaps there is nobody at all.

Do you come home to silence? Don't worry. I will come with you. I am the Moon, the lover of lunar creatures like yourself. I will embrace you when nobody is around, I will wrap you in your own glad feelings. If you let me, I will make the changes easy for you. I am the snake in the deep, the medicine of the herbs, the holy child of the mushrooms. I am the waters that seep through the earth. I wander alone and am content.

I know your body better than you do yourself. I know because I control the Moon inside you, your egg. She moves with mysterious majesty at my stimulation. I am the true opener of your womb. If you conceive a child, I will be with you. I am already an old intimate of yours. I wrote your fate before you were conceived. O my beloved, only look up into the sky and I will be your visible spirit guide, the obvious yet ever-changing constancy in your life. I will be true to you like no other.

You are so much like me! You wax and wane, just as I do. We both dance the dance of life. You may curse me, dissatisfied with your lot, but remember, this is how I teach you new ways. Hardship is my classroom, getting through those times is your challenge from me. But I shall never reject you, my beloved. You are my child. In you I have planted the seeds of humanity, the seeds of hope, and the seeds of love. In you I live on earth. I walk with your feet, I feel with your heart, and I am warmed by your blood.

In this season we come the closest yet. Feel me in your dreams, invite me to your hearth, read about me in your reflective times. Be my lover on the lonely nights—come into my arms like the orgasmic lover you are. The cold you feel in your heart is an illusion. I am always here. My love for you goes on. I dwell deep inside your brain and high above your head.

Do not think you are abandoned. I am in the laughter of your little ones, I am in the smell of the food that grew by my rays, I am the postcard somebody sent you because they thought about you. If you look at me at length, I will sing you sweet songs. If you light a white candle for me with your name written on it three times, I'll know that is your gift to me and I'll send you good luck.

I am the most beautiful mandala, your true star sister. My roundness and my strong silver light will heal you. Watch me sail. Watch me love you. My beloved, you are never alone.

## *Virgo Message*

This lunation brings a thirst for knowledge, energy that is relentlessly curious and wants to find out what makes things go. The Virgo Moon loves movement and physical involvement with the world. Dancing, hiking, climbing—all active sports attract you now. The love that this sign brings is of the body but not exclusively sexual. It has a holistic interest in the body, in human welfare and good health.

This is a good time to study the earth and herb lore, to take herb walks and enhance your understanding of the world around you. Take stock of your own body and her health. Buy some herbal remedies you promised yourself you'd try, take a course, pick up a hobby, get a medical checkup, get involved.

If you live in a climate that allows for two harvests a year, now is the time to sow cereals. Plant all things from which bulbs and roots are taken, and ornamental bushes, hedges, and trees. Lay out a flower garden. Do not plant Indian corn in this sign (lots of stem, no heads). Plant flowers for rich blossom. In Norway October 7 was the time by which everyone should have finished harvesting their cabbages. The bear was believed to get his den ready for hibernation at this time by lining it with dried heather. It is a good time to catch up on your household work. Start teaching, take classes, and learn something new. Deal in real estate—both selling and buying are favorable. This time is also especially advantageous for meditation and philosophy.

MOONTIDE

## *Unconditional Love*

Deep love has opened your heart, and you thought it would never again happen to you. Admit it, it is a surprise! You are feeling something you never felt before. Or you remember how you felt but it was many years ago, too long ago to really remember. You had given up on deep love. You had started accepting the idea that love comes only as a temporary guest, not as a well-deserved long-range companion. Yet here you are, and love is in your heart. Deep love fills you up, you are like an old river filled to the top of her banks, flowing slowly, majestically, washing the banks with your ample waters. You are like a river, and you know your love will always flow like this.

Your future is like a ship on this dear old river, a nice ship with cabins and accommodations for everyone. The green, happy river is old, the ship is new, and they go together. All the pieces of the picture are together as they should be. You have left the land of surprises, now you are part of the flow. Deep love makes you more conservative, you have so much more to lose. You have to be careful, measure your energy as if it were gold. You are the captain of your ship, and you feel responsible for protecting it. You make plans, you buy houses, you get dogs, and you plan for kids. The souls of your future children already surround you, hoping for reentry into the world through reincarnation with you. You are now the kind of parent you were looking for before your own birth. Happy, loving, having passed the stage of being "in love" to feelings of fulfillment and responsibility.

Deep love is what spouses feel, and now it is yours too. You are included in this much-envied company of well-matched people. Their hearts are united. They live longer than the rest of us mortals. They get sick a lot less. They are one. Deep love merges without hesitation, deep love is not insecure. Deep love is not about sex, it's about life, lifelong. Sex may have started it all, sex sparked it, but now you are content with or without sex. How can that be? Unconditonal love is good medicine.

## MOONSPELL

## *To Maintain Unconditional Love*

Every Full Moon light a white (blessing) and a pink (happiness) and black candle in gratitude to the Fates. View the Moon before you light them, then say:

> *The kind Fates have blessed my home,*
> *The kind Fates have blessed my heart,*
> *The kind Fates have blessed my loved ones,*
> *I offer thanks with a humble heart.*
> *I thank the Goddess for my life,*
> *I thank the Goddess for my love.*
> *I thank the Goddess for continued*
>    *blessings already on their way.*
> *Blessed be.*

Also burn some high-quality incense, the best you have. Do this each month to make your good fortune last.

## MOONTIDE

## *Guilt*

Guilt is a very popular feeling. Entire religions depend on your feeling guilt. You can confess your sins to somebody and ask forgiveness, or you can let the guilt fester until some self-destructive energy coming from yourself punishes you at last. Some savor their guilt, some really enjoy it. Guilt is very profitable for clergy and therapists.

Yet no one gets to go through life without hurting anybody at all. We give pain and we take pain. It doesn't make us into bad people, it simply makes us part of the happening that is life.

We feel guilt about not serving others more fully, about taking something for ourselves, be it time, love, or attention. The things we give ourselves should not make us feel guilty, but they often do. Women are the main consumers of guilt. Did we give enough? we ask. Were we selfish?

If you really hurt somebody and you have a chance to say that you are sorry, do so. If you hurt somebody and made them lose things—money, property, love, attention—try to make up for it. But after a while, if guilt is lingering in your soul just because you are used to it, try to make it go away.

Guilt is not a good friend for a woman. Guilt makes us do things we don't want to do. Guilt makes us allow things we really are against. Some people have developed guilt management to the point where they can make us feel guilty even if we have not done anything real to warrant it. Guilt mongers are not our friends.

## MOONSPELL
## *To Get Rid of Guilt*

*Left brain work:* Describe on a piece of paper what you feel guilty about, and why. Make a list of guilts. Confront the problem.

*Right brain work:* To purify yourself from guilt, first clean your house and go through your things, discarding anything that reminds you of the main guilts. If there are objects to which guilt is attached, give them away. It's good to get rid of things. Make a giveaway ritual of clothes and useful objects.

When the New Moon rises, when a cresent is showing, take a bath in green salt crystals. If you can't find any, use regular salt in your water. Also put a bag of hyssop in your bath, and get bath oils that smell like lemon. Take some lemon peel with you into the bath, and rub it all over your body. Say:

*My body, my mind, my body, my soul,*
*Purify with water, purify with salt.*
*A new phase is dawning, a new fresh clean life*
*I say good-bye to all the guilt,*
*I say good riddance, good-bye.*
*I am a good person*
*I am the angel of love*
*I bestow my blessings*
*On creatures large and small.*
*I bless my own body, and*
*I bless my own good soul,*
*So that wherever I tread,*
*Only good fortune will unfold.*

## *Fear*

This feeling is very dominant in our species. In the old days of our race, when we were relatively helpless, we feared the abundant predators of the wild. Today we are no less fearful, but the causes of our fears have changed. We fear fear itself, we fear love and intimacy. We also fear the enemies of the day: men fear women, women fear men's violence. The streets are battlefields—male against female and male against male. In no other species is there such brutal, persistent violence against the females and the young. Fear is our original sin.

To live in fear and with fear all the time is crippling our spirits. Excessive fear has become our entertainment. Horror movies, violent movies, TV news—all feed our fears.

To lift fear from your heart, use this moonspell.

When the moon is waning, get a red flannel bag, small enough to fit into your pockets. Pass it through some purifying smoke and call in the angels of protection to help you put your fears inside the bag. After you have lit a white candle say:

*I gather my fears into my red magical bag.*
*I include the black stones of apprehension.*
   *[place tiny black stones into bag]*
*I include the red stones of anger and dissatisfaction.*
   *[place red stones into the bag]*
*I include the gray stones of the fear of the unknown.*
   *[place gray stones into the bag]*
   *[close them and bless them]*
*As the Moon wanes*
*Let Grandmother take them away.*

Hang your little bag on a tree where nobody can get it. Forget about the entire matter.

# FESTIVALS OF THE MOON

## *Feast of Gauri*
### *First Day of Bhadra, New Moon — India*

Gauri ("Fair One") is the maiden aspect of Durga. She is a golden Goddess, sweet as honey, who gives intoxicating liquors (especially mead?) to humankind. At the New Moon of the month of Bhadri, sweets made with honey are eaten at bedtime to bring Gauri's sweetness and grace into the soul. This is a good time to pray for forgiveness and to do some forgiving yourself.

### Citua (Feast of the Moon)
### New Moon Nearest Equinox—Ancient Peru

In South America September is the time of the Spring Equinox. According to the Spaniards who described Inca customs, this was the month that women enjoyed most. The Citua festival began with the rising of the New Moon. First the men conducted a cleansing ritual to clear the city of sickness. Then everyone bathed. A paste of cornmeal (maize) was smeared on people's faces and on the lintels of their doors as a mark of purification. The festival continued with several days of feasting and dancing, culminating in the sacrifice of four llamas, whose lungs were examined for omens. In Inca mythology the sun was male, represented by the Inca emperor. Mama-Quilla, the Moon, was served by the Inca's sister-wife, the Coya. She was worshiped in a shrine ornamented with silver and served by priestesses.

One might speculate that women enjoyed this festival because at this time they were honored as representatives of the Moon Goddess, who made the crops grow. Possibly the men took over other chores in addition to the purification. In any case, women were probably released from the daily household grind during this festival. If you live in a coed household, you might work out a reciprocal agreement to honor your man on one of the solar holidays in exchange for his service on this feast of the New Moon. Have him cook you a feast of foods from the Americas (and do the dishes) or take you out to dinner at a South American restaurant.

### Birthday of the Harvest Goddess
### Eighth Day of Ninth Month,
### Waxing Quarter Moon—Ancient Russia

The birthday of the Goddess was celebrated with feasting and the exchange of gifts. Traditional folk embroidery motifs for the autumn season show women holding cups of wine and placing them on altars. Other embroideries feature an alternating line of wheat sheaves and women holding up cups or a larger Goddess figure holding out her hands to protect the harvest. In some places a young girl personifying the

Goddess Berehynia was carried through the fields draped in red cloths embroidered with traditional Goddess and sun symbols, her arms uplifted in the traditional pose; or harvest dolls with upraised arms were made from the last sheaf and carried through the harvested fields.

To share this celebration, decorate your altar with corn dollies, Eastern European embroideries (or color xeroxes of them from a book on folk crafts), and red candles. Fill your chalice with beer or apple cider and offer it to the Goddess with uplifted arms. Pour out some onto the earth and drink the rest. In the same way offer and eat a round loaf of whole-grain bread.

### Holy Cross Day
### *Full Moon of the Ninth Month — Medieval Europe*

Throughout Europe and the Near East, the festival that commemorates the finding of the true cross (of the crucifixion) by Helena, mother of the Emperor Constantine, seems to have inherited a number of older customs. In the village of Avening, Gloucestershire, the Sunday after the festival is known as Pig-Face Sunday, and pork sandwiches are served in the parish hall. Pigs' heads are displayed then eaten with apple dumplings.

One legend explains this as the commemoration of the slaying of a wild boar that was "ceremonially hanged from an oak in the village centre" and then eaten. Pigs were sacred to the earth gods all over Europe, from the Greek Demeter to the Norse Vanir. The hanged boar in particular recalls the Germanic custom of hanging sacrifices from sacred trees, of which the oak was one. Moreover, the boar was sacred to the Norse Goddess Freya. In Britain Holy Cross Day was also celebrated by gathering nuts in the woods. On the second Sunday in September, pigs that have been led in procession are ceremonially slaughtered at the shrine of Santa Maria delle Grazie in Italy.

Celebrate with a feast of roast pork (vegetarians can substitute maize), new wine, and fresh bread (and perhaps fruits such as grapes and apples), and set out a platter of offerings for the Earth Goddess in a wild place, where her representatives can consume them.

# MOON TALE

## *The Custody of Emily*

Once upon a time in the early 1970s, in the very early days of the women's spirituality movement when we didn't even know we were a movement, I went on my first Witchy Revival Tour.

This was my very first experience taking the Goddess on the road and teaching. The trip took place right after I had been tried for Tarot reading in Los Angeles (see the November story in *The Grandmother of Time*). I lost and was fined. I hate losing, which is why I don't even like to play cards or Monopoly. But in this case, losing was more important than winning my case in court. Had I won, the trial would have been of no historical importance. But since I was found guilty of having predicted the future by reading the cards, my loss was actually a vindication of witchcraft. The trial attracted a lot of publicity, and as a result I was asked to speak at a number of meetings and festivals.

This tale takes place near the Quiver River in Missouri, where they were having a festival of women dedicated to the Goddess and healing. A friend and I drove a borrowed Ford pickup from California across the Arizona desert and the plains day and night.

When we got there at last, I unpacked my three pillows and began to relax. I always travel with my pillows. They make a home out of a hotel room or a tent. I think there is something very moonish about a pillow. Hungarians have created an entire culture decorating, embroidering, and collecting pillows, using them in rituals, stuffing them with herbs as well as goose down.

This festival was small and cozy. We had cabins, there was a large eating hall, beautiful fields stretching in all directions, tall trees, balmy weather, and women in flowing shifts or nothing at all. Toleration of nudity is a measure of personal freedom in any society. The amount of the clothing worn (weather permitting, of course) is a direct indicator of how free women feel in a particular environment. When women feel totally at ease, they shed their twentieth-century clothing and run around comfortably.

At this time I specialized in blessing groups of women who were working together for some high moral goal. When asked to perform this bonding ritual, I would entwine the members of the group with red thread, symbolizing action, life, our blood. We raised power with songs, we called on the four directions in groups, and then in the name of the New Moon, which was riding overhead, I blessed their work and energy. These were very powerful rituals. Those I touched reported great changes in their lives, mostly very positive ones. Several women became teachers as a result of those bonding rituals. They bonded themselves to the Goddess as well as to the other women. At this festival I was blessing a group called HERA. They were therapists who were also activists—political and spiritual. The new breed. The fourth wave.

It was after the bonding ritual that a sad-eyed lady named Leslie came to me with some friends in tow.

"I need help with a custody case," she said. "It has to be a miracle, everything else has failed. As things are I don't have a chance. My ex-husband has hired a powerful and expensive attorney to take my daughter away from me. And it's all spite—he didn't even like Emily before. The problem is that he's an attorney himself. You can imagine how slim my chances of winning custody of my daughter are."

It was clearly a good mother's cry for help. Leslie's friends all testified that Emily really wanted to stay home with her mother. Everybody was still in ritual mode, so I gathered them all around a young sassafras tree. We had only water to offer to the Goddess, so we placed the chalice at the foot of the tree. We held hands and hummed like gathering bees.

My people in Central Europe often prayed to the winds, so I called on the four winds and asked Hera, the Goddess of Mothers, to help Leslie keep her daughter if it was the wish of both of them. All of us pronounced all kinds of positive magical blessings. We improvised. The blessings involved peace of mind for Emily as well as for the ex-husband. We thanked the spirits. We spilled out a libation of water on the ground, kissed the sassafras tree, and asked that its spirit speak well of us to the Great Spirit. I remember that the New Moon was in sight all during the short ritual. The silver crescent was rising over the trees. There was a feeling of assurance, a sense of the divine presence, and a calm afterward that I recognized as a divine good omen.

Then we had dinner and, except for a feeling that things would go well, the ritual passed from my consciousness. The festival went on to its conclusion and I forgot all about it, but just before we drove off a phone call came in.

It was Leslie.

"Witch!" she began, but her voice was celebrating. Anyway, I take being called a witch as a compliment.

"So what happened?" I asked.

"Imagine, my ex and his lawyer set out together for court, but they never arrived. Nobody knows where they went instead. I have won my case by default! Blessed be!"

"Blessed be!" I echoed, then asked her just to light a white candle as a thank-you note to the Goddess.

"You know I will. Here—Emily wants to say something to Z." The other end of the line crackled and I heard a little girl's voice giggling.

"Thank you, Goddess!" she said sweetly.

I could hear Leslie laughing in the background. The New Moon is quick with results and awesome in her solutions.

As far as I know, the case of the missing lawyer and ex-husband was never solved.

# TENTH LUNATION

*Time ‹ September–October*
*Sign ‹ Libra*
*Lunar Herb ‹ Oatstraw*
*Lunar Animal ‹ Cat*

# Blood Moon

## VIEW FROM THE MOON

*The Blood Moon rises red with the smoke of burning leaves. Below her, haze smudges the horizon and drifts across the emptied fields. As the balance of the days tips toward darkness, the woods are mellowing in shades of tawny and ocher and the dark red of old blood. Among the leaves the nuts are ripening and acorns fall to the ground. The beasts of the forest feast upon the bounty, storing up fat for the starving season that will come. The air is calm and still. It is a time of acceptance and completion. The Moon of Libra is the balance of the seasons; in her light the world finds rest.*

## THE GODDESS SPEAKS
# *Maat*

How many times we have met, you and I. One lifetime after another, my beloved, you come to me. We meet when your labors are done, when you have laid down your head and passed over to the other side, to me. With my twin sister I await you in this Hall of the Double Maat. Men say that we weigh your heart against an ostrich feather to see if your life made it heavy with guilt or light from charity and good deeds.

But we are not your judges. You are. If you harmed life more than you loved it, your own heart will give you away. The Moon that shines within you, your own soul, will reveal whether or not you have been mean or kind. It will show us if you killed instead of giving birth, if you took more often than you gave freely from what was your own. You alone know these things, and it is you who will betray yourself to us in the end.

We are the truth, the rhythm of justice. We simply confront you and all is known. We do not pronounce the fate that those who have been found "good" will walk victoriously among the dead. It is you who will determine that. You have the free will to decide the boundaries of your freedom after death, my beloved, not I. You will seek other souls to console in your loss, your own ancestors will claim you from the Hall of the Double Maat and lead you to your next world.

The dead are dead, my beloved. I have no hell or heaven. Like the harvest, you are brought in and weighed and accounted for. Balance is at last restored. In our realm there is no more blame. In our realm you all hold only one truth.

See me in the falling leaves, see me in the feathers left on the ground by the birds. See me in the shining Moon, the Hall of the Double Maat. The accounts of your lives must balance with the accounts of your death. The harvest has been gathered in. It is your time to rejoice, sing the wine songs, hold great dances in my honor, embrace those who love you, and give back beauty with your own creations.

# Libra Message

The energy of this lunation is that of comfort and beauty. The Libra Moon stimulates in us the sense of the romantic, a longing for partnerships in love and work. Create your environment in beauty now. Place cut flowers in vases every day to enjoy, pay attention to your clothes, get some new threads! This is a lucky time to fall in love with somebody special.

A sign that strengthens the desire for justice in us is the scales. The balance in nature under the rule of Venus brings fulfillment. This is the natural Tao. The energy of life revels in pleasure now, and the time for appreciation and practice of the arts and writing is favorable.

The Full Moon of September that rises nearest the Autumn Equinox was called the Harvest Moon because its light enabled farmers to work through the night. The position of the Moon relative to the earth at this time makes it seem very large, and it appears to rise slowly. This sign is wonderful for sowing grass. Drive the cattle out to pasture, but don't make hay when the Moon is in Libra (wait for the other signs this month)—the cattle won't eat it. Sow and plant things from which the blossoms are taken. During the Waxing Moon, plant trees and bushes. Among human activities, start physical projects now that can be quickly achieved. Traveling, partying, feasting, getting married, making new friends and business deals in general are great.

## MOONTIDE

# Pleasure

Pleasure is perceived through our five senses and with the sixth sense as well. But pleasure is so threatening to our industrial society that our entire professional lives are designed to kill it. Think about the nine-to-five pattern for making a living. Do we really need to work away most of our adult lives laboring for others? Our pleasures are confined to weekends and holidays. Can you really address the purpose of your life in two-week vacations?

To call for more pleasure in your life you must first make time for it. This is an act of will (yours) not an act of divine intervention. If you cannot make time for your pleasures, you don't really want them, you just say you do.

How much pleasure is enough? How much pleasure is appropriate? Imagine a life-style that would allow you to test the outer limits of your capacity for pleasure and then incorporate these experiences as an organic part of your life. In Tantra, a most ancient practice of the Oriental earth religion, the force of life is called Kali Ma, and her worship was practiced using all the senses.

"On my woman being satisfied, the whole world is satisfied" says the old Tantric mantram. "There is so much pain in the world, why not make religion pleasant?" says another.

One worships Kali Ma with thoughts, sounds, touch, smell, taste, vision, and sex. The same force that produces life, produces bliss and death. She is both wonderful and terrible. However, the cultivation of her presence in the world results in happier lives, increased resistance to illness, and longevity. Advanced Tantric exercises train one's body to connect the heart with the soul and the genitals. The control of sexual power stills the chattering mind, creates oneness with the Creatrix Matrix.

## MOONSPELL

## *For Pleasure*

Create an altar to Kali Ma on a table with a beautiful tablecloth, flowers, lovely candleholders with lit red candles, and a picture of the Goddess, as a triangle with a slit. She can also be represented as a conch shell, an open rose, a yoni image, the door of life, a woman's vagina. Imagine her to be your inner woman, the one that is most like an ancient form of your soul, nonverbal, attracted to pleasure and smells and food and beauty and sex. This same inner woman controls your life force, controls your mating habits, your social life, and the energy to live. You want to be on good terms with her.

When the Moon is full or dark (she likes both), after a purifying bath, go naked to your altar and light some incense—sage or sandalwood, frankincense or myrrh. Place some delicacies on the altar for taste, such as breads or sweets. Wine is sacred to her. A chalice filled with red wine is traditional. If you can't use alcohol, use grape juice and alter the prayer. Use bells for sound. She likes tinkling sounds.

Inhale the scent and chant a little mantram, "Kali Ma, Kalina Ma, I surrender to love," until you feel you have raised your temperature and you are not cold. Then take the glass of wine and offer it to her, saying:

> *As this liquid transforms*
> *Grapes into wine,*
> *I transform dullness to pleasure.*
> *As I drink this cup of wine*
> *My life fills up on your energy,*
> *My life force grows and attracts your pleasures—*
> *Kali Ma, Kali Ma, Kali Ma, Kali Ma*
> *I surrender to your flow.*

Now offer the food and then eat some.

> *As I eat this delicious food*
> *You are eating it with me. [ring the bell now]*
> *As I listen to this sound*
> *You are dancing within me. [touch yourself lovingly]*
> *As I touch myself*
> *You are loving me.*

This can take a while. Feminate, but do not allow yourself to reach the point of orgasm. When you are on the very edge, stop. Inhale deeply into your genitals and draw the breath into your heart. Feel your heart expand with life energy. Repeat this three times, then reward yourself with an orgasm.

See Kali Ma as a bountiful, beautiful woman, naked, dancing in your mind. Dance with her if you can. Finally, smell the flowers you placed on the altar.

> *As I enjoy beauty,*
> *You bring me more.*
> *As I enjoy life,*
> *You bring me more life.*
> *As I enjoy you,*
> *You bring me more of you.*
> *As I enjoy more of me,*
> *You propagate and sustain my pleasures.*

Now dress up and nip out your candles. Repeat this once a month. Kali Ma has brought me good luck and lovers. She gives fast results, so be careful what you ask for.

# FESTIVALS OF THE MOON

## *Rosh Hashanah*
## *New Moon of Tishri—Israel*

Rosh Hashanah, the "head" of the year, is the beginning of the ten-day time of spiritual renewal that begins the Jewish New Year. The Jewish calendar is based on phases of the Moon. In the old days, official moon-watchers signaled the rising of the New Moon, and from hill to hill the bonfires were lit to tell the people that a new month had begun. The Rosh Hashanah feast includes round challah eaten with honey and new fruits to symbolize hopes that the coming year will be "round, smooth, and sweet." Each food eaten has its individual blessing.

Whether you are celebrating the Jewish new year or a pagan harvest thanksgiving, be mindful of the unique qualities of each kind of food, and thank the earth for her abundance.

### New Moon of the Tenth Month
### (October) — China

In China veneration of the ancestors was a major part of family religious life. The living did their best to demonstrate that they still honored their ancestors, providing them with the necessities of life in the afterworld. The chief priest of this cult was the oldest surviving male of the family. The major feasts of the dead were in the spring, midsummer, and at the harvest season. The dead were buried beneath mounds in the fields, and during the Tenth Moon families would picnic nearby and tend the graves. At this time they offered their ancestors pictures of winter clothes and gifts of symbolic money.

### Durga Puja
### First–Fifth Day of the New Moon of Asvin
### (September–October) — India

The great Indian festival of the Goddess Durga honors her as divine Mother, the personification of energy. Durga is daughter of the Himalaya Mountains and notable in her own right as slayer of the buffalo demon. In Bengal it is a family festival. For four days the Goddess is worshiped, and on the fifth day her image is bathed in water. Families hold reunions. Children honor their parents, and quarreling neighbors make friends. Everyone dresses up to add to the gaiety. In northern India the festival is known as Dasahara and features plays from the life of Rama, who worshiped Durga before and after his successful struggle to rescue his wife, Sita, from the demon king Ravana. On the next day Lakshmi, Goddess of Fortune, is worshiped. Every house is lit, and the party goes on all night.

### Full Moon of Asvin — India

In Hindu mythology the Moon, which is the final result of all evolution, is the offering (*soma*) — that which is consumed and thus supports life. The

Moon is a reservoir of this divine nectar, and during the month of Asvin it is especially powerful. At that time, sweets and sweet drinks are exposed to the moonbeams in order to absorb the sweetness of the soma. It is believed that the power they absorb will cure diseases, especially those of the eyes. The sweetmeats are kept in an airtight jar and eaten a piece at a time for strength and to improve the complexion.

### Divali, Asvin 29–30 or Kartik 1/2
### Dark Moon/New Moon — India

Divali, the Feast of Lights, was probably originally a harvest and fertility festival that became associated with the coronation of Rama. The first day is dedicated to Lakshmi, Goddess of Rice and Prosperity. Traders close their accounts on this day and begin new account books. On the evening of the fourth day earthen lamps filled with oil are lit and set up in rows outside the houses. People exchange greeting cards, gifts, and sweets.

In Bengal the festival honors Kali, who is both primeval energy and destruction, the creative power of Siva, the absolute. Kali destroys evil in nature and in humankind, protects the good, and shelters her devotees. Her day is observed with fireworks and illuminations. In the mountains this is the occasion for burning all accumulations of old rubbish.

### Festival of Ciuateotl
### Full Moon — Ancient Mexico

For the Aztecs and Toltecs, the Full Moon of harvest was the snake woman Ciuateotl, grandmother of adversity, poverty, and toil, mother of the stars. She was called Obsidian Butterfly, and old Goddess of the Sweatbath. Her priests wore phallic emblems to attract her, and roaring, she appeared in her great green skirt to provide good crops. Later she was transformed into the Lady of the Americas.

### Children's Festival
### Full Moon — Vietnam

In the middle of autumn the Vietnamese celebrate a festival in which the children form a lantern procession in the moonlight and parade through the streets, making rowing or swaying motions. The following rhyme is sung:

> *Let's row in rhythm, not laugh at one another,*
> *for there are no branches free from worms.*
> *Let's row in rhythm, let's row in rhythm,*
> *If you don't ponder life now, you can't do it later.*
> *Let's row in rhythm.*
>     (Butler, *Skipping Around the World*, 63)

An excellent appeal for toleration.

### *Disirblot*
### *Full Moon after Autumn Equinox*
### *or October 14—Scandinavia*

This feast, also called Winter Nights, was the official beginning of the winter half of the year in the north (given the latitude, it was probably the real beginning of the winter season as well). It was one of the major feasts of the Norse year, whose focus was local and domestic rather than national. At this time folk celebrated the harvest and made offerings to the *dísir*, the female ancestral spirits who guarded the family line, and to Freya Vanadís, their chief. The Norse feast was part of the worship. Horns of mead and ale were dedicated to the gods and to the dead, who were invited to join the family at the feast. Pork was sacred to the Vanir, the elder gods. Apples, barley, and cabbage were eaten as well.

The dísir may have been something like the Gallo-Roman mother Goddesses called the Matronae, who granted fertility and prosperity. The dísir often appeared to warn their descendants of danger as well. Among the Germanic peoples, women were held to have great spiritual power. Queens were supposed to be experts in spellcraft, and heroes asked the ghosts of their mothers for magical protection. Women were also the primary practitioners of seidr, a form of shamanic divination.

# MOON TALE

## *The Last Swim*

I am a swimmer, and I used to swim at the Lions' Club pool in Oakland. Well, one day I missed my scheduled time and ended up with the senior swim. It was quite a surprise.

When you swim with the regular lap-swimming crowd, you silently get into your swimming suit, take a quick shower, jump into the pool and swim until your hour is up, go back to the locker room, silently change, shower, and go home. You may say an occasional "Excuse me" or "I am sorry" if you have bumped into somebody by accident or have to push past bodies to get to your clothes. A self-imposed code of conduct requires no personal contact in the dressing rooms. There is no female bonding like the kind of thing that occurs in a men's locker room, which is raucous with jokes and slapping towels. We the women have to protect ourselves from all this luscious nakedness and make sure that it doesn't bring us together. We in the adult female category are trying to deny our naked presence and our feelings this brings up by pretending to be alone.

The seniors could have come from a different country!

These women were in their sixties, their seventies, even their eighties, and they didn't care about proper manners anymore. And they were not afraid of their naked bodies. There were open glances, deep discussions about pies and husbands, operations and birthday presents while they were rubbing, rinsing, scrubbing, or soaping their bodies, private parts and all.

Fearing that they might eject me from the pool because I wasn't old enough, I hid from them in the dressing room by getting into the pool early, and once there I never took off my goggles. I just kept doing my laps, wondering how I could get myself into this seniors' swim period all the time.

The oldsters were friendly, they talked to one another. They called to one another across the water. Why, they even they knew one another's names!

"There is Jennifer!" somebody would call, and they all would stick their swim-capped heads out of the blue waters and check it out.

"Yes, that's her all right!"

"We haven't seen her in a while!" another voice would say.

"She was here last week. I wonder how her knee is doing," a third would chime in.

This friendly banter, the human cohesiveness and caring among them, was all normal procedure here in seniors' swim time. I was determined to join them. Somehow I had to make them accept me and let me come and belong.

But I couldn't figure out what I would have to do. For weeks I kept going, disguised in my goggles, really enjoying being there during senior swim time. I felt that maybe I could get in by osmosis—if I just kept coming long enough, they would not question my age. Years could go by, and they would just get used to me.

One day I was having such a good time and felt so confident among them that without thinking I took off my goggles, and Mildred, who was swimming next to me, saw my face. Mildred is an outspoken person.

"My gaaawd!" she cried. "You are not a senior!"

I was caught. I felt like a thief. I stood there in the water, a couple of decades short of qualifying for this warm community. Everybody was looking at me, questioning my integrity. What a dirty trick! they were thinking. Was I there because the seniors have to pay less for swimming?

There was a silence in the pool. All the eyes and goggles were trained on me.

Then I thought of one of those desperate nonsense responses that one never plans ahead but tries to get away with anyway. Only I didn't know if it was going to work. I pointed to my silver hair, prematurely white since my early thirties, and said, "That's true, but I have a lot of white hair!" Proudly I pulled off my cap and showed them my shock of wet silver tresses.

Mildred looked at my hair. It was white all right. She was coloring hers, and she had no white hair at all. Mine impressed her.

"She has silver hair!" Mildred announced to the others.

"Yes, silver hair. She has a lot of that," another voice agreed.

And so it was OK. I may have lacked about twenty years in age, but white hair I already had, and that's what was important. I was in.

I continued swimming there, openly now, just like the seniors. They learned my name, I learned their names. We talked a little in the dressing rooms after swims, we gave each other running showers when we were done, so the hot water didn't have to be adjusted all over again.

Then one day I came in and everyone was hanging onto the sides of the pool. There was no laughter and nobody was pushing the little blue floats for their tummy exercises as they had always done before. There was a sense of funeral in the air. Afraid to ask, I counted heads. A few were missing, but the oldest ones, the ones I kept an eye on, the over-seventy crowd, was here in numbers. So nobody had died, thank Goddess.

"What's going on?" I asked finally.

"This is the last swim," Hugh said gravely. "They cut the funds. They are closing the pool."

"What?"

Then the story came out. Even before I had joined them, this had been a perpetual danger. The seniors had been going to city hall for years to plead with the powers that be for their pool. The pool was the center of their lives, their meeting hall, and the main reason they were not in bodily pain. Most of these meetings at city hall went on all night, so the seniors took turns keeping a watch on the agenda while the others slept in their chairs.

And after all this effort, it was over. The decison had come down. After three years of fighting, the pool was going to be closed. Alma was crying softly. She was the most emotional because she was often the one who led the fight againt the bureaucracy. So many nights, year after year, all for nothing!

But what to do?

This was shortly after Reagan had been elected president. Many of these seniors voted for him, thinking he was "senior" identified. I told them he was "actor" identified, even "leading man" identified. But no, they insisted, the man was old like them. He had to have noticed this fact. But the first thing that happened after his election was that the funds for the pool were cut.

Because I am a witch, I felt it was up to me to come up with some kind of plan. It was also a way to repay the seniors for letting me into their blessed family circle, an extended family for me, where I could have access to twenty-nine mother figures. So often they had counseled me about my life. So often they gave me courage, saying, "You'll see, to-morrow it will be better!"

I prayed to the old, gnarly myrrh tree facing our pool. I held its branches, looking up at the Full Moon, and asked her to help us keep the pool. And then the plan came into my head, crystal clear and fully formed. It could work, provided the seniors played along smartly themselves. They had to be radical this time.

"We will call a press conference!" I announced.

The wet-suited seniors in the pool didn't even blink. I could tell they were open to all possibilities. They were miserable without their pool, they felt betrayed about losing it, and they were angry.

Saunders, who used to be a lifeguard, wanted to know more. Where would the press conference be?

"Here, in the pool," I said. "I will call the press, tell them it is the last swim."

"Nobody will come," Jennifer, aged seventy-two, objected. "Who would want to talk to a bunch of old fogies at a press conference?"

"That is always a possibility," I agreed. "But imagine that you are not just any seniors, you are seniors who swim every day and have been swimming for your lives since you were children and this pool was dedicated to you back in 1920."

"Well, it's true," Logan, who used to be a fireman, assured me.

"Right now Maggie Kuhn, the Gray Panther, is stalking the area, and in Washington, D.C., they are holding the first conference on aging. I will try to tie these strings together," I said.

It sounded better to them as I explained it. They gained some confidence. They started talking among themselves, making sure everybody understood this big undertaking. None of them had ever attended a press conference before, much less participated in one.

What I needed from them was what they had always done so naturally. The seniors used to bring little goodies to the pool, for snacking afterward. This was just one more reason I loved belonging to this group—they treated each other like family. Jennifer made her famous lemon cake slices, which were simply bliss in the mouth. Logan made very good gingerbread. Saunders was a meatman, and he usually broiled the hamburgers at our picnics, turning them over and over until they were perfect. We didn't need hamburgers, but he could also make good coffee. He carefully dripped gourmet coffee through brown paper filters into waiting cups.

They were all wonderful—Alma, the activist; Kathleen, the woman who swam a whole mile daily; Mabel, a heavyset woman who swam like an eel once in water; and Olga, who was from Germany and entered the senior Olympics every year and won medals for us all. Among the men there were handsome Hugh; Bob, who swam like a whale spouting water with every breath; and the old doctor, Herbert, who swam with a snorkel. (I always suspected he liked to look up between the ladies' legs underwater, the rascal.)

This was my plan: I would tell the press about the grandmothers' cookies and grandfathers' gingerbread and coffee. In my experience as a PR person I had found that the press cannot resist a good spread of sweets and eats.

But I also wanted the seniors to do something radical.

"I need a protest sign—something on a large sheet of paper. It should say, Seniors Fight Back!"

They engaged in a stimulating discussion about this in the pool, splashing with their feet as they talked about how they could make a large poster like that. The part about Seniors Fight Back—the radical part—didn't bother them at all. They had never protested anything in their lives. This was the silent generation, the obedient generation, and now the ripped-off generation.

I went home and took out my old radio and TV lists and made the media calls, always stressing that the seniors must swim for life, and that this would be the last swim unless we got some attention. I reminded the press that they too would be seniors all too soon, and I added coyly that the seniors were going to go all out with their baking and cooking, and there would be delights laid out for the press, unimaginably tasty morsels for grown-ups who have no grandmothers and grandfathers to bake for them.

More than any other angle, I think the sweet-tooth one worked.

On the morning of our press conference I could already smell the delicious scents of coffee and cake mixed together in splendor as I approached our pool. And there, on the fence where we usually had only a clock timing our laps, hung a large sheet of longish paper that said in Alma's handwriting, Seniors Fight Back. It looked great.

When I entered the pool, the seniors were all in the water, but I could tell that the women had donned their better suits, and everyone was on their best behavior. Even Sophie, the wild one (aged a mere sixty-four), refrained from doing her traditional belly flops from the trampoline, which always annoyed everybody because she splashed so hard and made so many waves and then just sank to the bottom of the pool like a stone. It was unnerving.

Then the press started arriving. They were coming in their vans full of equipment. They came like hungry children to the party. They nibbled and did interviews. They admired the seniors in their fine swimwear swimming or treading water.

I heard them repeat the line "We swim for life," which was true—they had just never mentioned it before. I could hear Logan (aged seventy) giving an interview. Jennifer too. Hugh, our best-looking male, gave his views on swimming and his health, and then Sophie talked to the press— her payoff for not doing the belly flops.

Then more press came. And more interviews were conducted. We unveiled even more of the delicious cakes and cookies, and Saunders ran a second pot of coffee out from the office. There was a contented hum to the whole affair, everybody comfortable with one another, the report- ers crouching at the side of the pool, the seniors slicing the water se- renely, unpretentious and unaffected by all this attention. The movie cameras recorded Jennifer swimming proudly with her brand-new nose clip. Once, Sophie got near the trampoline, but Alma caught her legs and held her in one place long enough to remind her of her promise, and Sophie shyly slipped back into the water and resumed serene swimming.

Then came the best part. We all went home and met again in the evening and watched the news. The seniors fighting for their pool got almost five minutes on local and even national news. We were on every channel. The seniors swimming in Californian blue waters was news! I was ecstatic and thanked the Goddess for our luck.

Our city hall, however, was not amused. There was an explosion, and somebody must have kicked somebody's ego because the next morning at the pool several offical-looking men were waiting for us with big smiles on their faces. They wanted another meeting. Suddenly there was a way to save the pool. They wanted another press conference.

But the information already imbedded in public consciousness could never be recalled.

Saunders had been magnificent copy. He looked sad yet dignified. His report was haltingly given, the words of somebody who is not in the habit of complaining. There he was, a tall, tanned older man pushed to the brink of rebellion by the cruel treatment of the powers that be.

Now those powers came to the pool, shamed.

Logan brought up the fact that he had voted for a senior for president, but now he thought this was a mistake, since this senior didn't care about the rest of them, cut lunch money from his grandchildren and funds from the grandfather's pool. Alma's emotion registered very well on TV. We wept with her when she explained how lucky she felt not being in pain every day, how her arthritis cleared up from regular exercise.

And the food was also photographed—the yellow and chocolate-covered cookies, the lemon cake (my favorite), the fruits and teas. How could anybody be so mean to such a nice bunch of people who made such excellent goodies, anyway? It just wasn't American.

The powers that be suggested a new plan. They suggested that we raise ten thousand dollars and keep it in a bank account so that if their funds got too low we could ante up the difference and the pool could stay open.

Well, through bake-outs, sales, and numerous garage sales, we did raise the money, and we keep it in the bank just in case. We spend the dividends from our money on outings, on chartered buses into the country. We also have dinners together celebrating our activism, now a ten-year-old memory, but a proud heritage.

The pool got saved, even though city hall honored the seniors only when they were fighting them on TV. It reminded me of a quote I heard from Florence Kennedy, the famous civil rights activist and feminist troublemaker: "Remember, if you do anything political and it isn't on TV, it didn't happen!"

And TV coverage doesn't happen without cakes and coffee. History finally always comes down to cookies.

There is some deep wisdom here somewhere. Only the old gnarled myrrh tree knows the truth. And the Full Moon.

# ELEVENTH LUNATION

*Time ‹ October—November*
*Sign ‹ Scorpio*
*Lunar Herb ‹ Nettle*
*Lunar Animal ‹ Snake*

# Mourning Moon

## VIEW FROM THE MOON

*A cold wind is blowing veils of cloud between the Earth and the Full Moon and then tearing them away. A land stripped of all that is not essential lies revealed in her chill light. Dry grass hisses; the bare bones of the trees rattle loudly as the wind picks up once more and clears away a rustling drift of fallen leaves. The bears are seeking caves to sleep in; the squirrels are hiding the last sweet nuts that fall from the trees. Through the open forest move stags with branching horns. Then they too seek shelter. Only the wind is left to lament the vanished summer beneath the Mourning Moon.*

## THE GODDESS SPEAKS
# *Selket*

The remains of the dead stand tall in their proud urns, but not all of them are in tombs. The dead are beneath your feet. They are everywhere. You are walking on the bones of your ancestors, they hear your footsteps, they count each beat of your heart. And so do I.

I am Selket, the Guardian of the Dead. My golden wings enfold a peace that is eternal. My outstretched golden hands protect the dreams of the dreamers. You have seen me, in short, secret moments when death was on your mind. When you walked by a cemetery or buried someone you loved, I was there. You have seen me when love died in your heart or when you had to kill a feeling that had no future.

You have seen me when you had to make a choice to give life or withhold it. I was there too.

I am always there behind the veil, standing in power, extending my blessings or my deadly blow. I am the force that withers life, not quickly and mercifully but slowly and painfully. I draw the life force from the living if they offend me. I pass through the veil and take what shall be mine.

I demand respect for the dead. I require that the graves be tended, that incense be offered in billowing stacks. I require that the names of the dead be remembered and blessed. I enforce the rights of the dead to memorials and remembrances.

I guarded the tomb of the young Tutankhamen. I hid the royal grave from robbers and scientists, which is almost the same thing. I worked my magic for centuries, until it was no longer potent, and then I cursed those who disturbed the peace, I destroyed the diggers, made sick those who supported the expedition half a continent away. Selket did it all.

I am the Scorpion Goddess. I wear Scorpio on my crown, and I command the scorpions in the desert. They are my pets. Fierce fighters, deadly adversaries, sun-drenched creatures—they are me.

When you die, you shall see me.

I am the golden outstretched hand who will send you a guide you can recognize. This guide will bring you to my chambers and dress you in fine silk robes of pure white, the color of the dead. It is I who will write your name on the list of those to be protected, ask you what you need, then cut your ties with the living world.

When you are in my realm, nothing shall hurt you. Not the lovers who left you or the lovers who never came, the husbands who struck you or the ones who weren't there for you. The ungrateful children who used you or have gone astray, even your own evil, the guilt and the pain—none of these shall hurt you anymore.

Your poverty, your ignorance, your slavery, and your sufferings—of these nothing shall remain. I wither all memories. You will be yourself, pure and new again. I enable you to gain back your strength, your self-esteem, your self-love. In my Scorpio affection you shall find pleasure you have never had before. In my fierce Scorpio mothering, you shall find opportunities you never thought possible. Opportunities for rebirth and reincarnation.

This too I am. I am the door of life and death.

You will tell me how long you wish to stay sheltered by my wings, how long you wish to enjoy my eternal peace. You will tell me how long you wish to go without feeling the pain of life. You will tell me how long you wish to be unconditionally loved.

If you say you are ready to go back, I am the one who will open the doors wide.

I shall release you into the world on the back of the north winds. They will carry you to your destination outside my realm, outside my queendom. There you shall no longer see me or sense me, for I shall cut away all your memories of me. You will forget the peace and the bliss I gave you so that you will not long to be with me anymore.

When I kiss you farewell, you shall begin to fear me, for you will only dimly remember that I ever existed, I, Selket, the Scorpion Goddess, underneath your feet, always in your future, never in your heart.

## Scorpio Message

This lunation brings us close to nature's death and rebirth. Now is the time to look within, to contemplate our mortality, to think about how we have spent our lives so far and how we are going to improve our habits so that we can make our life's dreams come true.

This is a time of deep sexuality and intimacy, the best antidotes to death. We stay indoors more, we celebrate with family and friends, we cook and nurture, we feel the need to be close to each other. This is a rich season of dreams, of all kinds of prophecy. Get your cards read, go to a psychic, practice divination with your friends.

In ancient and medieval Europe, the farm folk looked at their herds at this time and slaughtered those animals they could not afford to keep through the winter. The meat was smoked, made into sausage, or frozen. Now is the time to plant the healing garlic, the vitamin-rich leeks, and every vegetable from which leaves are taken. Spray plants, sow hops, poppies, and melons, cultivate fruits with pointed shapes, such as pears. But don't plant potatoes, and don't cut wood or hay. Wash your hair, cut toenails to prevent fast growth, but don't wear new clothes.

## MOONTIDE

## Courage

To help us face death we have been given a feeling, a quality, that can see us through hard times. It is worth more than gold. It is courage. How often have you found courage when you thought you had none left in your heart? How often did you call on courage when you knew you needed it but doubted you could find it?

Courage is the health of the soul. Without it history would not happen. Without courage nobody would ever get married, write a book, or win a prize. It is an essential feeling, it is ennobling, it is curative. Courage can heal all self-doubts, it can heal self-hatred, it can heal fear.

During this lunation especially, it is a good idea to call more courage into your life.

## MOONSPELL

## *For Courage*

Create a circle of golden candles, using as many as you feel comfortable with. Five is traditional, but seven is the number of lunar good luck, and again nine is the number of the Muses—take your choice.

In the middle of this circle place your own photograph or a voodoo doll representing you, or create the circle on the ground, and step into the middle of it yourself for this ritual.

Light a little sage incense or the herb artemisia, and let it burn until the space fills up with the sacred smoke. With your arms outstretched to the New or Full Moon, pray this way:

> *I invoke you, mother of the darkness!*
> *I invoke you, mother of the night!*
> *Let your angels of inspiration open my heart,*
> *Let your angels of courage fly inside.*
> *I shall make a golden cradle*
> *To make a place for courage.*
> *I shall make a golden fire*
> *To warm courage inside.*
> *I shall put my hands in your lap*
> *For you to bless and use.*
> *I shall put my heart in your lap*
> *To be caressed by your blessing hands.*
> *To grow courageous with your use*
> *To put high purpose in my heart.*
> *Inanna, Lady of the evening star,*
> *Inanna, Lady of the morning star,*
> *Study my words.*
> *May courage dwell inside my soul.*
> *As you have dwelt in the Great Above,*
> *May courage dwell in my soul.*

*As you have dwelt in the Great Below.*
*May courage dwell in my soul and in my destiny.*
*Make it so.*
*Make it so.*
*Make it so.*

Step out of the circle now or step back from your altar, nip your candles out with wet fingers. Do not blow out the candles. Repeat the ritual three nights in a row or seven or nine. You choose.

## MOONTIDE

# *Devotion*

I love this feeling. I seek it in others, I give it to others.

Devotion is a deep, searing passion on slow burners. It is steady, it is selfless, it is satisfying. It may or may not be sexual. It is impersonal as well. We hear a lot about devotion to God. It is like being in a state of prayer all the time, with every thought, with every deed, with every wish. Yes it does border on obsession. But while obsession is heavy and dramatic and often dark, devotion is lighthearted, freedom loving, generous.

I have devotion for my best friends, my close friends who taught me things about the world and myself. Those precious jewels I treat with devotion.

I have devotion for my Goddess work. I still work 80 percent of the time for free. I still donate a lot of myself to causes and to the earth. These are devotional works, for the good of all. This is where you can see the value and Tao quality of this feeling. To be devoted to a cause gives you energy. It gives you heightened self-esteem. However, if you overdo devotion, it can also make you angry and burned out.

But without devotion there is no prayer, because a true prayer is total practice; all the energies are one.

To be devoted to a man or a woman is very tempting, isn't it? But be careful with personal devotion. It may keep you from focusing on yourself. If you are devoted to each other, always remember to let the angels dance between you.

## MOONSPELL
### *For More Devotion*

Light a white candle with your name written on it three times. Place a picture or an image of the Goddess on your altar. A single rose would also do nicely. Light some vertivert herbs and inhale the smoke. You will find the scent is earthy and hardy and delicious. Say:

> *My Lady looks in sweet wonder from Heaven.*
> *My Lady of the moon is radiant.*
> *I devote myself to serve and manifest*
> *The Lady of the evening star,*
> *She who watches over all living beings*
> *And makes them hurry to their sleeping places.*
> *She is the Queen of Heaven, the Fairy Queen.*
> *I shall be her and She shall be me.*

Repeat this moonspell every Friday.

# FESTIVALS OF THE MOON

### *Festival of Osiris*
### *Moon of Choiac — Egypt*

Osiris was a vegetation god and lord of the underworld, seen as the night form of the sun or as the Moon, whose phases were his death and resurrection. During the month of Choiac, when the Nile flood was receding, the Egyptians commemorated his death and resurrection with a variety of customs and celebrations. The dramatized myth of the god involved a ritual fight in which Osiris was killed by his brother Set and his body dismembered. The people accompanied the mourning mother Isis in her search for the lost pieces and followed her to the temple with passionate mourning. Restored to life by the magic of Isis and her sister Nepthys, Osiris triumphed over death like the sprouting grain. His son Horus (magically conceived by Isis) then defeated Set in another ritual combat.

One practice was to plant barley in flowerpots and water it with water from the Nile until it sprouted. Images of Osiris with barley were floated down the Nile on barges with images of the other gods and 365 candles. Once the Nile inundation had subsided, planting could begin. At this time the image of Osiris was buried in a lunar-crescent-shaped coffin of mulberry wood. The image that had been buried the previous year was placed in the branches of Hathor's sacred sycamore tree. Elsewhere, models of the parts of the god's body were made of paste and grain, watered and tended for twenty-one days, embalmed and buried. When the body of Osiris was dismembered, the different pieces ended up in various cities of Egypt, each of which had its own cult of the god and version of the

celebration. His backbone was especially sacred and was represented as
the djed-pillar and erected with great ceremony.

In the marriage of Isis and Osiris, as in Hinduism, the male is passive,
and the female is the active power that works upon the world. Osiris
reigns beneath the earth, in the dark womb in which the seed is buried.
The magic of Isis enlivened his body enough for her to conceive by him.
He then became Lord of the Dead, while she gave birth to his son. After
that he stayed in the underworld while his son Horus ruled the daylight,
but Isis reigned as queen in the land of both the dead and the living. This
myth is one of many that illustrate the idea that the God dies and is
reborn, while the Goddess has many aspects but is eternal.

### Oschophoria Festival
### Full Moon of Pyanepsion — Ancient Athens

This was a festival of the autumn grape harvest. Carrying ripe grapes,
twenty youths raced from the temple of Dionysus in Limnae, Athens, to
the sanctuary of Athena Sciras in Phaleron. The winner received a drink
made of wine, cheese, meal, and honey and an honorary place in the
procession that followed. The procession, headed by two youths dressed
in women's clothing (originally priestesses, or perhaps this was a recognition of the transsexual aspect of Dionysus) and followed by a chorus of
singers, marched back from the temple of Athena to that of Dionysus. The
procession was followed by a banquet.

### St. Martin's Day
### November 11, Waxing Moon — Europe

The oldest Irish references to this festival describe the killing of a pig
for a feast on this day. Since the pig was sacred to the earth deities both
in the ancient Mediterranean and in northern Europe, one suspects that
the festival was originally in honor of the Earth Goddess as Goddess of
the Dead. This was one of the holidays on which no work could be done
that involved the turning of a wheel, such as spinning and grinding corn;

nor did farmers plow, perhaps to avoid interfering with the turning of the year.

According to tradition, blood should be shed on this day. Later on, a cow or a sheep or a goose, a turkey, or even a chicken would be sacrificed, and the threshold and four corners of the house were sprinkled with the blood to keep out evil spirits for the coming year. It was the responsibility of the wealthy to share the feast with the poor.

It is important to remember that all meat-eating cultures in the ancient world spiritualized the natural shedding of blood involved in butchering animals by periodically offering beasts to the gods as a sacrifice. Usually a portion of the animal was given to the earth, and the rest was shared among the community. In some places this was the only time that most people got animal protein at all. We who buy our meat wrapped in plastic and Styrofoam at the supermarket and never thank the creature that gave its life to feed us, or who eat no meat but use products that destroy the environment in which other creatures live, have no right to sneer at cultures that perform reverent sacrifice.

Women, however, have a source of blood offerings that harms none. To make the autumn sacrifice, perform the following ritual during your bleeding time in this Moon. Clean your house and put away or get rid of things you will not need during the coming winter. Then bathe and light a harsh, purifying incense, such as sage, and a red candle. Collect some of your menstrual blood in a bowl or on a sponge. Put the blood on your altar, and say:

> *Lady of Life and Death,*
> *As the year changes from summer to winter,*
> *As the Moon changes from new to full to dark,*
> *My own womb waxes and wanes.*
> *Accept this blood of my unused fertility,*
> *Blood that flows with the moon's changes*
> *Freely given as an offering,*
> *As I will give you my body and my spirit when the time comes,*

*As my womb is renewed each Moon,*
*In the proper season, let my spirit be reborn.*

Spend a few moments meditating on the Dark Goddess and feeling her love for you. Then take your blood and mark the corners of your house and your threshold (if there is enough, draw the three-cornered yoni symbol of the Goddess). Say, "The offering is made, the price is paid. Blood of Earth and Moon, protect this house."

You may also want to share a feast with your friends featuring your favorite kind of meat, nuts, and other autumn specialties. Be sure to thank the animal for feeding you. Afterward take a gift of canned goods to a shelter for the homeless.

### Festival of the Nine Lotus Leaves
### Nineteenth Day of the Eleventh Month
### Waning Moon—China

This was a festival of Kuan-yin, who is Lady of the nine lotus leaves— the nine realms of Buddhist philosophy. The nineteenth day of the Moon (about halfway between full and third quarter) is always sacred to Kuan-yin. The Persian Goddess Anahita was also honored on the nineteenth of the Moon. The Merry Maidens and several other megalithic circles in Britain have nineteen stones, and according to one version, nineteen nuns, or priestesses, of Brigid tended her sacred fire. One theory is that this number refers to a nineteen-year cycle of rising and setting positions of the Moon.

# MOON TALE

## *Requiem for Masika**

April 18, 1979

That day a free-floating anxiety overwhelmed me. Busy, busy, I was trying to drain off an almost unbearable tension, the way I felt before menstruation, but I had just finished. What was happening? Should I keep moving or . . . ? Nothing I did was enough. Inertia yawned at me and I fought back. All I could do was to keep moving thirteen times faster than anybody else.

I was worrying about my mother, Masika. Since my father had died there had been this threat that she would be next. But at sixty-three? *No, you will live, won't you?* I thought. *Forever? Let the old man go by himself.* She had cried no tears for him, she said. Neither did I. But after that her calls for me became more urgent. She dreaded the winter. "The winds shook the house last night," she wrote. "They howled like hounds in the house." Other things happened too.

One day she and her third husband were sitting in her studio, and

*Reprinted from *Womonspirit*, Spring, 1979.

CRASH, a giant sound shook the house. Masika thought that all her ceramics and glass had broken. But nothing was wrong. Kama, her husband, heard it too. When it happened on another occasion, she wrote to me about it.

"Were the doors between life and death being opened? Was that crash the sound between the worlds?"

All day I ran my Aries energies. I made phone calls, wrote, did laundry, did my temple exercises, swam about thirty-five laps. That calmed me down. I was supposed to go to a meeting that night with the Feminist Wicca sisters. I picked up my lover and drove up Laurel Canyon, searching for the house. We never found the house. As we came down toward the valley again, I began to shake as though I had a cold, a deep inner cold that nothing could warm.

☾ ○ ☽

*April 19*

In Budapest Masika woke up refreshed. It was spring, and she loved her wild garden. Everything grew there: acacia trees and dahlias, parsley and comfrey and scarlet poppies. She loved poppies in all colors.

During the night I was fine and woke refreshed too. But as soon as I rose, all my energy left me. *I have to clean the house,* I thought, but pushing a vacuum cleaner around suddenly became an insurmountable task. When a witch is tired, a witch goes back to bed. I slept deeply.

Masika said good-bye to Kama and Imre, her son, one to work, the other to school. Kama reminded her that her breakfast was ready on the stove. He always made breakfast for her before he left the house.

Just before he left she called a lawyer, an old friend, to change her will. She wanted her daughter included. Somehow she thought I might return someday and would want to live in the house she built. The lawyer was to come over the next day. Meanwhile she fixed Kama with her powerful blue eyes and said, "Don't forget I have two children, not one. When I am not anymore, you make sure Zsuzsika is in my will."

She knew the time was short. Masika left her entire art collection to the museum named after her in Celdömölk—a prosperous peasant town, with fields, air, and art-loving people. But her house, her only comfort and pride, she left that to her immediate family, Kama and Imre and me.

She ate her breakfast slowly, looking out the window. She preferred looking outside because lately she had begun to see faces looking at her in the studio, floating about—some friendly, some curious, some merely passive.

"I can see through the veil now," she wrote. "It's so strange how the warnings come."

Right after breakfast she had another attack, the thirteenth, the Big One. She had endured twelve without succumbing. She even joked about it. "None but the thirteenth will have me," she said. Nobody was home but the neighbor, who happened to come in to see her right after she threw up her breakfast. The neighbor helped her upstairs to lie down.

The second floor was her temple. Here rested all the pieces she had made over the years. It was a minor museum, smelling of clay and paint and wood. She always had freshly cut wildflowers in dove gray, hip-high vases, mixed with cattails. She had no more plans. She had raised a pagan Temple in the Modern Museum, her last show. She planned no more. She had said it all. She had expressed it all. Her "white period" was her last. I knew it too. But living without working would still attract her, I hoped. It didn't.

Kama was called and Imre too. They rushed home in cabs. Masika was lying with her head to one side. Kama trembled with fear for her. Imre cried while he called the doctor. He wasn't in. The doctor wasn't in, the one who had pulled her back from death's jaws often before. Keep calling! Call the ambulance!

Kama was packing Masika's things for the hospital, her toothbrush and her towels and her glasses. Masika lifted her head and looked at them and then said, "I do not want to go to the hospital anymore." She indicated that she wanted to bless them. They knelt down and she kissed her hands and put the kiss on their heads. It was done.

When the doctor finally arrived, she was gone and floating about the room. Imre remembered the incense I had sent and he lit some. Kama found white candles; they too were lit. Masika, the priestess, the artist, the Goddess in body merged with the Great Source she portrayed so often. She knew the way to Her. There was peace on her face. There would be no more winters. Only deep peace.

I woke in a sweat and in pain from head to solar plexus. I tried to get up and do something in the house. What was wrong? *I must have the flu,* I thought. *O Goddess! That's all I need when there's so much to be done! I'm tired of living,* I told myself. *I am tired of going on.* I was surprised at the great depression engulfing me. I crawled back to bed again, wishing I had my mother to fix me some tea and give me good words. Mother. Oh, I miss my mother.

In the evening I woke again, still depressed. I took some lobelia and cayenne. Maybe that would pick me up. I lit some red candles for energy. The flames on my candles took off violently, burning down the side, forming a new candle, both flaming high. It frightened me.

☾ ○ ☽

*April 20*

I felt very ingrown. My feelings were held tight inside me and now I made myself get up and go do my errands. I chanted and cleaned. I had a date to go to the movies; maybe that too would help. We missed the movie. Not meant to happen. My body temperature was finally rising. But I had a fever now. Let's go home to rest. And there waited a telegram for me.

*"Our mother is dead. Imre."*

Like an explosion of all my illnesses, agony erupted from me in a primal howl. I whirled around dizzily, clutching the wall as if it were my mother.

The wall between us must be climbed. I wanted to touch you again! The child in me was dying, and at thirty-nine the passage was painful.

"I never could show you the success of my career, my new house, Mother. I wanted more than anything to show you how well you taught me."

But she knew it, and never demanded "success" from me. Yet it hurt that I could not share that with her because she went too soon. Masika was mortal and now she was immortal. I should have rejoiced. I couldn't. Inconsolable. Deeply grieving. Crying nonstop for days. No amount of theology could cure my pain. None of the teachings about reincarnation made sense. Only that she suffered too much, and she did what she had to do.

Sister witches surrounded me with their naked bodies to hold me in a collective womb. I cried and cried. I knew this pain would never ebb. This pain would be mine until I saw her again. But when? I wanted my mama!

We then had a wake. Wine was bought and some bread and cakes were put out, and we settled at my altar, which was fully ablaze with candles I had just bought at The Wicca.

The Tarot served as our language. I took out my deck and shuffled above the telegram, as my last link with home. The cards felt ready.

Beth was visiting with her cat, Jupiter, a Siamese. She joined us, and her cat looked on from outside my room.

I lifted the cards three times, and the first card for the significator was Death. She is here!

The second card was the Three of Swords. Heart attack.

The third card was the Page of Cups. Beloved Youth. She hated to leave me behind. For the duration of this reading we were both alive. Blessed be the Tarot for giving me solace.

Overhead, in the position of the crown of her life, was the Six of Wands. Moral victory, achievement, high honor. She was a modern temple raiser. In her roots was the Chariot. The soul aiming higher, the deep mind was taking her to other planes. The past was the Hierophant. Yes, she took care of administrative duties. The wills, the works all protected and finished. Her divine self was Strength. Control over her destiny. She met death with dignity, not drugged out. The immediate future, the Seven of Swords. It was not over yet. The consciousness now had to overcome the attachments to the living. Her house was the Eight of Cups. Leaving behind earthly loved ones for higher love, higher goals. The card for the outcome was the Five of Pentacles. Oh, when you die, isn't it all solved either? Adaptation to her new situation was necessary. But don't feel lonely, please! Justice is the far outcome. A just outcome is hard to swallow. I want my mama back! It has unfolded as it should. But O Goddess, it hurts!

Suddenly the cat started mewing. Jupiter came into the circle, and I remembered that Mother loved cats. OK, let's ask the cat to pull a card!

"What is your path for the next three months?" I asked. The cat pawed as if he were playing with a ball, except it was the Tarot's Ace of Wands. A new life for Masika. The Six of Wands. More moral victory and achievement ahead. The Three of Cups. A happy issue, good divine choice, worthy of celebration.

Then Jupiter pulled Death, in case I had forgotten. "Yes, Mother, I am trying to accept it." The Chariot. Her destiny was yet to unfold. This was only one episode.

The pain didn't stop, but the heaviness left me the moment they cremated her body. It felt complete then. She had made it home.

☾ ○ ☽

*June 13*

Forty-nine days after her death we convened to celebrate her arrival in the spirit world. It is a pagan custom called the Feast of Parentalia. Only close friends are invited. My mother's place was at the head of the table.

This was our first Parentalia. Goddess, would she come? I had tried not to disturb Masika from her deep sleep until this day. Kirsten's mother, Dorothy, was present too. It just happened that she had flown in to visit her daughter. Although a very conservative lady, she understood Parentalia immediately and demanded that she cook the entire dinner for it.

I told stories about Masika, her memory revived. Pictures were assembled in a big leather book, from her childhood to her death. We passed it around and sent her love. No sign was given to us at this event. But I felt it was because Kristen's mother was her representative as a crone and she didn't want any psychic happenings. We ate and praised her. It was well. Every year now I have this same dinner date with Masika.

☾ ◯ ☽

*October 31, Halloween*

I have had only one dream of you since you died, and that has been sustaining me though this year like medicine. You were running upstairs from some deep place, dressed in a soft, full-length purple gown you never owned, and looking about thirty-five years old, the age you were when we still lived together. I was wringing my hands, begging you to stop—your heart! But you laughed a rich and free laugh, saying, "Hey, I can even fly!"

Why don't you come to me more often? I have some of your graveyard dust on my altar. I need to see you more. Why? Didn't we have a contract to aid each other even after death? Do you need anything from me? Nothing?

I feel that you have involved yourself with my book. Your art is in it. In *The Holy Book of Women's Mysteries*, we are a team. I feel your protection like a bulletproof window. Some jerk stole my car and I asked for your help, putting on your navy-blue dress Titi sent me as my heritage. The car was found within twelve hours, intact. I feel your voice, like a monologue inside me. You make me write more; you talk to me. But the pain won't go away. And for the first time in my life, I dare death for your scent. Your Goddess love. Please, help me live for now, and when the time comes, send me gentle death. I know that you will have the power to pull me through the veil. My ghostwriter, my mother, my sister!

This good-bye is only temporary.

# TWELFTH LUNATION

*Time ‹ November–December*
*Sign ‹ Sagittarius*
*Lunar Herb ‹ Motherwort*
*Lunar Animal ‹ Owl*

# Long Night's Moon

## VIEW FROM THE MOON

*The time of the longest nights has come, and the Lady of the Night, the Cold White Moon, rules supreme. She wheels through the heavens above a white world, as if her power were transforming the earth into her own image. Moonlight glitters from frosted branches, sparkles from fields of new-fallen snow. The air tingles with energy. Now, in this time of greatest darkness, the Moon is pregnant with light. The stars dance around her in the heavens, and Earth blossoms with a million points of brightness. Out of the darkness the new year is born.*

## THE GODDESS SPEAKS
# *Diana*

My name is written all over the mountains and rivers, the songs of my beauty ring in the hearts of the farmers. My magical deeds fill children's fairy tales. I am Diana, the fiery, protective huntress, the conceiver and deliverer of all babies. I am the free spirit of achievement, and this Moon I shall stimulate you to follow my dynamic lead. Set high goals and I shall help you to achieve them.

What are you so afraid of? Why are you cowering, stewing in inactivity? Listen to the sound of my trumpets! *Evoe!* I call to my sisters, *Evoe!* I call to my hounds and my wild stags! *Evoe!* A new future must be sown, *Evoe!* A new life must be forged from the old one. *Evoe!* Hear my trumpets calling to gather you all behind my banner.

You must get it into your heart that it is good to stand out, to be different. It is good to take risks, to push ahead. It is good to take your chances and see how far you can go. Women who emulate me are independent; I give them power to sustain themselves in hard times. Women who are assertive are my special daughters. I reward them with recognition for their efforts. Energy is my special ally, you generate it by deeds. The more you work, the more energy you will receive. But work must be physical, energy is physical, you will need to be strong. You must run with me outdoors under the trees and stars, you must run with me in races and marathons or swim laps in waters great and small. You must move and raise more energy—life is too short to wait around.

I am lusty. Do not think that chastity is rewarded unless it is itself a reward. Sexuality is fuel for your whole life, not just lovers' trysts. I urge you to love as much as you can, I urge you to embrace other hearts. Stay true to your lovers, it will make you stronger. I am Diana, Mistress of the Wild and the white archer's Moon of Sagittarius overhead. I love you as Amazon warriors love each other. I lead you as a sister and your peer, and I reward you with your own gifts fortified. Come and compete in the games of life! Be a player and my partner. The Sagittarius Moon is behind you, you cannot fail!

# Sagittarius Message

This lunation gives a surge of energy to us, we rebirth. Our juices start churning again, we get going, and in our New Year's resolutions we set high goals. Nature looks dead, but below the surface the Tao is shifting again toward life. The process of renewal has started already, we are moving toward the rebirth of light.

Take your studies very seriously—the future belongs to those who are informed and well read. The age of information is the next century, beginning at the end of this decade. In the age of information women will dominate because the work will have to do with knowledge and intuition, with smarts, not competition and brute force. Support your spirituality, expand and take chances. Build partnerships. In this sign harvest everything that is left in your garden.

## MOONTIDE

# Enthusiasm

This is a gift of good mental health or perhaps a gift of the stars. People who don't get enthusiastic miss a lot. This feeling makes you glow, it makes your blood run faster, it is the fuel that carries you to your goals. Motivation is another form of this feeling.

## MOONSPELL

# For More Enthusiasm

If you want to become more enthusiastic about your life, do this ritual every morning just after you get up and every evening just before you fall asleep.

Get a piece of green stone. It can be jasper, malachite, emerald, or jade. Rub it with your hands over the smoke from a little incense (your favorite) and say three times:

*Green stone, green star,*
*We grow, we reach,*
*We mind, we shine!*

Carry the green stone on your body at all times in a little pouch. Even
sleep with it under your pillow. The Little People who live in the earth
and are always enthusiastic will help you gain some of their magic.

## MOONTIDE
## *Apathy*

The death of the soul is apathy. When you have been beaten so long
and so much that you can no longer fight back, "they" have got you.
"They" in this case are whoever would benefit from your lack of participation in real life. Apathy is bad for your health, it is a form of
depression. Many people are depressed today, but I don't think they are
sick. I think that those who believe they can be completely healthy in an
environment that is unhealthy both culturally and ecologically are the ones
who are ill.

If you are still healthy enough to be discouraged, apathy is a state of
limbo. You can take a rest in it while you are waiting to get more wind
behind you. When you are ready to get out of it, here are some things
you can do.

## MOONSPELL
## *Against Apathy*

Since apathy means that you are not doing anything at all, spellcasting
is too hard. But you can begin by taking a tonic. I prefer Hypericon (St.
John's wort, which you can get at health-food stores), which is a nervine
and balancer. Its psychic effect is to heal overstressed emotions. Other
friends of mine use ginseng tea, another tonic and antidepressant.

You still have enough energy to wear a scent. Use lavender. It will
invigorate you. Wearing ylang-ylang will dispel negative moods and wake
up your kundalini. Scents influence the way we feel about ourselves and

the world. If you have problems with digestion, use burdock tincture. It makes the entire food-processing mechanism of your body run more smoothly, and if you improve your body, you are improving your mind.

## MOONSPELL

# *Against Depression*

When you are really depressed or have sunk into deep apathy, light a pink candle and watch it for a while. This is a high-vibration color that will call in your reserve energy. Pink is the color of equilibrium.

If you have gained some psychic energy, a magical bath is the easiest spell to use. Scrub your tub with salt. Light some pink candles and set them around the bathroom. Put in a bathbag some melissa, sweet balm, and hyssop. You put the herbal bathbag under the running water and allow your bath to become a kind of tea for you to sit in. It will also smell heavenly. Rub the herbal bag all over your body to improve circulation by making the blood rise to the skin. Burn pink candles in the bath as well.

Just before you are ready to get out of the water but are not cold yet, say:

> *By the power of the Goddess,*
> *By the power of all of nature,*
> *The stars, the clouds,*
> *the rain, and the herbs,*
> *I shall be healed,*
> *I shall be healed,*
> *I shall be loved,*
> *It is done.*

Do this seven nights in a row if you have enough energy. Otherwise, just watch the candle, burn some sandalwood incense, and let it be.

Once you have become functional again without having to use heavy drugs, you will need to examine the reasons for your depression. Is the cause psychological or physical? If the former, you may have to change your life, take a big risk, make a choice, and move on. Depression is a sign that you are not on your spiritual path, your spirit is not being nourished. The depression will return unless you take more power and put your life in better order. If that is impossible in the current environment, you must work for social change to create a situation in which it will be possible for you to flourish. Political activism is good medicine for a depressed person; you are constantly being reminded that your pain is shared by millions.

If your depression is the result of a chemical dysfunction, however, make contact with a mental-health worker, preferably someone with social awareness. Avoid self-righteous male doctors who would recommend electric shock treatments, heavy drugs, or brainwashing. Remember, your body can heal you with the aid of your spirit.

# FESTIVALS OF THE MOON
## *St. Andrew's Day*
## *November 29, Dark of the Moon — Eastern Europe*

Somehow this Moon speaks to love and marriage. On St. Andrew's Eve girls hold a black cat over (or in front of!) the fire, throw a handful of barley into the flames, and say, "Barley, burn! Cat, mew! And let my dear one come!" (Urlin, *Festivals, holydays*, 219). The dark of the Moon is indeed very good for prophecy, but this scaring the cat business doesn't appeal to me.

In Austria there was a tradition that if you wore a branch of apricot flower to Mass on St. Andrew's Day, you would be able to identify all the witches. But to me this also seems like a perverted love spell. Taking in branches of a plump tree elsewhere in the world means calling on your lover, making the blooms of love come faster.

In ancient times the last day of the month and the dark of the Moon were sacred to the Witch Goddess Hecate. The nordic Vanir were the deities of the old earth religion, which preserved so much of the ancient magic. Freya, whose cart was drawn by cats, was a Goddess of Love, Death, and Witchcraft, and her brother/lover Frey, of fertility and prosperity.

### Weatherworking
### (Poseideon, St. Nicholas's Day, Tunderman's Night)
### December 6, Waxing Moon — Europe

In ancient Greece the major feast of early December was held in honor of Poseidon. In the Mediterranean, coastal chapels are full of votive offerings that were formerly made to Poseidon and Neptune for safety from storms. This is the season when the winter storms are supposed to start rolling in, and the absence of snow and rain can be as disastrous as their violence. In the Shetland Islands the feast that follows Mother Night is Tunderman's Night — the feast of Thor the Thunderer, who brings the storms.

Whether you call him Poseidon, Nicholas, or Thor, honor the deity of sea storms on this day, and ask for gentle, regular rainfall. If the weather has been too violent, dance clockwise to bring a fair spell. In a drought, dance counterclockwise (widdershins) to bring the storms. Analyze the way you use water and correct any wasteful habits.

### Soyal
### Full Moon — Native American (Pueblo)

Midwinter has been one of the chief festivals of the Pueblos since the time of the Anasazi. The courts above the kivas at Chimney Rock pueblo are aligned so that the rising of the midwinter Full Moon can be observed through the double spires of Chimney Rock. Rising between the red rocks above a desert frosted with snow, the sunset-colored Moon is an amazing sight. In Zuni mythology, White Shell Woman persuades the Sun to return northward at the winter solstice. The rising of the Full Moon enables the chiefs to establish the date for the Soyal ceremony.

Soyal is the Hopi nine-day winter solstice festival that celebrates the return of the sun to his house. It follows the initiation of Hopi youths as adults in the tribe. Imagine if we had a winter solstice ritual where men could be part of a peaceful and strong role model. The purpose of the festival is to pray for health and prosperity in the new year and to open the way for the return of the kachinas, the protective ancestral spirits of the people, from their home in the underworld.

### Return of the Light
### New Moon after the Winter Solstice—Inuit (Eskimo)

In Inuit myth the Moon is male and the Sun is his sister. On the longest night, or the first New Moon after the longest night, all fires are put out in the villages. Then two shamans, one of whom is dressed as a woman (or who at times probably *was* a female shaman), go from hut to hut relighting them from their own ceremonially kindled flame and saying, "From the new sun comes light." This is followed by feasting, playing, and dancing to celebrate the return of the sun and the prospect of good hunting.

### Dianic Full Moon

Gatherings of women share good foods of the season in this feast to the Goddess. The circle of mothers is honored, those who have taken on the arduous task of bringing up souls from their waiting place and manifesting them in flesh. Befana, the good witch, is giving out her blessings, presents from her magical bag. Storyteller is taking us on a flight on the wings of the great Yule stag, who draws the chariot of the Moon. Arts and crafts fairies celebrate creativity; beauty is displayed.

# MOON TALE

## *Welcome, Grandmother*

I am not the kind of Californian who loves to sit limp in hot tubs, who enjoys hot saunas or seeks out steaming Turkish baths. I hate to be too hot or too cold. And I hate to sweat.

For my well-being I need Mediterranean temperatures, a little breeze, sunny skies, but not heat that is baking. My Native American friends introduced me to the sweatlodge many years ago, and I participated because the opportunity was offered kindly.

It is true that a good sweat can purify you, push you to confront your fears in the small dark womb of the sweat hut. But I never truly enjoyed the sweatlodge experience, especially when there were many women in the lodge and I had to wait for all of them to say their prayers, gasping for air in the meantime. Sitting with a bare butt on cedar twigs can also prove to be a very unspiritual experience. My city-girl rear end didn't appreciate the sharp pain of twigs digging into my skin.

This year I announced that I would lead an end-of-the-year retreat. It was going to be a purification from the old year/decade/century. In the enthusiasm of planning, we decided that we would start with a Friday night Full-Moon ceremony. The next day I would lead a sweat, and later that night we were going down into a 150-foot-deep cave (the California

Caverns in Calaveras County) to worship the Fates in a candlelight ceremony.

It sounded like a good plan.

But as soon as I saw all this in print, I started worrying about the sweat. O Goddess! That cooking my flesh again! The only thing that helped was that I would be leading it. I could make short prayers, decide on the number of hot rocks in the middle, have water right next to me, and otherwise keep things under control. So I was all right until it was actually time to begin.

The thirteen women all arrived safely, no small achievement, since we had to find this very private place in the western Sierras in the dark. The place is owned by Kala, my spiritual daughter (meaning that she is studying with me) and her life partners.

"Touchstone" has been in the making for fifteen years. These women love their land—180 acres of pristine California forest—and wanted to share it with other women. They built a redwood cottage, complete with meditation room and kitchen, toilets, two more rooms for sleeping, a lovely deck. The groundcover is bear brush here, friendly, no poison oak to stop the wanderer. There are some small ponds—we call them lakes— very low or totally dry now in the winter drought.

This was Touchstone's first professional Goddess retreat. Everybody was nervous. Kala was checking and double-checking the details. She would relax and start enjoying herself only to catch herself worrying again. We have all done this. Kala's extended family had turned into cooks and caretakers. Even little six-year-old Darsey, who is normally a pink terror, ran docile errands for her mom, telling the group when dinner was ready, finding the missing ones who had wandered away under the starlit trees.

The circle centered around the Full Moon and a large fire. The familiar smell of wood burning, the delicious inconvenience of the smoke, the stars and the Moon—all were soul enchanting.

Is this normal at last? I asked silently. Do women have enough community and resources to enjoy the worship of the Goddess in the open, in the presence of the brilliant Moon? I tried to send out my feelers to the whole world. Let it be, I prayed, let this presence give birth to this dream. Worldwide, when the Moon is full, let women pray for peace and health and wealth and wisdom.

I have a very easy job to do as the Medea, the Medicine woman. The way is what you perform for the spirits in worship.

I walked around the circle with a thick, locally picked smudge stick—a bundle of sage and cedar, the great purifiers, bound together. Each woman I confronted held out her hands and looked up at the Moon. I let the smudge stick flare up, and when its smoke was billowing generously, I fanned smoke into the auras around the heads of the women, one by one, washing them with the smoke, washing their whole bodies.

"I purify you from all anxiety, from fear and doubt. I bless your hands to do the Goddess work. I bless your body to enjoy life in strength and beauty. I bless your feet to walk in the Goddess path."

Finally I turned them around and smudged their backs.

"Blessed be your back so that you will be safe and healthy, with no enemies."

At this point my usual ideas about humming, power raising through chanting, all went out the window. Better to use those techniques indoors. Outdoors you need the drums and the rattles and the bells and more drums.

The night advanced. The Moon was close in our faces. The cool night was not bothering us, because the fire kept us warm. Some even took off their sweaters.

We drummed. We danced.

We invoked the corners of the universe. I always enjoy listening to participants' images, the way they call on the Goddess differently but with the same reverence. Some are simple, some are elaborate.

I called in the center, the ancestors.

Three beautiful red apples were my offerings. Red is the color of life and blood. The apples are the sacred fruit of dominion and disobedience—Eve's power.

"Come to us, O guardian spirits of the future! Angels of good luck and angels of effectiveness! Come into this circle, angels of the future! Inspire and protect us, transfuse us with your courage and lightness! Guide us into the next phase! Let us create with you together!"

In the circle the drums exploded with sound. There was no doubt, the Goddess was here!

I had the three red magical apples. The first one was for me personally, my love life, my health, my work. The second apple was the symbol for the successful continuation of the Goddess work, that which is good for all. The third was for Death, that she'll be kind and not too hasty. I offered them to the Moon, then I cast them into the roaring fire as a sacrifice. Baked apples for the Lady.

The other women passed a tray of cornmeal mixed with lentils, both traditional offerings to the Goddess. They each prayed silently and then cast a handful of cornmeal into the fire. We call this feeding the fire, an old tradition from the peasants in Central Europe.

What wishes can one really make for the future? That it will be great? That it will be a woman future? That there will be a future at all? We did our best. As usual, the women remembered everything and everybody— from children and men to the redwoods and the quality of life. The old Moon heard thirteen witches dancing in the new century.

Ah, but by early morning of the next day, I began to worry about the sweat.

I wanted to do something different, not the traditional praying to the four corners and chanting, but something that in my opinion would go better with the extreme heat. Like extreme pain, extreme heat (or physical stress of any kind) helps us to get down to the depths of our beings, to deal with the darkness.

Kala talked about the sweat in preparation. I appreciated this opportunity to recognize my fears about the tight, dark place, to tell everybody that this was the first sweat I had conducted, so they would know what they were getting.

I also mentioned that since Halloween I had not yet been able to meet my own spiritual needs. I priestessed the fifth annual Women's Sacred Dance, but there my energy always goes outward. There I cannot go along the transformational emotional path that I lead others on. Many women who come to the Halloween Women's Dance have an opportunity to deal with their own feelings. In the first part of our program, we listen to stories, we listen to songs, and then we listen to our own hearts. Here we find our pain, our losses, and our wounds, and we cry together, holding on to each other, no longer strangers. This catharsis has always been the product of my work, but I never feel it myself. After the Halloween circle, I felt lonely. Everybody else had such a good time—first they felt pain, then they were released from it. Sometimes when that happens, I feel betrayed somehow by my own talent. How did I get to be the giver instead of the receiver of this gift?

But here at Touchstone under the wide western sky, it was my time.

We entered the sweatlodge from the east, and as we entered we all said, "For my ancestors."

Inside, the red dirt floor was covered with cedar twigs, but I wisely brought my own towel to sit on. In this first sweat there were six of us. The first glowing-hot lava rock arrived on a pitchfork.

"Welcome, Grandmother!" we all greeted her.

Immediately the heat from the rock filled the space. The cedar added freshness. I felt perspiration form on my forehead. I was very aware of the six naked woman bodies and the hot, glowing rock in the middle of the small space. My claustrophobia stirred. It felt as if all six of us had crawled back into the womb at the same time.

As I became aware of this feeling, I released it. The fear passed. I realized then that the sweatlodge wasn't even all that dark, since the sun was shining outside and a little came in around the edges.

"I would like to dedicate this sweat to our life cycles," I said. "This is the end of a decade, also the end of a century. Let's go inside our souls and confront old pains, new pains, whatever we need to take care of, so that we can be purified."

Silently the women nodded. *What courage!* I thought. We just met last night, a random selection of participants, and today we were going to help each other to clean out our psychic garbage. Holy compost. Soul manure.

I started. It is always easier to lead by example. I called on the little girl within me, who was a toddler during World War II.

My inner child is always afraid she will get shot. She grew up in a war zone. She fears loud explosions, shotgun sounds, cannons even worse. She can never watch war scenes on TV or in the movies. She looks away, hides her face. She fears starvation, she is always eating for tomorrow.

It wasn't hard to cry. The heat was warming us all, but as my little girl became real to me, I felt the coldness of death again. I stuck a hand out under the tent flap and beckoned for more hot rocks. Another glowing lava stone arrived.

"Welcome, Grandmother!" we greeted her.

The heat grew. My pain melted slowly with the tears. How can you ever heal an ancient wound like the war? What happens to the veterans of revolutions? The little girl extended her hands over the fire, and sobbing, she settled down. "The war is over. You have enough to eat now. Don't worry, I will protect you!" my adult self assured her. The tears still flowed.

The next woman took up the task of soul cleaning. She was much younger. I noticed how beautiful she was; she had the body of a ballerina, or of a gymnast, as it turned out.

"I feel so sad about my little girl," she started. "She is so afraid of her daddy, especially when he drinks, then he beats on her and her mommy . . ."

The tears came naturally. Avoiding all philosophy and sticking to feelings, her little girl moaned her pain about sexual abuse, humiliation, poverty. She sobbed, rocking the tent, vomiting her pain like a psychic discharge.

The pain chilled the heat again.

"More stones, please!" Another glowing stone arrived. "Welcome, Grandmother!" we called out.

Now something interesting started happening in the sweatlodge. There were now three stones in the center, and as the last one arrived, their combined heat increased. I remembered the water and poured some on the rocks. The heat actually escalated. The roots of my hair dripped water now.

The sounds of weeping and remembered pain became part of the heat-filled environment. The sweatlodge was developing its own sound and taste. We still held one another's hands as we sat in the circle, but we started feeling more primal, more animal as we released our anguish over the unalterable past. We fed on one another's tears. Whether we were speaking or not, we cried.

In the modest hole in the earth before us, the three Grandmothers glowed with an earthy assurance of life fire.

Slowly a face began to form in the dim glow above it, a seventh woman's face, not one of ours. Her face was lined like the rocks, her eyes glowed like coals, her body was the darkness. But she was there. When the next woman spoke, she instinctively reached out to touch the old woman, disconnecting her hand from that of the woman sitting next to her. She kept reaching toward the old face in the middle, and the old woman kissed her hands.

"More rocks, please!" I called.

"Welcome, Grandmother!" we all said when the next stone was pushed in.

Now the heat really pushed me to the limits of my endurance. It was so hot my ears were dripping. I couldn't see because of the moisture flowing over them. But I could see the Grandmother in the middle. She got bigger. Now she had shoulders, and her arms were visible. It seemed as if the more rocks we placed in the middle, the more visible she became. I wondered if the others could see her. Clearly they could sense her.

The fifth woman started talking about the feelings she was carrying. She was another neglected child. A lost daughter. A daughter who was yelled at, who was unloved, who wasn't allowed to say good-bye to her own grandmother when she died. The ancient pain rocked her like an earthquake.

Grandmother seemed to envelop her like steam. For a moment her sobs were muffled, then they burst out with renewed power.

"I wanted to hold my grandmother so much!" she cried. "They didn't let me say good-bye!"

The sixth woman had trouble getting in touch with her feelings. She was the type who never cried, who always hid her feelings. When I saw her struggling to reach deep enough, I put some water on the rocks and the heat shot up again.

"My little girl was always such a good girl. She wanted to please everybody." She stopped.

Grandmother turned toward her and touched her face, touched her heart, and loosened her arms. Without any more words, a great sob rose through her and rocked her with elemental force. Everybody understood that something unspeakable had happened to the sweet little girl who wanted to please everyone to make her grieve like this.

"I feel for your little girl!" we said to her and cried with her. Grandmother gathered our feelings in her lap. I could see it as she swept them out of our hearts and into her skirts. She put them into the glowing stones.

She melted the grief out of our eyes. She melted it out of our memories. The six women were getting cleansed from pain. Grandmother was busy with us.

"Another stone, please!"

"Welcome, Grandmother!"

How do we ever make it to adulthood being abused like this? Didn't anybody escape the abusive hands of patriarchy? Was there ever a little girl who was happy and safe? Here there were six women. Three had been raped, one was abandoned, one was neglected and ignored, never touched, and one lived in a war zone. It is a miracle that we have any strength today.

Now I splashed us all with water. We shuddered and shrieked.

"Say good-bye to the little girl. Assure her that she will be heard again and again. But now we need to talk to our adolescent selves."

Things got a little better for most of us during adolescence. Of course I was now caught up in a civil war. I was shot at, my house leveled again, my friends killed. I walked on dead bodies on the streets.

The other women were still struggling, but you could hear how they were succeeding in beginning to change their situations. The sexually abused children ran away. It was hard but it was safer. The neglected child was still further neglected. The unloved one was still unloved by parents but made some friends.

More tears flowed, but you could feel that Grandmother was not packing away quite as much pain as before. She was still there, but she faded in and out of my sight. She was consoling us, stroking our wet heads, she kissed our faces.

We said good-bye to the adolescents within us, and I sprayed us with more water. We passed a jug and drank as well.

The last round was without tears. We assured each other that we would have strength and peace of mind. We were here together, we had overcome.

At the end I knew more about the five women who were with me than I knew about my best friend. I loved them all deeply and felt they were my friends.

We thanked Grandmother by throwing our sweat onto the stones. Then we touched the cool, red earth and smeared our faces and bodies with it.

"For my ancestors!" I greeted the sunshine outside as I left the tent.

When we all gathered together around the cool tubs to dunk our bodies and wash off, I looked around. We looked as if we had just come back from the Stone Age. Our faces were smeared with sweat and dirt; tear and sweat streaks made us look like warriors returning from the savage hunt.

For the first time in a very long time I felt I had taken care of myself emotionally while priestessing a ritual. The pain about the war and the revolution will accumulate again, but if I keep spooning it out to Grandmother, maybe I will get rid of it eventually.

> *We all come from the Goddess*
> *And to her we shall return*
> *Like a drop of rain*
> *Flowing to the ocean.**

*Song copyright © Z. Budapest, 1971.

# THIRTEENTH LUNATION

*Time ‹ Between the Years*
*Sign ‹ Your Sign*
*Lunar Herb ‹ Mugwort*
*Lunar Animal ‹ Butterfly*

# Blue Moon

## VIEW FROM THE MOON

*The round Moon pursues her orbit through the heavens, serene and unperturbed. But as she rolls onward, a new planet is rising before her, blue as lapis lazuli, veiled in wisps of cloud. How exquisite is this world in its roundness, how perfectly balanced, how rich in elements, protected by its fragile veil of atmosphere. The Moon is white and cold, but below, all is movement. The web of life that covers its surface is part of the glow. The Moon reaches out in love, and upon the planet, land and sea and all the creatures yearn for her in return. And still the Moon rolls onward, and the earthlight colors her whiteness with a blue glow.*

## THE GODDESS SPEAKS
# *Titania*

Rise from the unexpected mists, my fairy folks, my lovely flowers! I, the Queen of Nature, wish to recline here and be entertained by your follies. Come, my little goblins, my nimble elves; come, my butterfly men; come, my zephyrs and serious tree spirits. Surround me with your light-hearted chatter, with your musical offerings, the songs and dances you love to show me when I am in the mood.

It is our time again, it is the blessed Blue Moon, the Moon with no name but only a rare color. This is our magical surprise for the world, it is our private joke and pleasure to put an extra Full Moon in some months. It doesn't seem so long ago that some priests changed the way men reckon time from the silver lunar calendar to the golden solar one.

Ha! The Moon didn't fit in this way, so they are stuck now with the unexplainable, and the Blue Moon is even more magical than before. There are always thirteen Full Moons in my yearly cycle, not twelve. The gentle Moon was too threatening to the church; the Moon kept alive the fairy holidays that folk liked to celebrate with such joviality.

Now they have confusion. Extra days and extra nights are left over because only by the Moon is time measured in harmony with the natural world.

So, my fairies, let us dance! The Blue Moon is full and shining. You know its rays can heal the sick and cheer up the depressed. Hooting owls, how wonderful you sound! Baying wolves, how sweet is your sorrow! Chirping crickets and sweet nightingales, my pets, come to the Blue Moon's festivities, and let us dance the dance of life!

I remember many nights like this. The first to rise to the occasion is always my fairy daughter, the frog. See how she sheds her skin of green and brown, see how she is donning her silk cape and her silver crown.

"Will you kiss me?" asks the mortal man, longing for love.

"I will kiss you when you die," she answers with a smile.

"Then let me die now," yearns the mortal.

"You can't, you can't! It isn't your time yet!" chirp the insects in reply.

"If you will kiss me only when I die, let me die for you now!"

Oh, watch as the magical kiss is bestowed by the Princess of the Pond upon the mortal man who is full of longing for love. Watch him change into her partner, her mate. How happily they dance now. The kiss of life has transformed them both.

Under the Blue Moon you can change shape, you can visit other worlds, you can find true love. I, Titania, oversee miracles. I am the Fairy Queen, the nature fairy, the energy that makes it all work in perfect cycles. Look now under the big redwood tree—witches are coming in groups of threes and fours, making in all thirteen.

Will they feel me near?

"Could we see you, please?" Already they sense my presence. They are my grandchildren. I hoot back through my owl's throat. The witches sway, holding hands, they sway in rhythm. Then the youngest one speaks again.

"Can we please see you, O Goddess of the Woods?"

Oh, this is great fun! Titania is never bored. I have my magical tricks. I am the one they all adore.

"Yes, you may see me!" I say as a woman.

"Who said that?" they ask, nervous now. Deep down they know it was I.

"Titania!" they chant my name and the woods echo. "Titania! Blue Moon Goddess! Come to us!"

"I am already here!" I say through the throats of my stags.

"Did you hear? Did you hear that?" they ask each other excitedly. And I laugh. My laughter is the nightingale's song, rising from the grass.

"I need to sleep," says the youngest one now. "I think if I dreamed, I would really see her."

They all lie down on my mossy grass. I lie down with my witches, and I shall drip visions into their heads from a flower I carry in my bosom, the mugwort. So dream, my children, dream of me.

"I see her!" says the oldest now, deeply asleep, her lips wet with saliva from the sweetness of my visions.

"Ah, I see her now," whispers the middle-aged one, lifting her head a little to see me better.

"I see her now!" whisper the rest of the witches. Now they all are having visions of Titania.

"See even more, my grandchildren!" I whisper. Come see my family, the fairies, come look at their tiny, fragile wings, look at the iridescent, silky wings they have fashioned for themselves. Look at their tiny red shoes, which can help you climb mountains without any effort. Look at the mirrors they carry in their pockets—my fairies can look into them and see me and each other any time they wish.

"What is our future?" the witches are asking.

"The future is life," I answer, and they are satisfied.

Now the redwoods are quiet. The witches are sleeping and dreaming of me and watching the festivities as the late hours unfold.

"Mistress, Lord Oberon is looking for you!" says my little cricket servant.

"Let him look for me!" I say, smiling. "My lord Oberon knows where his mistress is." Soon he will appear in his naked beauty, my mate, who makes love to me under the Blue Moon.

"This is our night of tryst, my lady!" he says as he steps from the shadows.

"It is as it should be!" I answer. "Titania is ready, my lord."

He comes to me as a stag, his horns covered with virgin fuzz, to match the moss under his feet. O my Oberon, my child, my husband! I embrace him dearly, my white bosom like lilies, my pink arms like roses, my deep lap like the everglades' depths. My lips searching his lips are blushed with raspberries. He feels my enchantment, he breathes deeply as he serves my pleasure, he licks, he kisses, he whispers fantasies into my ears.

The Blue Moon is sailing overhead, Selene's chariot. I lie in my lover's arms and let him carry me to ecstasy. All of nature mates when I do. All of nature loves when I do.

My witches are shaking their heads.

"What's wrong?" I ask.

"Nothing. It's just the mating, mistress. You are with a man."

"My grandchildren, you are wrong. Male and female are all one in me. Just look at my Calla lilies, orchids, and date palms. Go back to sleep and do not worry."

The night is flying by. My pleasures fill up the emptiness in the hearts of all living beings. The new dawn will come and bring hope. Titania has celebrated her Blue Moon in full.

## Blue Moon Message

When there is more than one Full Moon in a month, we call it a Blue Moon. The Blue Moon gives us an extra chance to touch the divine, to do important crazy things, like reveling, dancing, going into the woods at night to offer the Fairy Queen cakes and wine. The time of the Blue Moon is a never-never land, a time more enchanted than any other, because it is rare. Because the Blue Moon is between times, the world between the worlds is never as easy to reach as under this Full Moon. Magical spells find their fulfillment faster and more strongly with this bewitchment behind them. Thoughts fly like the wind, reality bends in its wake.

## MOONTIDE

## Altered States of Consciousness

Our species, the lunar primates, have spent a great deal of thought on our consciousness and its content. The subject is a major obsession of our existence. No matter what cultures you study, you will soon find that the ancestors have developed many methods for shifting consciousness, from powerful consciousness-changing drugs to milder highs to methods that use no drugs at all. It seems to have been going on as long as our kind have lived on earth. We are the only species that takes drugs. This is such a remarkable thing to do that I am inclined to believe that our involvement with the natural world and its drugs is basic to our very lunar nature.

When you change your consciousness, you are changing your brain. You are taking on the responsibility of the divine, in directing your brain to pursue this or that purpose, to facilitate a biological process that yields spiritual dividends, to bind the mind and the soul together, to heal the divided, to talk to a sickness, to make a wound heal. We must have discovered the first narcotics in tending to our wounded, and we used them carefully, and ritualistically, as gifts from the gods.

Our species evolved because we developed our brains as other species might have changed their bodies or grown longer feathers to fly. We transformed our brains, and we developed a very complex computer between our two ears. If we tried to duplicate it, it would take up as much room as the state of Texas. Our minds became windows to other worlds, where we visited and found allies, from whom we learned and even received help.

I once saw a documentary about the Matses Indian tribe in the South American jungles, who take a snuff called nu nu, which consists of wild tobacco leaves and the inner bark of the macambo tree. They blow this into each other's nostrils. First it hurts with a blinding pain. The jaguar people (Matses) meet the animals in the altered state, then hunt for them, already knowing which are theirs to take.

An altered state is a truer reality. It is as if we had added other windows to our perceptions. Our normal perception allows us to see only part of the picture, the so-called reality is a fraction of what's going on. We are still in the throes of our chaos without the fuller view.

What is this bigger picture?

It is the world of the earth, her core and her crust, her top layer of animals, and the creatures of all sorts, who live in the water and in the air. To visit with these souls is the purpose of journeying in the alternative reality, making the shamanic journey of the self, to make our unity with animals certain, so that we will never hurt them again, remembering that they are souls like ourselves in different forms.

An altered state in which you approach the natural world with reverence will not allow narrow-mindedness. Our first human civilizations sprang from altered states, which focused the intense and culturally supported purposes of nations and tribes. We gathered regularly to achieve this altered state of consciousness when we celebrated the cycles of the Earth and the Moon, using fresh air and chanting and dancing. We used starshine and singing, drama and theater, and comedy. We used poetry. Today we use video, movies, and rock concerts. The global village. These are the new tribal gatherings, when you rejoice, dress up, and celebrate together with your fellow tribal members.

## *Hallucinogens*

Altered states have been achieved with many kinds of mushrooms, especially in the Americas. Many native traditions show the healing powers of the Holy Children, as Maria Sabina used to call her mushrooms. She took them to get the help of the Holy Children and cured people overnight by holding an all-night visit in these altered states and chanting.

European witches used the famous flying ointment, which was a mixture of powerful drugs, including belladonna. It produced the sensations of flying. The witches' bodies dropped to the ground, where their sisters watched over them while they were out of the body. Hounds, the sacred animals of the Moon, guarded their mistresses against disturbance until the dear one returned back into her own form. The witches reported that they flew with Diana and her thousands of companions to a mountaintop for a festival, where they ate and drank to their hearts' delight and made love. And nobody who made love on these journeys ever got pregnant. Naturally. Witches entered altered states sometimes to escape the persecutions of their enemies. Belladonna taken in overdose stops the heart instantly. It was a better death than burning.

Opium, a very popular drug in the last century, destroyed empires. It is a powerful drug, but when taken in ritual in small doses, it allowed prophetic visions to come.

We know that slabs of hashish were burned in the clefts of the earth above which the priestesses gave their prophecies. Marijuana is a ritual drug in Jamaica today; ganja is used in the worship of nature.

Marijuana became the most significant American drug during the 1960s. Sharing joints and being stoned altered a generation's consciousness. It allowed them to be counterculture, to question the status quo. The drug generation redefined society, rejected war, and celebrated creativity with a burst of the best music in the world. Marijuana became a drug of peace. Peyote buttons also came to be widely used for vision quests, the Native Americans' spiritual drug of communion with the Great Spirit.

LSD was a modern spiritual drug, when taken in carefully protected space at the right time with the right people. But the use of all of these modern drugs is merely a longing for the old revels and the old highs achieved in the union with nature.

## Legal Drugs

Today wine is a favorite drug. It is a symbol of transformation. A good wine is constantly changing. The wine is the blood of the grapes, it warms the heart and aids digestion. It also gets you high. I come from an old country where wine is a sacrament. We make it, we drink it. Hungarian wines are the best in the world. I was given wine as a child, for my health, they said. Sick people always got alcohol in some form in my country. I remember that we cured colds with garlic and rum—four parts rum to a clove of garlic.

In Hungary we get drunk just to talk to one another. It is a national custom to get drunk often. It is considered good manners. I hope some day the use of wine will become more temperate and the worship of wine will be a conscious act. Beer is sacred too. It used to be mead. Fermented barley, and hops, meads of all flavors, and malts were the ancient drugs of the European peoples.

Coffee is a powerful drug, although I can find no ritual in ancient times that used it. In fact it was even outlawed in Turkey, where they really brew a mean cup of coffee, just a century ago. Today we do many rituals with coffee, starting out the day early with a cup of the black brew. There is a ritual for brewing it fresh, or just boiling water, to enable us to handle our industrial and postindustrial life-styles.

Sugar is an ancient drug. Sugar was used often in magic in the form of honey. When you cast a spell to reunite people, you wrote their names on a piece of paper and smeared them with honey and then stuck them together face to face. This was to make them love each other. Honey was the carrier of health, good against colds, and sweet to children's taste. Cakes for the Queen of Heaven were always sweetened, offerings of ritual foods were often sweet dates and pears and sugary fruits.

Salt is magical; it stands for wisdom. It is used in spells such as the self-blessing ritual. It causes a somewhat altered state as it speeds up the metabolism.

There are scores of other drugs in nature that can produce highs; even poppy seeds and morning-glory seeds are narcotic in nature. Our lunar primate species must have tasted them all, tested them all. We got high on them all.

I think human beings will always seek mind-altering drugs. Each culture has always had its dominant drug. Today we have tobacco and alcohol and coffee. Tomorrow there may be another set of drugs that we will endorse. But there will always be a way to get our minds bent, as long as people are people.

I don't think approaching the subject with judgmentalism and a frown does any good. All things, especially mind-altering drugs, must be in the domain of the spiritual in order to be controlled. In times of spiritual bankruptcy, like the post-Christian era in our society, drugs turn on us instead. Still, they have helped us so much historically; perhaps a new spiritual relationship would be possible with mind-altering drugs if people were smart enough to claim it.

## *The Ultimate Drug Is the Mind*

When we sit around in a circle and a gentle hum rises from the women's breath, we are connected with the life force and the energy of the universe. This chant can rock us, this chant can excite us, make us fly high. The chant can center us, the chant can comfort us; our consciousness is altered by the chant. This energy is the cone of power upon which all prayers are directed to the Great Spirit. The chant physically affects our bodies by balancing out the electricity in our blood and connects all our chakras into one holistic unit. These nights filled with the chant to the Goddess suspend us in time; we are truly between the worlds, we touch the past and the future at once. Chanting is one of the oldest ways of altering consciousness, used by all cultures.

The drums are the sounds of the universal belly; the drums keep the heartbeat company; the drums have direct connection to the spirit and make the spirit rise, get happy or angry, defiant and rebellious, or dissolve us in ecstasy. Drums are a very powerful mind-altering tool. Without the drums there is no dance. The drums collect us and draw us into one group; the drums warn and foretell of activities to come, consummate the union of body and spirit. Drums are used in all cultures. The drum is the oldest instrument. The shaman's drum is not used for entertainment or even celebration. It is used to call the spirits and help the shaman travel through the worlds. The drum is called the horse of the shaman. It is decorated with sacred symbols that chart the path that the mind can follow in the communion of the spirits.

Dance is worship. When we put our bodies and our minds and our voices to the sound of the drums, we are ourselves the Goddess, dancing the dance of life, the ultimate metaphor for higher consciousness. When was the last time you danced in ecstasy? When was the last time you felt in your whole body the blending of rhythms and the feeling of celebration? Dancing is healing. Dance at least eight times a year with the Earth as she dances around the sun; dance also with every Full Moon.

Sacred dancers were ancient priests and priestesses of the Goddess and gods who reenacted her mythology, her cosmology, even her philosophy by assigning special movements to thoughts and feelings. See the priestess dance. She turns as the earth turns. She opens her arms to embrace the world. She touches the ground to send her energy back to the earth. She rises and reaches to the sky to bring the energy up from the earth and direct it through her body to the spirit. She opens her arms to bless; she closes her arms to protect; she bends to bring the energy back to the world again.

Celebrate beneath the Moon. She is the ultimate source of trance and ecstasy.

# FESTIVALS OF THE MOON
## *Celebrating the New Moon*

When the Moon is new, it means that she is between her sister Earth and the sun. This is what the ancients meant by "touching the astral planes." There is a certain psychic tension, a kind of drive that originates from this astral event. A new energy is born. When the Moon is new, your hair grows faster, the grass in your backyard comes up quicker, the cells in your body multiply more vigorously. You are sharing a universal energy that flows through all living things.

"Speak to me," I said to the New Moon, and she did.

"My silver crescent is outlined against the blue sky before the sun goes down and the stars appear. I am already watching you as you go about your life, not even thinking of me, unless in passing you wonder, *I haven't seen the Moon in a long time, I wonder if she is back yet?*

"I am back! You know I am back, because you have missed me. You have had too many dark nights. You don't like dark nights, they are scary. Now there will be light. I shall shoot my arrow across the evening sky, so early I am chasing the sun. Then the sun will set, and soon after, so will I. But each evening, as I get older and lazier, I will get up fifty minutes later.

"But when I am new, if you look up during the day, there I will be, chasing my sister the sun, riding over your cities and towns, stimulating, invigorating, and inspiring everything below.

"How do you feel?

"If you have felt hopeless for a long time, I am ending that now. Out with it! If you felt no energy during my absence, I will spill universal energy into your body like fresh water into a cup. If you had no new ideas, nothing to look forward to, or even if you suffered from a lack of purpose in your life, I may now reveal them to you, give a twist to your thinking, allow your mind and your body to cheer up and even laugh again.

"Here is what you need to watch.

"Be at peace with my stimulation. Stay in your body and don't try to race with your mind only, using up my mental energy but ignoring your beautiful body. Today we'll take a long walk together somewhere in your city, and like a girlfriend I shall walk beside you, holding your hand. Now, you worry far too much! When I give you this excitement, which is my own energy, you should not get more overworked, but use it sparingly, like good honey. Use this stimulation, consciously, and integrate yourself with it. Look up! I am here. No, it wasn't your own madness that spoke to you. It was me. See? I am flying overhead and speaking in your own mind. Relax. Take a few deep breaths. Release the tension in your heart. All is well.

"It is going to be interesting now. Complex new things will require your attention. Don't hold back. Approach it as if you have plenty of time (as opposed to worrying that you are too late, which will put you off the track and build up more useless tension). Focus like an athlete who is concentrating on the next world record. Deepen your concentration and then make your move. Put this restless New-Moon energy into industry but not self-oppression. Work hard when you work, and play hard when you play. It is a balancing act.

All things will grow that are inclined to grow. I am not talking only about your body cells, your hair, or your nails but also about some of your troubles, some of your bad habits, some of your negative side.

"People are always so unhappy because life offers energy, not content. You are responsible for the content, for the details. We in the heavens cannot figure out every little detail for you. We are overly involved with you as it is. So put your mind to work. Create for yourself a balanced life. When the troubles grow, act with vigor to solve them. Troubles do not come into your life to make you into a loser. Troubles are like universal shadows of your own mind—they teach you something. Nobody likes these lessons, but, you see, harmony is not favorable for human growth. Troubles are. See them as an opportunity, or just feel their misery, feel their terror, their loneliness and despair, burn them out, and then let them go away.

"Stretch your hope far with my energy and counteract your depression. Hope loves me, I am the mother of hope. Hope will look at you from every corner, even from the newspaper articles you read, even though they are never written to further hope but rather to increase fear. Your mind is mine, and she will perceive hope where others don't see any. Hope will tug at your heartstrings, hope will make you recognize alternatives you didn't consider before. Hope will grow in darkness and light.

"I am sending you desire, all kinds of desire—the good stuff, destiny, even falling in love. If you are married already, I am still sending you this same restless energy. Watch it. It starts new things. Channel it into fantasy or a new project. Channel it into a new beginning emotionally with your own loved one. It's fair. I am giving everyone this same charge, this same power. If you are single and your heart has been open, allow your feelings to grow. If you don't have anybody you are interested in to think about, ask a Moon witch for a love spell and perform it, using my energy."

*Diet at the New Moon*    When this Moon energy begins our cycle, it is best to eat very little. Exercise a great deal, go for walks. What you do eat must be nourishing and fulfilling. A Moon diet consists of two and a half cups of green salad material. (Use at least nine different kinds of green things, including wild foods, especially in the springtime. There are a number of good books to help you identify them.) Make sure it has many different colors in it. Add one cup of cooked vegetables and about five ounces of fish or protein. Fish is not a boring food. I eat fish almost every day. Today I am having halibut, tomorrow I'll have trout, after that I may eat some shark. One tastes very different from the other. I always broil my fish. Both my salads and the fish love a good squeezed lemon.

As the Moon grows I eat a little bit more every day. I add fruit for dessert, maybe some grapes or melons—whatever appears to be in season. Do not eat anything past 7:30 at night, or your stomach will be full when you go to sleep and deprive you of prophetic dreams.

The New Moon is celebrated around the world. The witches celebrate every New Moon with teaching circles, purification and blessings on new projects, new relationships, new ideas. Jewish women celebrate the New Moon with different themes chosen for each month.*

## *Celebrating the Full Moon*

When the Moon is full, she rises at sunset, and the last glow of the dying sun makes her blush with a rosy light. This is the time of fullness, of flowering. At this time in her cycle the Moon's power is greatest. Those who are sensitive may become unbalanced by so much energy, especially if they are under the influence of some other mind-altering substance. There are more accidents at this time of month. In mental wards the patients are more excited. But for those who are in harmony with the Moon's energy and know how to use it, this is the time of greatest power. This is the time when witches meet to do their most powerful magic.  Night travel is easiest when the Moon is bright, and this was another reason that witches traveled to their meetings on heath and hill at the Full Moon.

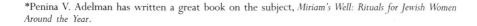

*Penina V. Adelman has written a great book on the subject, *Miriam's Well: Rituals for Jewish Women Around the Year*.

Just before the Moon reaches her fullest, do magic to manifest love, energy, creativity, prosperity. During the Full Moon, seek a wild place and dance to the drums until you are filled with the Moon's ecstasy. Lie on your bed before an open window, and let the moonlight fill you with power.

"Speak to me," I said to the Full Moon, and she did.

"In the time of my fullness let there be feasts. Let the cupboard be filled with delectable delicacies, let the milk and honey flow, let the wonderful fresh-baked bread rise, let yellow butter melt, let fruits be made into jams, apricots be dried, figs be made into sweet paste, and the good wine brought out and served in deep goblets in colors of gold and blood red. Let my feasts be celebrated everywhere.

"Let the women who come to my feasts be round like me and fear not their own flesh. Let the soft flesh on their hips imitate my curves, let their laps be soft and receptive, let their hands be firm yet warm and silky, and let them stroke their children with their soothing touch. Yes, let my women be round, let their fat bloom on their bones like the fruit on the vine, and let them take up space, a lot of space. In my honor let the women grow big and strong.

"Among the women let there be peace. Let hatred evaporate among them, and let the noose of self-loathing loosen. Let mothers and daughters come together without a sword between them anymore. I want to look down on merry gatherings, where the fine silver of the older women's hair will rival my own. I want to see the old ones dance and sing and teach their songs to the younger ones.

"Let the men in my sight be peaceful. Let their swords be used as magic wands from now on. Let the men bestow fine jewels on the ladies and their battle cries be exchanged for songs of love of life. Let their fighting spirit be transmuted into competition in sports and the arts. Let the roll of drums accompany ecstatic dances from now on and no longer be the drums of war. And let there be great rewards for those who please me.

"I am the Full Moon's magic. I make the desire in you rise like the sap. I govern with eternal change. I will be your boat when you die and take you across the rivers of life and death and teach you how to be with me, little bird, little flower, clever human. But tonight we feast and grow fat."

## *Celebrating the Waning Moon*

The second part of the lunation is the resting time. Now we grow slower, now we rush less, now we finish that which has been started earlier. The time of the Waning Moon is important to preserve energy, culture, excitement. The Waning Moon is good for mourning, cleaning, putting things in order, organizing.

Sleep more during this time and eat less and less as the Moon wanes. Every day just eat a little less food, fewer fruits, fewer sweets, until you end up fasting on the last day. Drink water and juices, herbal teas, take your tonics.

I asked the Waning Moon to speak to me, and this is what she said:

"Sleep deep on my nights, eat very little so I can come and give you dreams of the future. Together we will work out your problems in dreams and raise your hopes."

"On my nights burn a black candle with the name of your troubles written on it three times, or gray candles to neutralize that which is hurting you. Clean out your mind and soul, work on your conflicts to arrive at resolution."

# MOON TALE

## *How Grandmother Made a Pact with the Devil*

Once, when I was but a child, I went with my grandmother to the land we owned in Dósza Sürü to do the plowing. Grandmother held the plow's head, and I was walking in front of the oxen. We plowed row after row, going back and forth, until about noon. Then I started seeing something jumping ahead, in and out of sight. It was like lightning, an apparition.

"What was that?" asked Grandmother, sensing something weird.

"I don't know what it could be. But I think I saw goat feet and a tail, and I think it had horns as well."

Grandmother came around to the front with her bullwhip and started hitting the air where she sensed the thing to be.

"Don't you dare to hit me!" the voice said now. "You hit me with that whip and you will get trouble!"

"Who are you, and where are you?" Grandmother bellowed at him.

"I am the grandchild of Pluto, a little devil," said he, revealing himself. He was small and dark, part animal, part human, part divine. But he was a speculating kind of devil.

"I came to make a contract with you!"

Grandmother stood there wiping her hands on her apron, staring in surprise.

"What kind of contract are you talking about?" she asked suspiciously. Clearly she wasn't going to sign her soul away.

"I want to make a contract with you that when in the autumn you are harvesting your crops, I get half and you get half. If you don't agree, I will burn your fields." He was laughing behind his hand, already looking forward to his harvest riches.

This made Grandmother mad.

"You are a lot of trouble!" she said to the grandchild of Pluto. "But since you are asking for a contract I'll give you one. Whatever grows on top of the earth, all that will be yours. And everything that grows within the earth will be mine. Is that fair?"

"That will be fine!" rejoiced the little devil. "I'll be back in the fall to get my share."

Grandmother decided we were going to plant potatoes that year because they grow under the earth. We planted them really well. Twice we went out and cultivated the fields, and the rains were good that year. Soon it was autumn and we started taking the potatoes out of the ground. Pluto's grandchild knew about it and came right away to claim his share.

"Here are the potatoes' leaves, they're all yours, take 'em away!" said Grandmother. With this she gave all that grew above the ground to the little devil.

He was very disappointed. He saw that he had made a bad deal. His tail was standing up in the air, and he was threatening us with his horns.

"I want a better contract with you!" said the little devil.

"We can make another contract if you wish, but it will have to be for next year."

"That is fine with me," said the devil.

"So what should the new contract say?" Grandmother was still holding fast to her whip.

"The new contract should be that I get all that grows below the ground and you will get what grows above the ground.

"Very well," said Grandmother. "Come back a year from now and we will share the harvest."

The devil disappeared in the blink of an eye.

Next year Grandmother decided that the entire land should be sown with wheat. When the wheat had ripened, we cut it down and started bringing the sheaves in. Grandmother was waiting for the little devil. She knew that he would sense her harvesting.

And sure enough, he bobbed up from behind a bush and started running up and down, looking for his share.

"It's about time you showed up!" said Grandmother. "There is your share, the whole thing! I am taking only what was above the ground. Your share is all there." She pointed to the fields.

The devil started digging into the earth.

"Ay, but there is nothing in there but the roots from the wheat."

"That is true. You wanted only what was underneath the ground. Now you have it," answered Grandmother with the most innocent expression imaginable.

The devil kicked the earth, spat at us, and muttered things between his gnashing teeth. But he had to admit he had been made a fool of. From then on the devil stayed away from Grandmother, and never ever asked her for any more contracts. We have never seen any more little devils since.*

*Based on the story "Apo es a Ordogfloka" from the book *Villám Palkò* by Ráduly János (Bucharest: Iou Creangōr Könyrkiadò, 1989), 116.

# BIBLIOGRAPHY

Adelman, Penina V. *Miriam's Well: Rituals for Jewish Women Around the Year.* Fresh Meadows, NY: Biblio Press, 1986.

Allen, Paula Gunn. *The Sacred Hoop: Recovering the Feminine in American Indian Traditions.* Boston: Beacon, 1986.

Allen, Richard Hinckley. *Star Names: Their Lore and Meaning.* 1899. Reprint. New York: Dover, 1963.

Atwater, Donald. *The Penguin Dictionary of Saints.* 2d ed. Harmondsworth, England: Penguin, 1985.

*The Beltane Papers.* 1984–88. P.O. Box 8, Clear Lake, WA 98235.

Berger, Pamela. *The Goddess Obscured: Transformation of the Grain Protectress from Goddess to Saint.* Boston: Beacon, 1985.

*Better Homes and Gardens Heritage Cookbook.* Des Moines, IA: Better Homes and Gardens Books, 1975.

Bodde, Derk. *Festivals in Classical China: New Year and Other Annual Observances During the Han Dynasty, 206 B.C.–A.D. 220.* Princeton, NJ: Princeton Univ. Press, 1975.

Borghese, Anita. *The International Cook Jar Cookbook.* New York: Charles Scribner's Sons, 1975.

Butler, Francelia. *Skipping Around the World: The Ritual Nature of Folk-Rhymes.* New York: Ballantine, 1989.

*Calendar of Irish Folk Customs, 1984.* Belfast: Appletree Press, 1983.

Carlyon, Richard. *A Guide to the Gods.* London: Wm. Heinemann/Quixote, 1981.

Casella, Dolores. *A World of Breads.* 1966. Reprint. Port Washington, NY: David White, 1977.

Clark, Ella E. *Indian Legends of the Pacific Northwest.* Berkeley: Univ. of California Press, 1953.

Collins, June McCormick. *Valley of the Spirits: The Upper Skagit Indians of Western Washington.* 1974. Reprint. Seattle and London: Univ. of Washington Press, 1980.

Cooper, J. C. *The Aquarian Dictionary of Festivals.* Wellingborough, England: Aquarian Press, 1990.

Cunningham, Donna. *Moon Signs.* New York: Ballantine, 1988.

Deramer, Percy, Ralph Vaughan Williams, Martin Shaw. *The Oxford Book of Carols*. 1928. Reprint. London: Oxford Univ. Press, 1975.

Dexter, Miriam Robbins. *Whence the Goddesses: A Sourcebook*. Elmsford, NY: Pergamon Press, 1990.

Durdin-Robertson, Lawrence. *The Year of the Goddess: A Perpetual Calendar of Festivals*. Wellingborough, England: Aquarian Press, 1990.

Ekstrand, F. E. *The Ancient Norwegian Calendar Stick (Primstav)*. Seattle: Welcome Press, n.d.

*Engwall's Journal: A Newsletter for Coffee Connoisseurs* 1, 6 (Fall 1987). *Engwall's Journal*, Letter Drop, 120 Brighton Rd., P.O. Box 5221, Clifton, NJ 07015.

Friedrich, Paul. *The Meaning of Aphrodite*. Chicago and London: Univ. of Chicago Press, 1978.

*From the Lands of the Scythians: Ancient Treasures from the Museums of the USSR, 3000 B.C. to 100 B.C.*. Exhibition catalog. New York and Los Angeles: Metropolitan Museum of Art, Los Angeles County Museum of Art, 1975.

*Funk and Wagnall's Standard Dictionary of Folklore, Mythology, and Legend*. Ed. Maria Leach. 1949. Reprint. New York: Harper & Row, 1984. Cited in the present work as *F & W*.

Gimbutas, Marija. *Goddesses and Gods of Old Europe, 6500–3500 B.C.: Myths and Cult Images*. Rev. ed. Berkeley: Univ. of California Press, 1982.

*Goddesses and Their Offspring: Nineteenth- and Twentieth-Century Eastern European Embroideries*. Exhibition catalog. Binghamton, NY: Roberson Center for the Arts & Sciences, 1986.

Graves, Robert. *The White Goddess*. Rev. ed. New York: Farrar, Straus & Giroux, 1966.

_____. *The Greek Myths*. Vols. 1 and 2, 1955. Reprint. Harmondsworth, England: Penguin, 1983.

Greenberg, Florence. *Florence Greenberg's Jewish Cookbook*. 1974. Reprint. Secaucus, NJ: Chartwell Books, 1980.

Grimal, Pierre, ed. *Larousse World Mythology*. London: Paul Hamlyn, 1965.

Harding, M. Esther. *Woman's Mysteries*. New York: Harper & Row, 1976.

Harlan, William. *The Horizon Cookbook and Illustrated History of Eating and Drinking Through the Ages*. New York: American Heritage, Doubleday, 1968.

Harrison, Jane Ellen. *Prolegomena to the Study of Greek Religions*. 3d ed. New York: Meridian, 1955.

Harrison, Kenneth. *The Framework of Anglo-Saxon History to A.D. 900*. Cambridge: Cambridge Univ. Press, 1976.

Hendricks, Rhoda A. *Mythologies of the World.: A Concise Encyclopedia*. New York: McGraw-Hill, 1979.

Hope, Murry. *The Way of Cartouche*. New York: St. Martin's Press, 1985.

Hultkrantz, Ake. "The Religion of the Goddess in North America," in *The Book of the Goddess, Past and Present*. Ed. Carl Olson. New York: Crossroad, 1985.

Jobes, Gertrude and James. *Outer Space: Myths, Name Meanings, Calendars*. New York and London: Scarecrow Press, 1964.

Kavasch, Barrie. *Native Harvests: Recipes and Botanicals of the American Indian*. New York: Random, First Vintage Books, 1979.

Kimball, Yeffe, and Jean Anderson. *The Art of American Indian Cooking*. Garden City, NY: Doubleday, 1965.

Knightly, Charles. *The Customs and Ceremonies of Britain*. London: Thames & Hudson, 1986.

Krieg, Saul. *The Alpha and Omega of Greek Cooking*. New York: Macmillan, 1973.

Krupp, E. C. *Echoes of the Ancient Skies: The Astronomy of Lost Civilizations*. New York: New American Library, 1983.

Lurker, Manfred. *The Gods and Symbols of Ancient Egypt*. Trans. Barbara Cumming. 1974. Reprint. New York: Thames & Hudson, 1980.

Mikalson, Jon. *The Sacred and Civil Calendar of the Athenian Year*. Princeton, NJ: Princeton Univ. Press, 1975.

Monaghan, Patricia. *The Book of Goddesses and Heroines*. 1981. Rev. ed. St. Paul, MN: Llewellyn, 1990.

Murphy, John. *Traditional Irish Recipes*. Handscribed by Margaret Batt. Belfast: Appletree Press, 1980.

*Octava: Newsletter for the Eight Feasts, TBP's*. 1986–. P.O. Box 8, Clear Lake, WA 98235.

Ouei, Mimie. *The Art of Chinese Cooking*. New York: Random House, 1960.

Palmer, Martin, ed. *T'ung Shu: The Ancient Chinese Almanac*. Boston: Shambhala, 1986.

Potts, Billie. *Witches Heal*. Ann Arbor, MI: Du Reve Publications, 1989.

Robinson, Herbert Spencer, and Knox Wilson. *Myths and Legends of All Nations*. Totowa, NJ: Littlefield, Adams, 1976.

Rush, Anne Kent. *Moon, Moon*. New York: Random House, 1976.

Santa Maria, Jack. *Indian Sweet Cookery*. Boulder: Shambhala, 1980.

Sojourner, Sabrina. "From the House of Yemanja: The Goddess Heritage of Black Women," in *The Politics of Women's Spirituality*. Ed. Charlene Spretnak. Garden City, NY: Anchor Press, Doubleday, 1982.

Spicer, Dorothy Gladys. *The Book of Festivals*. New York: Woman's Press, 1937.

Stein, Diane. *The Goddess Book of Days*. St. Paul, MN: Llewellyn, 1988.

Stewart, Katie, and Pamela Michael. *Wild Blackberry Cobbler and Other Old-fashioned Recipes*. Salem, NH: Salem House, 1984.

Stone, Merlin. *Ancient Mirrors of Womanhood: Our Goddess and Heroine Heritage*. Vols. 1 and 2. New York: New Sibylline Books, 1979.

*The Time-Life Holiday Cookbook*. New York: Time-Life Books, 1976.

Thompson, William Irwin. *The Time Falling Bodies Take to Light*. New York: St. Martin's, 1980.

Thorsten, Geraldine. *God Herself*. New York: Avon, 1980.

Tun Li-ch'en. *Annual Customs and Festivals in Peking*. Trans. Derk Bodde. 1900. Reprint. Peiping: Henri Vetch, 1936.

Urlin, Ethel L. *Festivals, holydays, Saints' Days, A Study in Origins and Survivors in Church Ceremonies and Secular Customs*. 1915. Reprint. Detroit: Gale Research, 1979.

Walker, Barbara G. *The Woman's Encyclopedia of Myths and Secrets*. San Francisco: Harper & Row, 1983.

Weed, Susun S. *Healing Wise*. Woodstock, NY: Ash Tree Publishing, 1989.

Wohlgenanut, Hermann. *Der Mond*. Bregenz: Teutsch, 1988.

Zimmerman, J. E. *Dictionary of Classical Mythology*. 1964. Reprint. Toronto: Bantam, 1980.

# INDEX

# ABOUT THE AUTHOR

Born in her namesake city of Budapest to an artist witch mother, Zsuzsanna was raised among models, painters, sculptors, professors, and psychics. Postwar Europe, poverty, and illness marked her early years. At sixteen, she experienced the Hungarian Revolution, coloring her consciousness forever. When the revolution was crushed, she left the country with 64,000 other Hungarians and went to study language in Vienna. Still filled with passion for the revolution, she went to school at the University of Chicago to further her study of communications. There she discovered Second City in its infancy and studied improvisation under the esteemed Viola Sills and later studied theater at the American Academy of Dramatic Arts in New York.

From Hungarian emigrant to feminist witch, her road was marked by politics, revolutions, and spirituality. She married and gave birth to two sons who are now grown—and her friends.

Z became a feminist at thirty, bringing to feminism her unique family heritage of creativity and her knowledge of improvisation. She founded the first feminist witches coven in 1971 and led open rituals on Malibu mountaintops and beaches, in backyards and living rooms for ten years, thereby initiating the spiritual emergence of the women's movement. Arrested in Los Angeles for reading the Tarot, her trial marked the first time a witch was persecuted in this country since Salem. More importantly, it was the first time the witch defeated the law.

Making the San Francisco Bay Area her home base, Z has continued to be a strong voice in the feminist and pagan communities. She has traveled extensively in this country and in Europe, teaching about the Goddess and her holy days. She has published hundreds of articles and several books, most notably *The Holy Book of Women's Mysteries* and *The Grandmother of Time*.

Z stars in her own cable TV show called "13th Heaven," which is syndicated in the San Francisco Bay Area and features Goddess artists, speakers, and sacred animals. When you write to Z Budapest about a problem you have, she will put your letter on the Full Moon altar, but she will not cast a spell for you. If you want to book an event with Z, write to P.O. Box 11363, Oakland, CA 94611.